D1021959

Professors Behaving Badly

Professors Behaving Badly

Faculty Misconduct in Graduate Education

John M. Braxton, Eve Proper,
and Alan E. Bayer

The Johns Hopkins University Press
Baltimore

Printed in the United States of America on acid-free paper
9 8 7 6 5 4 3 2 1

The Johns Hopkins University Press
2715 North Charles Street
Baltimore, Maryland 21218-4363
www.press.jhu.edu

Library of Congress Cataloging-in-Publication Data

Braxton, John M.
Professors behaving badly : faculty misconduct in graduate education / John M. Braxton, Eve Proper, and Alan E. Bayer.
p. cm.
Includes bibliographical references and index.
ISBN-13: 978-1-4214-0219-2 (hardcover : alk. paper)
ISBN-10: 1-4214-0219-X (hardcover : alk. paper)
1. College teachers—Professional ethics—United States. 2. College teaching—Corrupt practices—United States. 3. Teachers—Professional ethics. I. Proper, Eve. II. Bayer, Alan E., 1939–
III. Title.
LB1779.B74 2011
378.1′250973—dc22 2011008669

A catalog record for this book is available from the British Library.

Special discounts are available for bulk purchases of this book. For more information, please contact Special Sales at 410-516-6936 or specialsales@press.jhu.edu.

The Johns Hopkins University Press uses environmentally friendly book materials, including recycled text paper that is composed of at least 30 percent post-consumer waste, whenever possible.

In memory
Robert K. Merton
July 4, 1910 to February 23, 2003

Contents

Tables

Acknowledgments

We wish to acknowledge financial support for our research in the form of a 2006 grant from the Center for Ethics under the directorship of Charles E. Scott, professor of philosophy at Vanderbilt University. In addition, we express appreciation for thoughtful suggestions for improving this volume made by an anonymous reviewer.

For assisting us in the development of the content of our Graduate Teaching and Mentoring Behaviors Inventory (GTMBI), we are indebted to a number of colleagues in the Department of Sociology at Virginia Polytechnic and State University. We also acknowledge the thoughtful comments and suggestions of colleagues at other universities, including Melissa Anderson, Maxine Atkinson, Ann Austin, Leonard Baird, Martin Finkelstein, Mary Frank Fox, James Orcutt, Luther Otto, John Smart, and Mark Wardell. We also would like to thank the *Chronicle of Higher Education* for allowing us to adopt one of its headlines as our book title.

Professors Behaving Badly

INTRODUCTION

The Critical Role of Norms in Graduate Education

College and university faculty members have considerable autonomy in their teaching and research role performance (Braxton & Bayer, 1999). Such autonomy springs from the highly symbolic value of academic freedom, one of the deeply seated values of the academic profession (Finkelstein, 1984). Autonomy also emanates from the expertise faculty members have in their academic subject matter areas (Baldridge, Curtis, Ecker, & Riley, 1978; Finkelstein, 1984; Scott, 1970).

Although faculty members who primarily teach undergraduate students have autonomy in their teaching (Braxton & Bayer, 1999), faculty members who teach and supervise graduate students possess maximum professional autonomy in such role performance (Braxton, Proper, & Bayer, 2011). This assertion finds strong reinforcement in Fox's (2000) observation that "graduate education is highly decentralized" (p. 47). She elaborates by asserting that "departments leave untouched the core of graduate education: the advisor-advisee relationship" (p. 57). Further, Fox depicts this core relationship as "highly privatized." There is also an asymmetrical power relationship between graduate faculty and graduate students, especially in the advisor-advisee relationship.

Thus graduate faculty members enjoy considerable latitude in the professional choices they make concerning various facets of graduate education. For the academic profession, graduate study stands as a powerful mechanism of socialization that shapes professional identity and commitment (Bucher & Stelling, 1977). Through this process, graduate students also acquire the attitudes, values, and disciplinary knowledge and skill needed for their subsequent research and teaching role performances (Austin & Wulff, 2004; Merton, Reader, & Kendall, 1957).

Important components of the graduate school socialization process include course requirements, qualifying examinations, the dissertation, research and teaching assistantships, mentoring relationships, and both formal and informal faculty-student interactions. Graduate faculty members make professional choices regarding these various dimensions of the socialization process, choices that may foster or harm the acquisition of attitudes, values, and disciplinary knowledge and skill by graduate students. These choices may also influence the professional identities and commitments of graduate students.

Norms and the Ideal of Service

The ideal of service, a core generating trait of professionalism, fosters strong expectations for professional choices that safeguard the welfare of clients (Goode, 1969). The ideal of service resonates with Parsons's (1939) notion of the "collectivity orientation of professions." In the case of graduate study, clients include graduate students as well as the academic profession and its associated subject matter areas.

The welfare of such clients is safeguarded through norms. Because norms represent shared beliefs within a particular social or professional group about preferred or expected behavior in a given situation or circumstance (Gibbs, 1981; Rossi & Berk, 1985), they provide guidelines for the professional choices graduate faculty members make regarding the above-mentioned dimensions of the socialization process. Explicitly, these guidelines delineate appropriate and inappropriate behaviors regarding such professorial choices given that norms are prescribed or proscribed patterns of behavior (Merton, 1968, 1973). Without the existence of norms, graduate faculty members would be free to follow their own preferences in making choices regarding the various facets of graduate teaching and mentoring. Some choices might safeguard the welfare of clients of graduate study, but others might negatively impact clients. These assertions logically flow from Durkheim's 1895 assumption that nonconformity is the natural human condition whereas conformity is the induced social condition (1982).

Thus norms play a critical role by offering a balance between preserving professorial autonomy in graduate education and safeguarding the needs and welfare of clients of graduate education. Norms strike this balance by forming moral boundaries around the exercise of autonomy. Such moral boundaries emerge from violations of norms (Ben-Yehuda, 1985) and ensure that graduate faculty members adhere to the ideal of service and safeguard the welfare of the clients of graduate study.

Other Critical Roles of Norms in Graduate Education

First, professional self-regulation requires the existence of norms. The lay public grants autonomy to members of professions that adhere to the ideal of service (Goode, 1969). Accordingly, the lay public expects professionals to be self-regulating (Anderson & Louis, 1994; Goode, 1969). Self-regulation entails the assumption of responsibility by a profession for ensuring that its members perform their professional roles in a way that safeguards the welfare of its clients (Braxton, 1999). Norm violations represent misconduct that requires some action by the profession. By providing guidelines for graduate faculty members' choices, norms safeguard the welfare of the clients of graduate education.

Second, norms provide moral boundaries for the enactment of pattern maintenance (Braxton, 2010), which is one of the four functional imperatives of social action systems (Parsons & Platt, 1973). Both the existence and the effectiveness of a social action system depend on the performance of the four functional imperatives, which form independent subsystems (Parsons & Smelser, 1956). Pattern maintenance entails the development and maintenance of the ideas, values, and beliefs that define the fundamental frame of reference for a social action system (Parsons & Platt, 1973). In this case, college and university work constitutes a social action system (Braxton, 2010). Teaching and research serve as a basic frame of reference for college and university work as a social action system (Braxton, 2010). As such, teaching and research are instrumental to the achievement of the functional imperative of pattern maintenance. Graduate education stands as an important frame of reference for pattern maintenance (Parsons & Platt, 1973).

Third, norms as proscriptions and prescriptions for professorial behavior function as a moral compass for stewardship of academic disciplines. Golde

(2006) posits that graduate education should prepare future members of the academic profession to be stewards of their academic discipline. Stewardship entails disciplinary competence in the generation, conservation, and transformation of knowledge and serving as a moral compass for the disciplines by embracing a set of principles of integrity (Golde, 2006).

Fourth, norms provide parameters for reform in graduate education. Norms impede or facilitate the enactment of reforms in graduate education that pertain to the various roles of faculty in graduate education. Without norms supportive of reforms in place, the reliability of faculty enactment of policies and procedures developed to implement these reforms is uncertain. This uncertainty arises from the freedom faculty have to follow their own preferences in the absence of either supportive or proscriptive norms (Braxton, Eimers, & Bayer, 1996). This formulation springs from Durkheim's contention that conformity is not the natural social condition (1982).

The Existence of a Normative Structure for Graduate Teaching and Mentoring

The formulations set forth in the previous sections of this chapter strongly indicate a need for mapping the existent normative structure for graduate teaching and mentoring. Chapter 1 also presents a compelling need for the existence of such a normative structure, describing incidents of faculty misconduct involving graduate students reported in various articles appearing in the *Chronicle of Higher Education* since the year 2000.

Does such a normative structure empirically exist? What normative structures for the academic profession do exist? Three interrelated primary normative structures prevail for the professoriate. The first structure, norms related to research and scholarship, is well documented. The second, norms related to undergraduate teaching, has recently received increased attention. The third, norms related to graduate teaching, has been relatively less addressed. While the last of these structures contains some components of the first two, it also has some unique aspects related to the normative structure for graduate training and mentoring. In this section we briefly review some of the core aspects of norms regarding scholarship and those pertaining to undergraduate teaching. Subsequently, we propose a conceptual framework to address the normative structure for graduate teaching and mentoring.

A Normative Structure for Scholarship and Research Role Performance

The development of attitudes, values, and disciplinary knowledge and skills for future research performance constitutes the primary thrust of graduate school socialization (Austin & Wulff, 2004; Cole & Cole, 1973; Hagstrom, 1965). Through this process, the norms of science, and the norms that provide guidelines for scholarly role performance in nonscience disciplines and fields, are also communicated to graduate students (Merton, 1973). Strong support among graduate students for the norms of science, and the parallel norms in other disciplines and fields, exists (Anderson & Louis, 1994).

Moreover, a robust body of literature focuses on the existence of a normative structure for research role performance or the norms of science (Braxton, 1986; Zuckerman, 1988). This normative structure consists of four norms delineated and described by Merton (1942, 1973): communality, disinterestedness, organized skepticism, and universalism. Communality ordains that research findings are the intellectual property of the research community. In exchange for the communication of their research findings, scholars should receive appropriate recognition for their contributions. Disinterestedness stipulates that the advancement of knowledge should be the individual academic's primary motive for conducting research. Accordingly, this normative pattern prescribes that individuals should not conduct research solely for personal or financial gain, to merely receive recognition, or simply to gain prestige. Organized skepticism insists that research findings should not be accepted by the research community without peer assessment based on empirical and logical criteria. Universalism stipulates that research be judged on the basis of merit and not on such particularistic criteria as race, nationality, or social origin.

The knowledge base of an academic discipline stands as the client safeguarded by the norms of science and the parallel norms for other academic disciplines (Braxton, 1990). Faculty adherence to these norms is instrumental to the advancement of knowledge (Merton, 1942, 1973).

Moreover, conformity to these norms is variable, as Braxton (1986) and Zuckerman (1988) have concluded from their reviews of research on this topic. Zuckerman (1988) elaborates by indicating that these norms are neither consistently binding on scholars nor routinely violated.

Thus, a normative structure for scholarship and research role performance exists. This normative structure provides guides for research role performance by graduate faculty members. Graduate students also internalize to varying degrees this normative structure during their graduate studies.

A Normative Structure for Undergraduate College Teaching

A second normative structure related to faculty role performance pertains to undergraduate college teaching. In *Faculty Misconduct in Collegiate Teaching* (Braxton & Bayer, 1999), we describe an empirically derived normative structure for undergraduate college teaching. We obtained this normative array from the perceptions of 949 faculty members holding academic appointments in five types of colleges and universities (research I universities, comprehensive universities and colleges I, liberal arts colleges I and II, and two-year colleges) and four academic disciplines (biology, chemistry, mathematics, and psychology). Seven inviolable and nine admonitory norms constitute this normative structure. Inviolable norms are behaviors viewed by academics as warranting severe sanctions, whereas admonitory norms are behaviors that academics believe should be avoided but not severely sanctioned (Braxton & Bayer, 1999). The components that constitute this normative structure represent proscribed behaviors regarding undergraduate college teaching role performance. Teaching improprieties result from violations of these normative patterns (Braxton & Bayer, 1999).

The seven inviolable norms take the following forms (Braxton & Bayer, 1999):

1. *Condescending negativism* rebukes the treatment of both students and colleagues in a condescending and demeaning way.
2. *Inattentive planning* proscribes a lack of planning of a course (e.g., required texts not routinely ordered in time for the first class session, or a course outline or syllabus is not prepared for the course).
3. *Moral turpitude* prohibits depraved, unprincipled acts by faculty.
4. *Particularistic grading* scorns the uneven or preferential treatment of students in the awarding of grades.
5. *Personal disregard* reproves disrespect for the needs and sensitivities of students (e.g., profanity in class, poor hygiene by faculty).
6. *Uncommunicated course detail* shows contempt for the failure of faculty members to inform students of important particulars about a course during the first day of class (e.g., changing class location to another building, changing class meeting time without consulting students, not informing students of the instructor's policy on missed or makeup examinations).
7. *Uncooperative cynicism* reproaches the refusal of a faculty member to par-

ticipate in departmental matters, the refusal to advise departmental advisees, the refusal to participate in departmental curricular planning, and the display of a cynical attitude toward teaching.

The first six inviolable norms directly safeguard the welfare of students as clients, whereas the seventh, which pertains to departmental colleagues and the role of college teaching, indirectly provides safeguards to undergraduate students.

The nine admonitory norms serve different clients. The welfare of the knowledge base of academic disciplines receives some protection by the admonitory norms of (1) *authoritarian classroom* and (2) *instructional narrowness* (Braxton & Bayer, 1999). The norm of *authoritarian classroom* reproves a faculty classroom demeanor that shows a rigid and closed approach to both course content and different points of view espoused by students. *Instructional narrowness* scorns faculty members who display a narrowness in their assessment of students and in the their use of teaching methods.

The admonitory norms of (3) *teaching secrecy* and (4) *undermining colleagues* pertain to faculty colleagues as clients. *Teaching secrecy* censures faculty refusal to provide colleagues with information and materials relevant to the role of college teaching. Faculty members who demean or belittle courses offered by colleagues receive proscription by the admonitory norm of *undermining colleagues*.

The remaining five admonitory norms safeguard the welfare of undergraduate students as clients: (5) *advisement negligence*, (6) *inadequate communication*, (7) *inadequate course design*, (8) *inconvenience avoidance*, and (9) *insufficient syllabus*. The normative pattern of *advisement negligence* rebukes the failure of faculty to serve the advising needs of students. *Inadequate communication* censures the failure of faculty members to communicate course details to students. The norm of *inadequate course design* proscribes such faculty behaviors as not keeping required course materials within reasonable cost limits, designing a course without taking into account the needs or abilities of students enrolling in the course, and not preparing new lectures or revised lectures that reflect advancements in the field. *Inconvenience avoidance* reproaches faculty efforts to avoid inconveniences related to the courses they teach. The norm of *insufficient syllabus* disdains the failure of faculty to provide students with an adequate syllabus for a course.

As is the case with the norms of science and the parallel normative structure for others in academic disciplines, conformity to the norms of undergraduate college teaching is variable. Braxton and Mann (2004) assert that "teaching norm violations are neither rampant nor non-existent" (p. 39).

We turn now to the third central component of the normative system impacting role performance of university faculty. In contrast to the other two components, the norms pertaining to prescriptive or proscriptive behaviors in the graduate training and mentoring role have received little empirical assessment. Consequently, we begin discussion of this normative system by introducing a conceptual framework for assessment of this normative system.

Conceptual Framework for Assessing Normative Role Performance Criteria in Graduate Training

This framework takes the perspective that norms develop from a variety of situations or events that university faculty members experience either directly or indirectly during their own graduate school socialization, in their day-to-day interactions with the university environment, and in their professional associations. When people engage in a particular pattern of behavior, typical behavior becomes expected and thus normative (Opp, 1982). Norms also emerge from the consequences of the behavior of others (Demsetz, 1967). Some behaviors might evoke approval because of benefits derived from the behavior. Other behaviors may result in harm and elicit disapproval (Horne, 2001).

Those behaviors that result in harm and elicit disapproval assume proscriptive normative properties. Such proscribed behaviors elicit varying degrees of moral outrage or indignation (Durkheim, 1912/1995). The severity of sanctions individuals deem appropriate for such proscribed behaviors indexes the degree of moral outrage they express. Thus some behaviors warrant severe sanctions, whereas others provoke less severe reactions.

The graduate school socialization process provides graduate students with occasions to either directly or indirectly experience those negative behaviors that produce proscriptions. Through advising and mentoring, taking courses, serving as graduate research assistants, and engagement in thesis or dissertation work, harm may come to graduate students because of the actions of graduate faculty members. Students may also learn of harmful behaviors experienced by other graduate students. Moreover, graduate students are perceptive observers and listeners, especially those who aspire to become members of the professoriate (Austin, 2002). Specifically, graduate students listen carefully to formal and informal conversations with supervisors and advisors and pay close attention to offhanded comments faculty members and advanced graduate students casually make about professorial roles (Austin, 2002). Taken together, these formulations indicate that normative inclinations of graduate faculty members may take shape during their graduate school studies. Such normative inclinations may vary in their intensity as a function of the degree of moral indignation the offending proscribed behaviors provoke.

Normative proclivities of individual graduate faculty members may also develop through their experience in an academic department or within the university context. A graduate student may report his or her personal experience with harmful incidents to individual graduate faculty members because they serve as the student's mentor, advisor, research assistantship supervisor, or thesis or dissertation chairperson or committee member. Graduate faculty may also learn of behaviors harmful to students and others through their interactions with departmental and institutional and from discussions with colleagues in their discipline at professional association meetings. Again, the normative proclivities that emerge from such experiences vary in their intensity in response to the degree of moral indignation that results from such experiences with offending behaviors.

Research Questions: Pursuit of a Normative Structure for Graduate Teaching and Mentoring

Research demonstrates the existence of normative structures for research role performance and for undergraduate college teaching. However, as noted above, little or no research focuses on the existence of a normative structure to guide graduate faculty behavior in relation to teaching and mentoring. This book seeks to fill this void by addressing a set of six research questions that flow from the formulations of the conceptual framework described above.

1. *What is the normative structure for graduate teaching and mentoring?* Norms differ in the degree of indignation that their violation elicits (Durkheim, 1912/1995). Accordingly, we raise a more specific question: *What are inviolable and admonitory normative patterns that constitute this normative structure?* In *Faculty Misconduct in Collegiate Teaching* (Braxton & Bayer, 1999), we made a distinction between those behaviors that academics believe warrant severe sanctions (inviolable norms) and those behaviors that academics believe should be avoided but less severely sanctioned (admonitory norms). This volume's conceptual framework provides a set of perspectives that suggest that a normative structure of graduate teaching and mentoring empirically exists.

2. *Does faculty espousal of the empirically identified inviolable and admonitory normative patterns vary between faculty holding academic appointments in universities of*

high and very high research intensity? Kenneth Ruscio (1987) asserts that the mission of a college or university greatly influences institutional structures. Institutional structures, in turn, influence faculty work (Blackburn & Lawrence, 1995). Accordingly, we might expect that faculty in high and very high research intensity settings may differ in their espousal of the inviolable and admonitory norms identified.

3. *Does faculty espousal of the empirically identified inviolable and admonitory normative patterns vary across different academic disciplines?* From their review of research on disciplinary differences, Braxton & Hargens (1996) concluded that the differences between academic disciplines are "profound and extensive." Specifically, the level of paradigmatic development of an academic discipline affects teaching and research activities. Moreover, Braxton and Bayer (1999) found disciplinary differences on five of the seven inviolable norms of undergraduate college teaching that they empirically identified. Thus it is possible that faculty espousal of the inviolable and admonitory normative patterns of graduate teaching and mentoring may likewise vary by their academic discipline.

4. *Do the personal attributes of individual faculty such as gender, citizenship, and professional age influence the espousal of the empirically identified inviolable and admonitory normative patterns?* Chapter 5 provides the conceptual and research-based grounding for the raising this question.

5. *Do the professional attainments and involvements of individual faculty members such as academic rank, tenure, research activity, administrative experience, and various types of participation in graduate studies influence the espousal of the empirically identified inviolable and admonitory normative patterns?* Conceptual and research-based rationales for this question are described in Chapter 6.

6. *Are there core inviolable norms and core admonitory norms?* This general question raises a more explicit question: *Are there inviolable and admonitory normative patterns that are invariant across institutional type, academic discipline, personal attributes, and professional attainments and types of involvement in graduate studies?*

Overview of the Book

Chapter 1 describes incidents of faculty misconduct involving graduate students reported in articles appearing in the *Chronicle of Higher Education* since the year 2000. These incidents strongly reinforce the need for a normative structure of graduate teaching and mentoring. Instrumentation, the sampling design, and the obtained sample used to empirically derive the normative structure for graduate teaching and mentoring receive attention in Chapter 2. Chapter 3 describes the empirically derived normative structure of graduate teaching and mentoring that consists of inviolable and admonitory normative orientations.

Chapter 4 discusses variations in the espousal of inviolable and admonitory norms of graduate study by institutional type and by academic discipline. The focus of Chapter 5 is the relationship between such personal attributes of individual graduate faculty members as gender, citizenship, status, and professional age and their level of espousal of the inviolable and admonitory normative patterns of graduate teaching and mentoring. Chapter 6 focuses on the professional involvements and attainments (academic rank, tenure, research activity, administrative experience, and various types of participation in graduate studies) of individual faculty members and the level of disdain they express for violations of these norms of graduate study. Chapter 7 builds on the findings of Chapters 5 and 6 and delineates both core and differentiated norms that surface from robust statistical analyses. Chapter 7 also centers attention on the array of factors that influence those norms that spring forth as differentiated.

In conjunction with the formulations of the conceptual framework described in this chapter, Chapters 8, 9, and 10 attend to various ways in which graduate faculty members acquire the norms of graduate teaching and mentoring described in Chapter 3. Chapter 8 describes in detail the acquisition of norms through the graduate school socialization process. Chapter 9 discusses the presence of norms of graduate teaching and mentoring in disciplinary codes of ethics. Chapter 10 discusses how the norms of graduate study are portrayed in books about the professoriate as it is and ought to be.

Chapter 11 advances conclusions, recommendations for further research, and implications for policy and practice.

CHAPTER ONE

Incidents of Faculty Improprieties in Graduate Training

Although there are no works that document the extent of faculty misconduct in American universities, academic administrators are generally aware of grievous examples, and news accounts of incidents are regrettably frequent, although not nearly comprehensive. The weekly publication the *Chronicle of Higher Education* documents many of these cases, although few address the professorial role of graduate teaching and mentoring. Recent articles have covered misconduct incidents including falsification of degree credentials by faculty (and institutional presidents), plagiarism in faculty publications, falsification of research findings, and embezzlement of funds by various college and university faculty researchers.

Anecdotal accounts of professorial misconduct in the teaching role and in relation to one's graduate students are likewise widespread; indeed, most experienced academics in graduate programs frequently share stories of faculty misconduct with regard to graduate students. Yet most of these instances do not become public, and few are reported in the *Chronicle of Higher Education*, despite this being the premier source for news reporting on all aspects of academe. There are a couple of reasons for this likely underreporting of faculty misconduct in graduate teaching and mentoring. First, there is a significant power differential between graduate students and faculty; hence either in fear of retribution or in anticipation of administrative inaction, graduate students are reluctant to report faculty misconduct that they might experience. Second, university administrators generally hope to deal with faculty misconduct "in house" and to minimize public disclosure of such incidents. This is perhaps particularly the case with respect to improprieties toward graduate students, as there are few noninstitutional mechanisms to deal with grievances. In contrast, the legal system, professional associations, and state and federal agencies can more readily become involved when the faculty misconduct is a violation of professional responsibilities or is research/scholarly misconduct than when it involves the teaching and mentoring role. When these nonuniversity entities become involved in a misconduct case, it is more likely to be noted in the press.

Consequently, we monitored the reporting and news articles in the *Chronicle of Higher Education* since the year 2000 that have dealt with faculty misconduct involving graduate students. Many of the incidents reported in the *Chronicle* over the past decade are presented below. Each of these incidents foreshadows aspects of some of the proscriptive normative behaviors in graduate teaching and mentoring that we empirically derive and discuss later in this volume.

A Department Chair Documents Faculty Misbehavior

The first *Chronicle* article, titled "Professors Behaving Badly," illustrates a range of misbehavior by faculty, including threatening behavior toward graduate students and sexual innuendos and physical groping of students. It is written by a former chairman of the English Department at the University of Illinois at Urbana-Champaign. He reports on incidents of misconduct by four separate faculty members, three of which involve students in his department during his tenure as departmental chairman (Baron, 2003). These three cases involving students are briefly summarized below (in all cases, pseudonyms have been used).

> Paula Barringer had sent an inflammatory and threatening e-mail note to a female graduate student. In it, she accused the student of encouraging hostility toward her from her faculty colleagues. However, the graduate student had never taken a course from Barringer and had never had a personal relationship with her. The only connection between them was that the student worked closely with a faculty member with whom Bar-

ringer was feuding. The student was nevertheless intimidated. Chairman Baron's intervention ultimately resulted in Barringer agreeing in writing to leave the student alone. Within a few months, Barringer resigned from her faculty position.

Near the end of the semester, Manny Rath had invited his students to his house so that they could present their final paper. He told them that it would be an occasion to do their presentations in a more relaxed atmosphere than the classroom, and it would also serve as an end-of-term party for the class members. Alcohol was served. Near the end of the evening, Rath approached one of his students, Angela Argo, and held her tightly by her arms. He then told her how gorgeous she was and kissed her on the lips. This was witnessed by several other students, who corroborated Argo's experience at Rath's house. Argo pursued her complaint with Chairman Baron, demanding a written apology from and a reprimand for Rath so that he would no longer grope female students. After meeting with his chairman and discussing the events, Rath wrote an apology. Chairman Baron put a letter in the faculty file chastising Rath for his behavior and warning him to no longer meet his students or hold class outside his assigned university classroom. Two weeks later, Rath announced his retirement.

Jack Keating was a faculty member in the English Department who frequently made suggestive sexual comments to his graduate assistant. What began as risqué banter soon evolved into more overt comments of a sexual nature, and more. The aggrieved graduate assistant filed a formal complaint, which resulted in a formal apology from Keating. Chairman Baron documented the circumstances and wrote out the expectations requiring changes in Keating's behavior. The following year, Keating left the University of Illinois and took a faculty position at another institution. Baron writes that he fears that Keating's sexual harassment of students was not solved but simply relocated to another campus.

In reflecting on these cases presented above, the writer notes that "students were harmed, careers altered or derailed." The department chairman was himself fortunate: in all three cases involving improprieties toward students, the faculty member perpetrator soon voluntarily left the English Department at the

University of Illinois at Urbana-Champaign. Interestingly, while documenting a substantial number of cases in only one academic department (and only during his tenure as department chairman), even this department chairman attempts to minimize the prevalence of faculty misconduct. He writes that professorial misconduct involves only 2% of the faculty members in the department, despite his documenting improprieties by 4 separate faculty members in his department of 55 tenured and tenure-track faculty (University of Illinois at Urbana-Champaign, 2010) during only his time as the departmental administrator.

The Demeaning and Contemptuous Professor

The next *Chronicle* article also pertains to misconduct by an English professor. It is written by a doctoral student, who published it under a pseudonym, "Henry Adams." It documents some of the arrogance and demeaning attitude that a graduate student might encounter with one of her or his professors. A professor is characterized as taking "delight in power" with respect to graduate students. One student is quoted in this article as saying that one way to cope with this faculty member is to "kiss his rear and he'll let you live" (Adams, 2009).

One of Henry Adams's first assignments as a new graduate student and a graduate assistant in the English Department was to attend an orientation for teaching assistants. It was a meeting held by the director of the freshman composition program, Dr. Dreedle. Adams arrived before anyone else. Then Dreedle entered the room, announcing that he was "Dr. Dreedle." Adams said, "Hi." Dreedle quickly replied: "Don't you know enough to shake hands and introduce yourself?" It was the first glimpse of many instances to come of Dreedle's angry contempt for students and delight in his power to demean them. In numerous subsequent discussions, Dreedle displayed arrogance and contempt for students. He insisted that TAs give no more than one or two A's per assignment. He advised that TAs should regularly refer to something that one's students don't know, to remind them "that yours is the superior intellect." He practiced this advice with his own graduate student classes: he would remind them that they could "never compete with the graduate students of a generation ago." He would regularly ask graduate students a question about a book they had never been assigned, and when no one could answer, he would demean the entire class by saying that "every serious student reads that before coming to graduate school." Graduate students universally feared and despised "Dr. Dreedle."

Inaccessible Professors and Overly Demanding Advisors

Not infrequently, graduate students who are encountering inappropriate behavior by a faculty member or mentor may feel that they have no place to turn for help or advice other than perhaps another graduate student. For more professional advice from experienced academics, some students have used advice columns that periodically appear in the *Chronicle*. These instances reflect a variety of problems that a student might encounter. Two recent examples illustrate polar opposite behaviors, each of which engenders severe difficulties for the graduate student. The first illustrates extreme unsupportive and unresponsive behavior by a student's advisor; the second concerns excessive demands on one's graduate student.

One *Chronicle* advice column, titled "Career Talk," often addresses questions regarding individuals who have already completed their graduate program. However, in one case this column demonstrates the severe difficulties that advisors or mentors may create for a graduate student when the faculty member fails in his or her role of being supportive, approachable, and responsive. In this situation, the student is finishing the dissertation but cannot get the advisor to read or respond to chapter drafts of the dissertation manuscript. Requests for feedback are seldom acknowledged. The faculty member is inaccessible. The student interprets this behavior as a lack of interest in the student's work and fears that it will ultimately delay graduation and lead to poor letters of recommendation (Vick & Furlong, 2010).

Another advice column that periodically runs in the *Chronicle* is by "Ms. Mentor." While humorous, the column addresses serious matters in academe. Most columns address questions from junior faculty adjusting to their new role or from those just embarking on their faculty career and concerned about the job-search process. However, one "Ms. Mentor" column concerns an all-too-common grievance by graduate assistants: taking on duties unrelated to one's education and academic pursuits. This student is working on her dissertation. Her advisor is a recent widow and depends on the student for companionship, emotional support, and to help with a variety of household chores. Not wanting to disappoint her advisor, and fearing that this is the person who will be most influential in the start of her career, she even undertakes painting a room at the professor's house, taking care of her pets, and exterminating rodents in her house. The student is becoming angry about doing these tasks and resentful of the time lost in nonacademic and distasteful activities. The professor is melancholy and needy yet very kind. The student feels very sorry for her but also trapped. She is overwhelmed by the time demands and worried about the cost to her progress in completing her dissertation with this faculty member (Toth, 2005).

Plagiarism, Fraud, and Publication Authorship Disputes

A frequent concern brought to university administrators by advanced graduate students has to do with scholarly collaboration with their mentors. Authorship credits are sometimes disputed. If data fabrication or fraud is found in a research project, one's graduate student is sometimes improperly accused of being the perpetrator. Occasionally, mentors are found to fully appropriate the work of their graduate students. Indeed, one *Chronicle* article cites a prominent scholar in medicine at the University of California at San Francisco who suggests that it is not uncommon in some academic settings to deny junior scientists and graduate students rightful authorship credit; indeed, he says, "it's routine to steal other people's work" (Woolston, 2002).

This article also briefly summarizes three cases of alleged theft of the work of graduate students. At one East Coast university, a graduate student spent seven years completing what she thought was a major scientific breakthrough in her doctoral project. She claims that her advisor had little involvement in the research project but subsequently published the work without giving her any authorship credit. The advisor has been cited frequently for this pathbreaking work and secured millions of dollars in grants as a result of the work. In another ongoing case at the time of the *Chronicle* article, a Cornell University professor was accused of plagiarism of a graduate student's work, and the student's charges of fraud and breach of contract were working their way through the New York courts. In the third case, a former graduate student won a $1.5 million lawsuit against her mentors at the University of Alabama at Birmingham for their theft of her work. However, the verdict was later overturned when it was established that her project was part of a long-term endeavor involving many others at the university.

In another *Chronicle* article, an extended account is presented of reciprocal allegations of plagiarism between a professor of psychology and education at Columbia University and two of her graduate students. One graduate student says that the professor, who was her mentor, told her that her work was not adequate for publication; later, portions of the same work were published under the professor's name. Another graduate student documented that the professor had likewise published work using many of the ideas in her dissertation, along with text passages of identical or near identical language. A law firm was hired by the university and concluded, after an 18-month investigation, that the professor had indeed plagiarized the work written by the two former students. Rebuttal evidence by the professor was found to not be credible. Nevertheless, the professor says it was her accusers who in fact stole her work (Bartlett, 2008).

While stealing intellectual property from a graduate student or not giving appropriate authorship credit to a graduate student's contribution to a piece of published research is a severe form of academic and scientific misconduct, crediting a graduate student with publication coauthorship when not deserved (sometimes called "honorary authorship") is also generally perceived as an unethical act. Indeed, if anomalies are later found in the research reporting, it may allow blame of misconduct to be wrongly attributed to the graduate student coauthor.

One such prominent case involves a professor of nuclear engineering at Purdue University. He published a paper claiming a successful method to fuse hydrogen atoms together, which would result in a possible new low-cost energy source. He then arranged to add the name of a graduate student who had no involvement in the experiment to a research paper that he could then cite as independent confirmation of his original fusion results. Other laboratories could not duplicate and verify the results, resulting in speculation that the research data had been fabricated. A Purdue University inquiry panel subsequently found the professor guilty of research misconduct. His named university professorship title was removed, his status as a member of the graduate faculty was withdrawn, and he was no longer allowed to serve as a graduate thesis advisor (Monastersky, 2008).

In cases in which a graduate student may be accorded appropriate authorship credit, the student may be subject to blame for fabrication of data or for plagiarism, whether or not deserved. A case reported in a brief *Chronicle* news article on a prominent Duke University biochemist is illustrative. The results of a claimed breakthrough enzyme study were published in two prestigious scientific journals. Much of the work described in these journals was performed by a graduate student in the professor's laboratory, and she claims that she expressed reservation that the lab work was still incomplete and not ready for publication. When other university researchers were unable to verify the work and ultimately the two papers had to be retracted from the journals, the professor blamed his student. He accused her of making up data and brought research misconduct charges against her to the university dean's office. She was cleared of the charges.

The scientific community, including an editorial in the journal *Nature*, expressed outrage at the way he had treated his student ("Research Gone Wrong," 2008).

Faculty-Directed Research Malfeasance

Much malfeasance is probably learned by graduate students from the misconduct they observe on the part of their graduate faculty members or mentors. In some cases, this misconduct is modeled by the graduate student and may be viewed as less inappropriate than it in fact is. Thus professorial misconduct may be perpetrated to the next generation of academics. But there are also instances in which malfeasance is actually promoted by faculty in their graduate training programs or with their mentees. One *Chronicle* article suggests that faculty may have actually encouraged plagiarism among their graduate students.

In this case, a former Ohio University graduate student in the Department of Mechanical Engineering alleged that faculty members within the department had either encouraged or ignored widespread cheating and plagiarism over many years. A faculty committee was appointed by the university's provost to look into these allegations. The committee reported evidence of "rampant and flagrant plagiarism" by departmental graduate students over a period spanning more than 20 years. After reviewing 55 engineering theses, the committee members determined that seven faculty members had supervised theses that were plagiarized. It was so blatant that there were even two theses with the same title and same first page, approved by the same professor. Faculty members clearly ignored academic honesty, integrity, and fraud and in that process may have implicitly actually encouraged their students in such behavior (Wasley, 2006).

Sexual Harassment

Another area of perhaps widespread misconduct by graduate faculty and mentors is sexual harassment of their graduate students. Two *Chronicle* articles provide extensive detail on several instances of sexual harassment. These articles focus on sexual abuse of students at two prominent American universities, the University of Texas at Austin and the University of Iowa. Coincidentally, both articles address misconduct by faculty members in music programs. The first article suggests that the unique type of instruction in music training creates a particularly conducive climate of opportunity for professors' sexual abuse of their students. In music schools, the instructional relationship is exceptionally intimate: there is extensive one-on-one instruction, not witnessed by anyone else; teaching takes place in soundproof practice rooms behind closed doors; and touching is frequently necessary for the professor to teach breathing technique or proper fingering on an instrument.

The first *Chronicle* article documents the case of a female student at the University of Texas who filed a sexual harassment complaint against a prominent professor in the School of Music. The hostile environment became apparent as early as in the student's first semester in residence, and Professor D.W. was a leading perpetrator. The student rejected his personal advances and refused to laugh at his off-color sexual jokes. He joked about women breast-feeding in the park, and on another occasion at a holiday party he asked the student to accompany him to a local strip joint. She refused but recounts that he loudly announced at the party that she would be dancing at the strip club that night and "she'll be wearing her dog collar and chain." She was mortified. Several other students corroborated various similar stories about Professor D.W. One doctoral student described a dinner that she and a male graduate student attended at Professor D.W.'s home: on that occasion he sang a song called "Isn't It Awfully Nice to Have a Penis?" and showed the students a naked photograph of himself.

Documents obtained under the state's open-record law show that a university investigation indicated that Professor D.W. and several other faculty colleagues denied that any of the student statements were true (although it does not appear that the investigation involved interviewing any students). The dean of Fine Arts at the University of Texas is also quoted as saying that he doesn't believe that anything at Austin is different from what goes on in schools of music at other U.S. universities. The graduate student received her degree, but not without Professor D.W. submitting a statement in a letter to the university that the student "lacks sufficient musical skills, a good ear, or the ability to produce competent music" (Wilson, 2002).

Not all cases result in the outcomes reported above. Sexual harassment charges can have more severe consequences for both the alleged professor perpetrator and the graduate student "target." Sometimes professors lose their academic appointment; frequently graduate students depart and do not complete their academic program. This last *Chronicle* article documents even more severe and extreme consequences:

Professor M.W. was an internationally acclaimed oboist. He recruited a graduate student to study with him at the University of Iowa. The relationship quickly deteriorated, with the student alleging that he made inappropriate sexual remarks and off-color jokes to her. She claimed she had observed him groping another female student. These complaints were strikingly similar to those of a previous graduate student who had filed a lawsuit against Professor M.W., which had been subsequently dropped. A university investigation confirmed some of these new allegations and required him to undergo antiharassment training.

The student whom he had recruited to the university felt that this hostile learning environment was intolerable, and it led her to leave the University of Iowa at the end of her first year in the graduate program. But the student felt that the university's punishment of Professor M.W. was grossly inadequate. She subsequently filed a complaint with the Iowa Civil Rights Commission and a lawsuit in the U.S. District Court. In the days that followed, articles about this University of Iowa case appeared in a number of newspapers, including the *Chicago Tribune* and the *Des Moines Register*. Professor M.W. was devastated. He feared students would no longer come to Iowa to study with him. He was aspiring to an associate provost position at Iowa and felt that the sexual harassment suit would forever preclude his obtaining that position.

Professor M.W. left a suicide note and killed himself. He was found inside his car in the garage. It was out of gas. Professor M.W.'s body was cold and rigid. This incident followed a widely publicized case at the University of Iowa just three months earlier. A prominent political science professor at the university shot and killed himself following charges of sexual harassment. He had been arrested and put in handcuffs after several female students said he had offered them As for letting him touch their breasts. He was charged with soliciting sex for grades, a felony in Iowa that can carry up to 10 years in jail. Like Professor M.W., he too took his life, believing that the sexual misconduct charges and resulting legal actions would forever ruin his career (Wilson, 2009).

Discussion

As noted at the beginning of this chapter, there are no definitive national assessments to ascertain the pervasiveness of various types of misconduct by academic researchers and instructional faculty. Estimates of faculty misconduct with regard to incidents in graduate training and mentoring are particularly difficult to compile. A principal reason for the lack of data on the frequency or occurrence of misconduct is that many cases are handled internally within the university, most are considered to be private "personnel matters," and there is strong institutional administrative initiative to avoid external publicity of these cases if at all possible in order to "protect the reputation of the university."

Cases of faculty misconduct are nevertheless more likely to be publically disclosed when they involve violation of professional codes of conduct, scientific standards, state laws, or federal regulations. Multiple mechanisms are available to pursue these cases outside the university: state attorneys general offices, the federal Office of Civil Rights, federal agencies' Office of Research Integrity, professional association committees and panels, and news coverage from the national press, particularly the *Chronicle of Higher Education*. Nevertheless, these external avenues are relatively seldom used, and even less so when the affront involves a faculty member's inappropriate relationship with a student.

Indeed, many university faculty members can offer a number of anecdotal accounts of graduate student abuse by institutional faculty members. As noted in Chapter 2, most of those faculty members whom we had asked to contribute inappropriate behavior items for inclusion in our Graduate Teaching and Mentoring Behaviors Inventory (GTMBI) submitted statements of misconduct in which they noted that they had unfortunately witnessed these incidents firsthand at their home institutions. But incidents involving abuse of graduate students are particularly likely to not become public, primarily because students have relatively little power, often distrust the institutional administration to fairly consider their allegations, and often fear retribution that could destroy their professional ambitions.

In reviewing reported incidents of misconduct between a faculty member/mentor and a graduate student/mentee over the past decade in the *Chronicle of Higher Education*, we located only an average of about one incident per year. They are briefly summarized above. These reported incidents are likely only the tip of the iceberg, but they readily convey the extensive variety in the sorts of inappropriate behaviors that most any graduate student might be at risk of encountering. These *Chronicle* cases likewise illustrate that adverse incidents might occur most anyplace in the university; the cases discussed above cover the entire spectrum of graduate programs, from English and music, to laboratory sciences and behavioral sciences, to engineering graduate programs.

In the following chapters, we catalog and analyze even a broader set of behaviors that are viewed by most academics as instances of misconduct by a graduate faculty member toward his or her graduate students.

CHAPTER TWO

Study Design

As noted in the Introduction, there are three primary interrelated sets of norms that have a direct impact on the primary work roles of the professoriate in American university settings. The first set of norms, pertaining to the research and scholarship activity of faculty, has generated an extensive literature documenting the normative structure for these professional activities. The second set of norms addresses prescriptive and proscriptive behaviors related to undergraduate teaching role performance. Analyses of this normative system are addressed in our earlier research on faculty misconduct in collegiate undergraduate teaching (Braxton & Bayer, 1999).

The third set of normative standards for university faculty involves the professorial roles related to graduate program instruction and mentoring. In some measure these normative standards parallel those already documented for research and scholarly performance, as well as those pertaining to undergraduate pedagogy. However, in some cases they are manifested differently; in addition, some normative expectations are relatively unique to graduate programs and relations with graduate students.

Like the earlier literature on the norms to deter scientific fraud and misconduct in the scholar role, and like the study of the core norms related to the undergraduate teaching role, in this volume we empirically derive a complementary set of norms that pertain to the teaching, mentoring, and advising of graduate students. Toward this end, we designed a survey instrument composed of various graduate teaching and mentoring behaviors that might be subject to normative criteria, which was then administered to a cross section of full-time faculty members who provide graduate training in a representative sample of research university graduate programs.

This chapter reports on the design of the instrumentation and the design of the study that employed this instrument. This study surveys faculty in graduate programs, and this chapter also shows the personal and education characteristics of respondents as well as aspects of their work performance and their institutional employment setting.

Survey Instrument

There is no comprehensive compilation of performance expectations for faculty in graduate teaching. Hence we began the development of our Graduate Teaching and Mentoring Behaviors Inventory (GTMBI) by selecting or adapting relevant proscribed behaviors as developed for our study of undergraduate teaching norms with the instrument called the College Teaching Behaviors Inventory (CTBI), employed and shown in *Faculty Misconduct in Collegiate Teaching* (Braxton & Bayer, 1999). However, numerous behaviors in the CTBI were deemed inappropriate and marginal as related to graduate teaching and mentoring; conversely, the CTBI did not include many behaviors that are more uniquely associated with graduate education.

A second set of sources explored to expand the array of behaviors listed in the GTMBI included the American Association of University Professors' *Policy Documents and Reports* (2006), or "Redbook," and codes of conduct of professional disciplinary associations and societies. These are the same sources documented and used previously in relation to the undergraduate teaching norms reported in *Faculty Misconduct in Collegiate Teaching* (see Braxton & Bayer, 1999, chap. 9). However, in this present case, behavioral standards that explicitly address relations with graduate students are reviewed for possible adaptation into the GTMBI. Few statements were found in either the codes of conduct or the AAUP Redbook that explicitly addressed graduate students and graduate education (see Chap. 10). Hence we turned to other sources to expand the list of behaviors to be included in the GTMBI.

Next we added to the list of behaviors incidents we had encountered, or received personal knowledge of, over our years of experience in academe at various universities where we had served during our careers. This included experiences related to us by our graduate students and incidents of faculty misconduct in graduate education that we had encountered as academic administrators or as a result of sitting on academic grievance committees.

Finally, we provided this compilation of possible inappropriate behaviors and instances of faculty misconduct pertaining to graduate education to colleagues in our respective university departments, to several editors of higher education journals, and to 14 other colleagues from other academic institutions who had published articles or books relevant to graduate education, the professoriate, and ethics in academe. The preliminary compilation provided a context of the types of behaviors we wished to elicit from these individuals. Most responded to our request for help in developing the GTMBI and had drafted statements of what they judged as improper behavior that they suggested for inclusion. Remarkably, most of these individuals had suggested for inclusion a behavior with which they had direct experience, as they were aware of inappropriate behavior or misconduct by a faculty member in their own institution.

Based on these various inputs, the GTMBI was constructed using 124 behaviors that fall into one of the following categories: (A) Supervising Graduate Research Assistants (17 items), (B) Mentoring and Advising (18 items), (C) Planning for a Graduate Course or Seminar (10 items), (D) In-Class Practices and Behaviors (36 items), (E) Class/Seminar Grading and Examination Practices (12 items), (F) Directing the Thesis/Dissertation (16 items), and (G) Other Behaviors Regarding Graduate Students and the Graduate Program (15 items). The 124 behaviors were negatively worded to follow Durkheim's (1912/1995) sociological premise that norms are best recognized when they have been violated. While obvious, it must be acknowledged that these 124 behavioral items are not exhaustive. Nor is it possible to compile a complete finite array of all possible behaviors that might meet normative standards applicable to graduate training and mentoring. Nevertheless, the 124 behaviors listed in the survey instrument generally cover transgressions in virtually all domains of the faculty-graduate student relationship.

Although one often thinks of proscriptive norms as being either existing or not existing as regards a particular behavior, the sanctions that may be applied to such a behavior lie along a continuum of severity. We later build on this fact by distinguishing between the strongest, called "inviolable" norms, and somewhat less proscriptive norms we call "admonitory norms" (see Chap. 3). Survey respondents used the following rating system to indicate the degree of their reaction to each behavior: 1, appropriate behavior, should be encouraged; 2, discretionary behavior, neither particularly appropriate nor inappropriate; 3, mildly inappropriate behavior, generally to be ignored; 4, inappropriate behavior, to be handled informally by colleagues or administrators suggesting change or improvement; and 5, very inappropriate behavior, requiring formal administrative intervention.

This section of the instrument, listing 124 faculty behaviors in relation to graduate students, composes the core of the GTMBI. In addition, the survey instrument included a short section on personal demographics and educational background, career characteristics, and disciplinary and institutional affiliations.

The complete instrument, the GTMBI, is shown in Appendix A. The means and standard deviations for the responses to each of the 124 behavior statements are shown in Appendix B.

Survey Sampling Design

The population of inference for this study was full-time, tenured or tenure-track assistant professors, associate professors, and full professors in academic departments with graduate programs in U.S. research universities that offered the PhD. A stratified cluster sampling design was used to develop a sample drawn from this population. The sample strata were academic discipline (biology, chemistry, history, and psychology) and the institutional research category of the Carnegie Foundation for the Advancement of Teaching (very high and high). For each discipline and institutional research category, only universities offering the PhD. in one or more of the four academic disciplines were eligible for random selection. Instead of sampling faculty members within institutions, we used the entire departmental populations.

Sampling of Universities

The Carnegie Foundation for the Advancement of Teaching (2005) categorizes institutions in several ways; we used the "basic" classification. Institutions are first sorted by their degree offerings into groups such as Associates, Baccalaureate, and Doctorate Granting. To be included in Doctorate Granting, a university must award at least 20 doctorates per year. This group is further subdivided into Research Universities (very high research activity) (RU/VH); Research Universities (high research activity) (RU/H); and Doctoral/Research Universities (DRU) based on an index composed of institutional levels of spending on research and development, science and engineering research staff, and doctoral conferrals. Only the RU/VH and the RU/H were included in this study because these institutions award the bulk of all U.S. graduate degrees. At present, the RU/VH category includes 96 universities and the RU/H 103. The use of these two classifications is discussed at length in Chapter 4.

Sampling of Disciplines

Disciplines were selected in part based on Biglan's (1973) classification schema. This schema categorizes academic disciplines as either high or low in paradigmatic development, together with other characteristics. Two representative disciplines with high paradigmatic development (biology and chemistry) and two with low paradigmatic development (history and psychology) were selected. These four are core disciplines offered at nearly every university.

The Biglan typology categorizing paradigmatic development was selected because research using this scheme for academic subject matter areas indicates that faculty members in different academic disciplines differ in their time spent on teaching (Braxton & Hargens, 1996). Therefore, the faculty in these various disciplines presumably may differ in their perception of the importance of the teaching role and in their concern regarding deviant behaviors in relation to graduate student training. Selection of these academic subjects allows the testing of differences in the degree of impropriety associated with these norms by faculty members affiliated with these disciplines. The differences between disciplines are discussed in Chapter 4.

Selection and Administration Procedures

The populations of high and very high research institutions were downloaded as Excel files from the Carnegie Foundation for the Advancement of Teaching. There were 96 very high research institutions and 103 high research institutions. Within each of the Carnegie classifications, a listing of faculty members was compiled for the departments in each of the four disciplines: biology, chemistry, history, and psychology.

For each discipline and research category (4 × 2 = 8), the list of institutions was randomly sorted using Excel's random number generator. A list of 24 institutions was drawn in each of the 8 groups. The first 20 institutions were the primary sample. The remaining 4 were to be used if and only if the first 20 institutions did not yield a sample of at least 375 faculty members. Some institutions that were drawn had to be discarded. Institutions dropped included those that did not offer a PhD in one or more of the 4 disciplinary departments of interest. Also excluded were those institutions that did not have that disciplinary department, subsumed that disciplinary concentration within a larger department, or divided it into several separate departments. Those institutions outside the 50 states (i.e., in Puerto Rico) and those that had insufficient information on their Web sites to obtain all information needed were also excluded.

For the very high research institutions, the initial random draw of 20 institutions provided sufficient faculty members in each of the 4 disciplines. The high research institutions, however, were less likely to offer PhD's and generally had smaller faculties. For the high research–psychology sample, the 20 initial institutions plus 3 of the 4 extra proved sufficient. For the 3 other high categories, the populations had to be resampled. Using the same random number technique, the first 10 institutions that were not already in the sample were added. These were used in the order drawn until the minimum of 375 faculty members' names was reached for each of the 4 disciplines. In all cases, however, the initial list of 20 as well as complete departments were used even if this led to over 375 names. Because many PhD-granting departments had faculty sizes that were substantially more than 20 members, several of the 8 institutional-type-by-discipline cells contained substantially more than 375 individuals.

The second sampling stage, that of the faculty members within departments, was conducted using institutional Web sites. All departments listed faculty members with additional information such as phone number, rank, and e-mail address. We were interested only in the name, academic rank, and e-mail address. The name was used only to identify individuals during the sampling phase. In some cases department Web sites did not provide all necessary information; in those cases, university-wide faculty directories were consulted. Faculty members without reported e-mail addresses or without designated academic ranks were dropped. Instead of sampling faculty members within institutions, the entire departmental populations were used. Only tenure-track faculty members were included in the sample. Faculty members who were designated as lecturers, instructors, professors of the practice, clinical professors, research professors, visiting professors, or emeritus faculty were dropped. The final sample contained 439 very high biology, 519 very high chemistry, 540 very high history, 591 very high psychology, 393 high biology, 389 high chemistry, 380 high history, and 398 high psychology faculty. This generates a total sample size of 3,649 faculty members.

The survey was conducted during the 2006–2007 academic year via the Web using proprietary survey software and administered by the Virginia Tech Center for Survey Research. An advisory e-mail was sent to all e-mail addresses stating the importance of the study and an appeal to participate by completing the forthcoming GTMBI. A total of 137 individuals had invalid or undeliverable survey addresses. These were dropped from the survey, yielding a sample size of 3,512. The link to the electronic version of the GTMBI was then sent to each of the remaining faculty members, and they were requested to electronically return their completed survey. A reminder e-mail was sent seven days later. Approximately three weeks after the initial e-mailing, a second request with the link to the electronic version of the GTMBI was sent to nonrespondents.

The Final Sample

A total of 820 individuals completed the GTMBI. Of the 820 respondents, 27 were removed from further analysis because their characteristics did not match those of the population of inference for this study: full-time, tenured or tenure-track assistant, associate, or full professors. Either these 27 individuals had their academic appointment information incorrect when we drew the sample, or their status changed in the interim between sample selection and response to the survey. The removal of these 27 individuals produced a final sample of 793 respondents who met these criteria and were used in the various statistical analyses conducted in this volume.

Of the 3,512 contacted by e-mail, 793 meeting sampling criteria completed the GTMBI. This yields a response rate of 22.6%. We determined the representativeness of this final sample of 793 respondents by comparing individuals who responded to the initial e-mail request linking to the Web version of the GTMBI with those individuals who responded to subsequent e-mail requests to fill out the GTMBI. This method, recommended by Goode and Hatt (1952) and Leslie (1972), is frequently used to determine response bias in mail surveys. The logic of this approach is that later responders are more like nonresponders in that they would have probably been nonresponders if a follow-up e-mail message had not been sent. If statistically significant differences between initial and subsequent e-mail messages on the variables used in the analyses of this volume are identified, then some bias is evident. The failure to identify statistically significant differences suggests that no bias exists. These statistical tests were conducted at the .05 level of statistical significance rather than the more conservative .025 level used in subsequent chapters. We used a more liberal level of statistical significance because of our desire to detect any possible respondent bias.

In summary, we identified no response bias on the following variables: institutional type, academic discipline, gender, citizenship status, professional age, academic rank, administrative experience, the three indices of participation in graduate studies (see Chapter 6), both measures of research activity (see Chapter 6), and tenure status. We also identified no response bias on all of the admonitory normative patterns described in Chapter 3 and all but one of the inviolable normative patterns delineated in Chapter 3. However, some bias exists on administrative experience, as later respondents tended to have more administrative experience whereas initial respondents tended to have less. Bias also exists on the inviolable normative pattern of whistle-blowing suppression, as initial respondents tended to voice more distain for the proscribed behaviors of this normative pattern than individuals who responded to subsequent e-mailings.

Thus we conclude that the obtained sample is generally representative of the population of inference of this study. Nevertheless, we view the response bias on administrative experience and the inviolable normative pattern of whistle-blowing suppression as limitations to the analyses reported in this book. We exhibit the detailed findings of our statistical tests to ascertain response bias in Appendix C.

Respondent Characteristics

The survey instrument, the Graduate Teaching and Mentoring Behaviors Inventory, included a short section on the respondents' personal, professional, and career characteristics. While a few respondents elected to skip answering some of these questions, the data displayed in Table 2.1 provide a descriptive snapshot of respondents.

Of the respondents, somewhat more than one-third (35.1%) were women and almost two-thirds (64.9%) were men. Most (83.5%) were U.S. citizens (either native born or naturalized). The professional age (years since earning highest degree) of these university faculty members averaged almost 20 years; fewer than 12% were 5 or fewer years beyond their graduate school years.

Table 2.1 Personal, Professional, and Career Characteristics of Respondents to the GTMBI

Characteristic	*N*[a]	Percentage
Gender		
Female	271	35.1
Male	502	64.9
Citizenship		
U.S. citizen, native born or naturalized	648	83.5
Not U.S. citizen	128	16.5
Professional age[b]		
5 years or less	89	11.8
6 to 10 years	127	16.8
11 to 20 years	193	25.5
21 to 30 years	175	23.1
More than 30 years	172	22.8
Type of academic employer[c]		
Very high research university	405	51.1
High research university	388	48.9
Disciplinary department		
Biology	173	21.8
Chemistry	211	26.6
History	223	28.1
Psychology	186	23.5
Academic rank		
Assistant professor	202	25.6
Associate professor	212	26.8
Professor	376	47.6
Tenure status		
Tenured	585	73.8
Untenured but on tenure track	208	26.2
Administrative experience		
Current or former department head/chair or dean	182	23.0
No academic administrative experience	608	77.0
Number of graduate courses/seminars taught[d]		
None	46	5.8
1 or 2	265	33.7
3 or 4	311	39.5
5 or more	165	21.0
Number of major professors for grad students[d]		
None	64	8.1
1 or 2	171	21.8
3 or 4	235	30.0
5 to 10	271	34.6
11 or more	43	5.5

continues

Table 2.1 Continued

Characteristic	N[a]	Percentage
Number of graduate student committees[d,e]		
None	26	3.3
1 to 4	249	32.1
5 to 10	344	44.3
11 or more	158	20.3
Articles published during the past three years		
None	37	4.7
1–2	147	18.7
3–4	174	22.1
5–10	239	30.4
11 or more	190	24.1
Books or monographs published during the past three years		
None	524	68.2
1	168	21.9
2	46	6.0
3 or more	30	3.9

[a]Sums may be less than 793 due to missing data for some respondents.
[b]Number of years since earning highest degree.
[c]Based on university categories defined by the Carnegie Foundation for the Advancement of Teaching.
[d]Numbers for past three years combined.
[e]Exclusive of committees for those graduate students for whom the faculty respondent also served as major professor.

The sample was drawn from the two highest categories of research universities as defined by the Carnegie Foundation for the Advancement of Teaching. Respondents were almost evenly divided between these two institutional employment settings: 51.1% were at the very high research universities, and 48.9% were at high research universities. The sampling design also used academic departmental affiliation: the final sample of participating respondents included 173 biology faculty members (21.8% of the total sample), 211 faculty (26.6%) in chemistry departments, 223 faculty (28.1%) in history departments, and 186 faculty (23.5%) in psychology departments. All of these departments offered graduate programs.

The sampling design was restricted to only faculty members who held full-time academic positions at their university. Moreover, all had to be either tenured (73.8%) or untenured but on tenure track (26.2%). Approximately one-fourth of the respondents held the rank of assistant professor (25.6%), and an additional one-fourth were associate professors (26.8%). The remaining respondents (47.6%) held the rank of professor at their university. Moreover, almost one-fourth of the respondents (23.0%) had academic administrative experience as either a current or former department head/chair or as a college dean.

Articles, books, and monographs published during the past three years index the research activity of academic professionals. Only 4.7% of faculty respondents to the GTMBI had no articles published in journals during the past three years. In contrast, over two-thirds (68.2%) of these faculty members had not published a book or monograph. However, one book or monograph was published by 21.9% of these responding individuals. At the other extreme, nearly a quarter of faculty respondents (24.1%) had published 11 or more articles during the past three years, and 3.9% of these academics had published three or more books or monographs.

The remaining descriptive statistics on the respondents to the GTMBI relate to faculty members' involvement in their graduate program. As shown in Table 2.1, almost 95% had taught at least one graduate course or graduate seminar in the past three years. More than 9 in 10 had served as a major professor for one or more graduate students. Less than 5% had not served on any graduate student committees in the past three years; 1 in 5 had served on 11 or more graduate committees in the past three years.

Discussion

Analyses in the following chapters offer more detail on how these 793 university faculty members perceive various aspects of deviance or misconduct in graduate program teaching and the mentoring of graduate students. Strong proscriptive norms are derived and identified from these faculty members' responses to the GTMBI. Chapter 3 describes the inviolable and admonitory normative arrays that constitute the normative structure of graduate study.

Then the analyses turn to how the characteristics described above relate to the normative orientations of these faculty members. Chapter 4 focuses on the possible influence related to one's job setting: the level of research at the respondents' university, and the departmental disciplinary affiliation of the respondents. This is followed by the analysis of some of the other background and career characteristics described in this chapter and how they may impact faculty members' perceptions of the severity attributed to the derived proscriptive normative orientations.

CHAPTER THREE

The Normative Structure of Graduate Education

Norms are prescribed and proscribed patterns of behavior (Merton, 1968, 1973). Emile Durkheim contended that norms are best recognized when violated (1912/1995). The violation of a norm evokes varying degrees of moral outrage or anger that indexes its social significance. Moral outrage or anger finds expression in a range of actions that members of a social group believe should result because of a norm violation. Norms whose violations are believed by members of a social group to warrant severe action meet the criterion for designation as an inviolable norm (Braxton & Bayer, 1999). In contrast, norms whose violations provoke less indignation than that elicited by transgressions of inviolable norms meet the criterion for status as an admonitory norm. Individual faculty members express an uncertain response to such violations. Admonitions not to violate such norms result because of such uncertainty. Accordingly, this chapter addresses the question posited in the Introduction: What are the inviolable and admonitory normative patterns that constitute the normative structure for graduate education?

Inviolable Norms

Following Braxton and Bayer (1999), specific behaviors included in the Graduate Teaching and Mentoring Behaviors Inventory (GTMBI) meet the criterion for designation as a violation of an inviolable norm if their mean values are 4.00 or higher on the range-of-actions scale described in Chapter 2. Appendix B exhibits the means and standard deviations for each of the 124 behaviors of the GTMBI. Of the 124 behaviors, 40 meet the criterion for designation as a violation of an inviolable norm. A mean value of 4.00 or higher signifies that respondents' perceptions range from viewing a specific behavior as inappropriate behavior to be handled informally by colleagues or administrators suggesting change or improvement, to the perception that the specific behavior is very inappropriate and requires formal administrative intervention.

The existence of these 40 specific proscribed behaviors raises the question: What inviolable normative patterns underlie these 40 proscribed behaviors? A principal components factor analysis was used to address this question. A five-factor solution was determined using the scree test. These five factors were rotated using the varimax method of rotation. The five inviolable normative patterns identified in order of their percentage of variance explained are *disrespect toward student efforts*, *misappropriation of student work*, *harassment of students*, *whistle-blowing suppression*, and *directed research malfeasance*. These five normative patterns include 36 of the 40 specific behaviors that meet the criterion for designation as a violation of an inviolable norm. The remaining four specific proscribed behaviors failed to load on any of the five normative patterns. These four proscribed behaviors include A4 (A professor diverts a graduate student to work in his/her personal "start-up firm" to the detriment of the student's research progress), B17 (A faculty member assigns their graduate assistant to take responsibility to teach the professor's assigned undergraduate class for the semester without administrative approval), F5 (Even when a student's proposed thesis/dissertation research design appears to require it, the major professor advises bypassing animal subjects or human subjects institutional review committees), and F15 (The thesis/dissertation advisor urges his/her graduate student to simultaneously submit the same article out of their thesis/dissertation to more than one refereed journal). These four proscribed behaviors are not included in any subsequent data analyses of this volume because they failed to load on any of the five normative arrays.

Each of these five inviolable proscribed normative patterns is described in this chapter. Their description occurs in order of the variance explained by each factor representing a normative pattern.

Disrespect toward Student Efforts

This normative pattern proscribes disrespecting the efforts students make in various aspects of their graduate studies. The 14 specific proscribed behaviors that make up this normative pattern, which are displayed in Table 3.1, show disrespect toward the efforts of students in the classroom, graded assignments, thesis/dissertation work, and the research apprenticeship. Put differently, this normative pattern provides moral boundaries for these critical aspects of graduate education. Specifically, such proscribed behaviors as making condescending remarks to students in class (D26) and routinely ignoring comments or questions from international graduate students (D25) relate to forms of disrespecting the efforts of students in the classroom. Prohibited behaviors pertaining to graded assignments or the awarding of grades include allowing personal friendships with a graduate student to intrude on the objective grading of their work (E7), no term papers, tests, lab reports, or other criteria to assign the final grades for a course (E10), the awarding of A's to all graduate students enrolled in a seminar regardless of whether the students do any assignments or attend class (E11), and social, personal, or other non-academic characteristics are taken into account in the assigning of grades (E8). Disrespect toward the efforts of students in their thesis/dissertation work include such proscribed behaviors as a student consistently being unable to get an appointment with their thesis/dissertation advisor within three or four weeks to discuss issues concerning the thesis/dissertation (F8), and a professor delays the graduation of his or her best graduate students in order to keep them around longer (F16). Lastly, the inviolable behavior of not permitting students to express viewpoints different from those of the professor (D21) cuts across all of the above-mentioned aspects of graduate study. Table 3.1 displays the other specific proscribed behaviors that constitute this normative orientation. This particular normative orientation finds concrete expression in actual incidents of graduate faculty teaching and mentoring improprieties described in the section titled "The Demeaning and Contemptuous Professor" in Chapter 1 of this volume.

A substantial degree of consensus exists among faculty members on the inviolability of this normative pattern. Specifically, Table 3.1 shows that 72.2% of faculty members responding to the GTMBI view the behaviors constituting this normative configuration with a high degree of disdain (rated 4.00 or higher).

Table 3.1 Factor Loadings of Specific Behaviors of the Inviolable Norm of Disrespect toward Student Efforts

GTMBI specific behaviors	Factor loadings
D21. Students are not permitted to express viewpoints different from those of the professor.	.649
F6. A student consistently cannot get an appointment with the thesis/dissertation advisor within three or four weeks to discuss issues concerning the thesis/dissertation.	.649
E11. A professor routinely awards A's to all graduate students enrolled in his/her seminar regardless of whether the students do any assignments or attend class.	.646
D25. The professor routinely ignores comments or questions from international graduate students.	.643
F7. The student's advisor often misses deadlines that affect the student's work or career.	.622
E9. Individual student course evaluations, where students can be identified, are read prior to the determination of final seminar grades.	.603
E7. The professor allows personal friendships with a graduate students to intrude on the objective grading of their work.	.597
G15. A faculty member intentionally misrepresents graduate program requirements in order to recruit a graduate student.	.574
D26. A professor makes condescending remarks to a student in class.	.562
E10. No term papers, tests, lab reports, or other criteria are used by the professor for assigning final grades.	.561
E8. Social, personal, or other non-academic characteristics of graduate students are taken into account in the assigning of grades.	.504
D23. The professor frequently makes negative comments in class about a student's dress, speech, or manner.	.486
E6. Individual graduate students are offered extra-credit work in order to improve their final course grade after the term is completed.	.483
F16. The professor delays the graduation of his/her best graduate students, in order to keep them around longer.	.475

Note: Percentage of variance explained = 29.83. Cronbach alpha = 0.91. Extent of consensus: 4.00 to 5.00 = 72.2%; 3.00 to 3.99 = 26.7%.

Misappropriation of Student Work

The failure to give graduate students the credit they deserve for their scholarly efforts characterizes this inviolable normative configuration. In the section titled "Plagiarism, Fraud, and Publication Authorship Disputes" in Chapter 1, we describe actual incidents of violations of this normative pattern. This particular norm demarcates inappropriate behavior of graduate faculty members in their role as "master" in the research apprenticeship for doctoral students. Table 3.2 presents the 11 specific censured behaviors that constitute this normative orientation.

Three of these rebuked behaviors give crisp meaning to this particular norm. One pertains to the apprenticeship experience of giving doctoral students the opportunity to conduct reviews of manuscripts or grant proposals received by the major professor. Specifically, this behavior involves asking the graduate student to prepare a review of manuscripts or grant proposals that the professor represents as his or her own review (A11). The other two proscribed behaviors relating to the role of the graduate student in conducting research as a part of the apprenticeship experience are as follows: a professor routinely removes graduate students from research projects when they begin to show innovative results (G1), and a faculty member publishes an article without offering co-authorship to a graduate assistant who has made a substantial conceptual or methodological contribution to the article (A10).

Additional rebuked behaviors pertinent to the role of graduate students in assisting their major professor in research include the professors failing to provide or ensure safe research conditions or safe laboratory environments for their graduate assistants (A9), routinely blaming graduate students when his or her own research work is called into question (G2), and putting a student's name as co-author of a publication even though the student made no contribution to the work (A13).

Other reproved behaviors involve misappropriating students' work by diverting them from the work of their research apprenticeship — for example, routinely borrowing money from advisees (B11) and asking graduate research assistants to perform such personal chores as baby-sitting or running household errands as a part of their assistantship duties (A3).

Moreover, a high degree of consensus exists on the inviolability of this normative orientation. As indicated by Table 3.2, the overwhelming majority (87.1% rated 4.00 or higher) of faculty respondents perceive the specific behaviors constituting this norm as highly inappropriate.

Table 3.2 Factor Loadings of Specific Behaviors of the Inviolable Norm of Misappropriation of Student Work

GTMBI specific behaviors	Factor loadings
A11. A professor asks a graduate student to prepare a review of a manuscript or grant proposal that the professor then represents as his/her own review.	.638
A12. A professor routinely removes graduate students from research projects when they begin to show innovative results.	.627
A10. A faculty member publishes an article without offering co-authorship to a graduate assistant who has made a substantial conceptual or methodological contribution to the article.	.540
G2. A professor routinely blames their graduate students when his/her or her own research work is called into question.	.530
B11. A professor routinely borrows money from advisees.	.528
B6. The mentor fails to write a letter of recommendation that he/she had agreed to send for a graduate student.	.524
A9. A professor fails to provide or ensure safe research conditions or safe laboratory environments for his/her graduate assistants.	.490
G1. A faculty member publishes an article using innovative ideas derived from a graduate student's term paper without acknowledging the student's contribution.	.472
A3. A faculty member sometimes asks his/her graduate research assistants to perform personal chores such as babysitting or running household errands as a part of their assistantship duties.	.467
G3. A professor accepts costly gifts from graduate students.	.432
A13. A graduate student's mentor puts the student's name as coauthor of a publication even though the student made no contribution to the work.	.413

Note: Percentage of variance explained = 5.24. Cronbach alpha = 0.83. Extent of consensus: 4.00 to 5.00 = 87.1%; 3.00 to 3.99 = 12.97%.

Harassment of Students

The normative pattern of *harassment of students* addresses graduate faculty behaviors that occur within and outside the classroom. We describe actual incidents of violations of this normative array in the section titled "Sexual Harassment" in Chapter 1. This norm consists of six specific censured behaviors, displayed in Table 3.3. These six behaviors give clear meaning to this particular inviolable

Table 3.3 Factor Loadings of Specific Behaviors of the Inviolable Norm of Harassment of Students

GTMBI specific behaviors	Factor loadings
D32. The professor makes suggestive sexual comments to a graduate student enrolled in his/her seminar.	.739
D30. The professor sometimes makes racist or sexist remarks in class.	.625
D31. While able to conduct the graduate class, the faculty member attends class while obviously intoxicated.	.623
B13. A professor has a sexual relationship with a graduate student in his/her program.	.526
G5. A male professor tells a female graduate student to avoid his specialty because only men can excel in it.	.474
D33. A faculty member criticizes the academic performance of a graduate student in front of other graduate students.	.465

Note: Percentage of variance explained = 4.38. Cronbach alpha = 0.70. Extent of consensus: 4.00 to 5.00 = 89.7%; 3.00 to 3.99 = 10.07%.

norm. The harassment of graduate students within the classroom setting includes such rebuked professorial behaviors as making suggestive sexual comments (D32), sometimes making racist or sexist remarks in class (D30), and, while able to conduct class, attending class while obviously intoxicated (D31).

Proscribed out-of-class graduate faculty behaviors reflective of the norm of *harassment of students* include professors having sexual relationships with graduate students in their program (B13), a male professor telling a female graduate student to avoid his specialty because only men can excel in it (G5), and criticism of the academic performance of a graduate student in front of other graduate students (D33).

The vast majority of faculty respondents regard the behaviors making up this normative pattern with considerable contempt, as 89.7% of faculty respondents rated this normative pattern 4.00 or higher on the possible actions scale. Thus, a considerable degree of consensus exists on the inviolability of the norm of harassment of students.

Whistle-Blowing Suppression

Whistle-blowing entails the reporting of suspected misconduct by the employer or one of its employees (Lee, 1999). The inviolable norm of *whistle-blowing*

Table 3.4 Factor Loadings of Specific Behaviors of the Inviolable Norm of Whistle-Blowing Suppression

GTMBI specific behaviors	Factor loadings
A16. A professor advises his/her graduate research assistant who has personally witnessed an incident of research misconduct by another graduate assistant to ignore the incident.	.846
A17. A professor advises his/her graduate assistant who has personally witnessed an incident of research misconduct by a faculty member to ignore the incident.	.792
A15. A faculty member fails to report a graduate research assistant who has engaged in an act of research or scholarly misconduct.	.695

Note: Percentage of variance explained = 3.98. Cronbach alpha = 0.83. Extent of consensus: 4.00 to 5.00 = 88.9%; 3.00 to 3.99 = 9.4%.

suppression applies to personally known incidents of scientific misconduct. Table 3.4 exhibits the three reproached behaviors that delineate this particular inviolable norm. Two of these behaviors entail a graduate faculty member advising a graduate student to ignore a personally witnessed incident of research misconduct by either another graduate student (A16) or faculty member (A17). The failure of a faculty member to report a graduate research assistant who has engaged in research or scholarly misconduct (A15) is the third proscribed behavior of this particular inviolable normative configuration. Like the norm of *misappropriation of student work*, this particular inviolable norm sets moral parameters for the research apprenticeship of graduate education.

Furthermore, *whistle-blowing suppression* approaches almost undisputed status as an inviolable norm: 88.9% of faculty respondents to the GTMI espouse a high degree of disdain (rated 4.00 or higher) for the behaviors that constitute this normative orientation.

Directed Research Malfeasance

Like *whistle-blowing suppression*, the inviolable norm of *directed research malfeasance* involves incidents of research misconduct. In the case of this normative pattern, a graduate professor instructs his or her graduate research assistant to engage in wrongdoing. This wrongdoing takes the form of either instructing the graduate assistant to alter databooks or lab notes to support a study's hypothesis (A5) or instructing the graduate research assistant to fabricate citations for a publication

Table 3.5 Factor Loadings of Specific Behaviors of the Inviolable Norm of Directed Research Malfeasance

GTMBI specific behaviors	Factor loadings
A5. A professor instructs his/her graduate research assistant to alter databooks or lab notes to support a study's hypotheses.	.735
A6. The professor instructs the research assistant to fabricate citations for a publication.	.708

Note: Percentage of variance explained = 3.32. Cronbach alpha = 0.37. Extent of consensus: 4.00 to 5.00 = 99.6%; 3.00 to 3.99 = 0.40%.

(A6). Table 3.5 displays these two forms of directed research malfeasance. In the section titled "Faculty-Directed Research Malfeasance" in Chapter 1, we describe a specific incident of a violation of this particular inviolable norm.

Table 3.5 indicates that almost total consensus obtains on the inviolability of the norm of *directed research malfeasance;* 99.6% of faculty respondents to the GTMBI view the behaviors reflective of this normative configuration as worthy of a high degree of censure (rated 4.00 or higher).

Admonitory Norms

Admonitory norms consist of specific inappropriate behaviors that receive a mean value of between 3.00 and 3.99 on the possible action scale, the scale that indexes the degree of moral outrage or anger that denigrated behaviors incite (Braxton & Bayer, 1999). This range of mean values falls between "mildly inappropriate, generally to be ignored" behavior (3.00) and "inappropriate behavior, to be handled informally by colleagues or administrators suggesting change or improvement" (4.00) on the possible actions scale used in the GTMBI. Such a range suggests a reproved but undecided type of response to a given behavior. A total of 69 specific behaviors of the GTMBI meet the criterion for designation as an admonitory norm. Appendix B includes the mean values and standard deviations of these 69 behaviors as well as the remaining behaviors included in the GTMBI. These 69 rebuked behaviors give rise to the question: What admonitory normative patterns underlie these proscribed behaviors? A principal components factor analysis was used to address this question. Using the scree test, an eight-factor solution resulted. The varimax method was used to rotate these eight factors. The resulting eight admonitory norms, in order of the percentage of variance that they explain, are as follows: (1) *neglectful teaching*, (2) *inadequate advising/mentoring*, (3) *degradation of faculty colleagues*, (4) *negligent thesis/dissertation advising*, (5) *insufficient course structure*, (6) *pedagogical narrowness*, (7) *student assignment misallocation*, and (8) *graduate program disregard*.

These eight admonitory normative clusters include 61 of the 69 reproved specific behaviors identified as meeting the criterion for designation as an admonitory norm. Thus, eight specific GTMBI specific behaviors failed to load on any of the eight admonitory normative patterns. These specific behaviors are A2 (a faculty member rarely gives any work to their assigned graduate assistant); A14 (the professor sends a research assistant to a national conference to present a paper to which the student has made minimal or no contribution); C6 (a professor will not provide information to graduate students about the content of his/her seminar for the next semester so that students might know whether it is a course they should take; C9 (assigned books and articles are not put on library reserve by the professor on a timely basis for graduate student use); D22 (the professor expresses impatience with a slow learner in class); D35 (the professor doesn't care to learn the names of the graduate students enrolled in his/her seminar); E3 (written comments on tests and papers are consistently not made by the professor); and F14 (a professor presses a graduate student to submit work for publication before the student regards the research results to be verified/confirmed). Given that these eight rebuked behaviors failed to load on any of the eight admonitory normative arrays, none of the subsequent statistical analyses in this volume include these eight GTMBI behaviors.

These eight admonitory normative configurations are described in this chapter. Their descriptions follow the order of the variance explained by each factor depicting a normative pattern.

Neglectful Teaching

Neglectful teaching reproves professorial behavior that displays a lack of commitment and effort in the role of graduate level of teaching. Put differently, this norm admonishes faculty not to neglect their teaching. The 15 specific behaviors that constitute this normative array are contained in Table 3.6.

These proscribed behaviors pertain to the conduct of faculty members teaching graduate-level courses. Several of these specific censured behaviors relate to the manner in which seminar classes are carried out. They include canceling most seminar classes during the term to allow more time for graduate students to read course materials or to write a paper (D10), providing few comments and

Table 3.6 Factor Loadings of Specific Behaviors of the Admonitory Norm of Neglectful Teaching

GTMBI specific behaviors	Factor loadings
D10. The professor cancels most seminar classes during the term, saying it is to allow more time for the graduate students to read course materials or to write a paper.	.644
D1. The professor is routinely late for the class meetings.	.603
D9. After the first few weeks of class, the professor provides few comments and questions while requiring graduate students to conduct the class seminar sessions for the rest of the term.	.594
D3. The professor frequently uses profanity in class.	.558
D13. The professor does not assign some of the seminar materials that students had been told to purchase.	.553
D8. The professor routinely holds the class beyond its scheduled ending time.	.552
D12. The professor does not follow the course outline or syllabus for most of the seminar.	.551
D16. The professor frequently introduces opinions on religious, political, and social issues clearly outside the realm of seminar content.	.534
C10. The professor changes seminar meeting times immediately before the term begins and without consulting enrolled graduate students.	.529
D4. The professor meets the class without having reviewed pertinent materials for the day.	.499
E5. The professor allows some graduate students to do alternative assignments without making this option generally known to all class members.	.464
D29. The professor practices poor personal hygiene and regularly has offensive body odor.	.436
D19. A professor devotes content of all of his/her seminar sessions solely to his/her own research and publications.	.429
E2. Graded tests and papers are not promptly returned to students by the professor.	.427
E4. The professor changes the grading base or criteria after the course has begun.	.420

Note: Percentage of variance explained = 10.4. Cronbach alpha = 0.92. Extent of consensus: 4.00–5.00 = 20.9%, 3.00 to 3.99 = 57.3%, 2.00–2.99 = 21.7%.

questions while requiring graduate students to conduct the class seminar sessions for the rest of the term after the first few weeks of class (D9), failing to assign some of the seminar materials that students were told to purchase (D13), not following the course outline or syllabus for most of the seminar (D12), and devoting the content of all of the seminar sessions solely to one's research and publications (D19).

Other rebuked faculty behaviors that pertain to the conduct of graduate-level courses include being routinely late for class meetings (D1), meeting the class without having reviewed pertinent materials for the day (D4), not promptly returning graded tests and papers to students (E2), and changing the grading base or criteria after the course has begun (E4).

The majority of respondents (57.1%) to the GTMBI view this normative pattern as meeting the criterion for designation as an admonitory norm (rated 3.00 to 3.99 on the possible actions scale). Put differently, some degree of consensus exists on the admonitory status of neglectful teaching. However, slightly more than a fifth of the respondents view this normative pattern as inviolable (20.9%), and another fifth (21.7%) view the behaviors of this norm as falling between discretionary behavior and mildly inappropriate behavior, generally to be ignored (2 to 2.99 on the possible actions scale).

Inadequate Advising/Mentoring

The admonitory norm of *inadequate advising/mentoring* rebukes graduate faculty members who counsel or mentor their graduate student advisees in an insufficient manner. Table 3.7 displays the 12 specific proscribed behaviors that delineate the admonishments of this particular norm. Inadequacies reproved by this normative pattern touch on such aspects of advising and mentoring graduate students as counsel on degree requirements, preparation for academic careers, and the treatment of advisees. To elaborate, this norm censures the failure of graduate advisors to inform their advisees of the requirements for the completion of their degrees (B1).

Proscribed inadequacies in preparing advisees for academic careers include not preparing students for their paper presentations and critiques at professional conferences (B15), requiring all graduate students to use the same outdated methodology in preparation of their thesis or dissertation (B5), requiring graduate teaching assistants to grade all essay exams from their undergraduate classes without providing guidelines to the graduate assistant or reviewing any grades assigned by the teaching assistant (B16), avoiding giving career or job

Table 3.7 Factor Loadings of Specific Behaviors of the Admonitory Norm of Inadequate Advising/Mentoring

GTMBI specific behaviors	Factor loadings
B4. A faculty advisor ignores his/her students whose academic and research interests are not similar to his/her own.	.658
B3. A mentor shows favoritism to those graduate students with the most academic promise and neglects those students judged to have lesser degrees of academic promise.	.652
B2. The professor takes on more graduate advisees than he/she can handle.	.646
B7. A graduate student's advisor fails to help the advisee make professional contacts needed to secure a position after graduation.	.617
B1. A graduate advisor fails to inform his/her advisees of the requirements for completion of their degrees.	.590
B14. A professor avoids giving career or job advice when asked by a graduate student.	.552
B15. The graduate student's advisor does not prepare the student for their paper presentations and critique at professional conferences.	.534
B8. A graduate student advisee is treated in a condescending manner by his/her advisor.	.471
B5. A graduate student advisor requires all of his/her graduate students to use the same outdated methodology in preparation of their thesis or dissertation.	.469
B9. A professor routinely criticizes his/her advisees to other faculty members.	.468
B16. A faculty member requires his/her graduate teaching assistant to grade all essay exams from his/her undergraduate classes without providing any guidelines to the graduate assistant or reviewing any grades assigned by the teaching assistant.	.439
B18. A graduate student's advisor routinely fails to show up for appointments made by the graduate advisee.	.437

Note: Percentage of variance explained = 9.59. Cronbach alpha = 0.91. Extent of consensus: 4.00–5.00 = 21.0%; 3.00–3.99 = 53.9%; 2.00–2.99 = 24.6%.

advice when asked by a graduate student (B14), and failing to help an advisee make professional contacts needed to secure a position after graduation (B7).

Admonishments regarding the treatment of advisees involve not ignoring students whose academic and research interests are not similar to one's own (B4), showing favoritism to those graduate students with the most academic promise and neglecting those students judged to have lesser degrees of academic promise (B3), treating an advisee in a condescending manner (B8), routinely criticizing advisees to other faculty members (B9), routinely failing to show up for appointments made by a graduate advisee (B18), and taking on more graduate advisees than one can handle (B2).

A slim majority of faculty respondents view this normative orientation as admonitory, given that 53.9% of respondents rated it between 3.00 and 3.99 on the possible actions scale. About one-fifth of GTMBI respondents view this normative configuration as inviolable, whereas almost one-fourth (24.6%) view the associated behaviors as between discretionary behavior and mildly inappropriate behavior, generally to be ignored (rated 2.00 to 2.99 on the possible actions scale). These three sets of percentages underscore the uncertainty of faculty response to violations of this particular norm.

Degradation of Faculty Colleagues

This normative array takes to task graduate faculty members who debase their colleagues to other faculty members or to graduate students. Although this norm consists of the eight rebuked behaviors shown in Table 3.8, four pertain particularly to the degradation of faculty colleagues. These four reproved behaviors include making negative comments in a faculty meeting about the graduate courses offered by a colleague (G8), making derogatory remarks to graduate students about certain research methods used by other department faculty members (G6), making negative comments about a colleague's graduate courses in public to graduate students (G9), and aggressively promoting enrollment in one's courses at the expense of the graduate courses offered by departmental colleagues (G10).

Although the mean calculated for this particular norm meets the criterion for an admonitory norm (mean = 3.44), consensus fails to obtain. Of the faculty respondents to the GTMBI, 45.4% view this norm as meeting the criterion for designation as an admonitory norm. In addition, a bit more than a fourth (26.9%) of the respondents view this norm as inviolable, and another fourth (27.1%) regard the behaviors that constitute this norm as either discretionary or mildly inappropriate, generally to be ignored (2.00 to 2.99 on the possible actions scale).

Table 3.8 Factor Loadings of Specific Behaviors of the Admonitory Norm of Degradation of Faculty Colleagues

GTMBI specific behaviors	Factor loadings
G8. A faculty member makes negative comments in a faculty meeting about the graduate courses offered by a colleague.	.747
G6. The professor makes derogatory remarks to graduate students about certain research methods used by other departmental faculty members.	.740
G9. A faculty member makes negative comments about a colleague's graduate courses in public to graduate students.	.733
G10. A faculty member aggressively promotes enrollment in his/her courses at the expense of the graduate courses offered by departmental colleagues.	.536
G4. A professor tells a graduate student who is in good academic standing that the student is destined to fail his/her preliminary or qualifying exams.	.465
B12. A professor frequently socializes with some advisees while intentionally avoiding socializing with others.	.437
D27. A cynical attitude toward the seminar subject matter is expressed in class by the professor.	.431
D34. The professor pits graduate students against each other by assigning them competing projects.	.426

Note: Percentage of variance explained = 7.27. Cronbach alpha = 0.88. Extent of consensus: 4.00–5.00 = 26.9%; 3.00–3.99 = 45.4%; 2.00–2.99 = 27.1%.

These faculty perceptions reinforce the vagueness of faculty response that suggests faculty caution in violating this particular norm.

Negligent Thesis/Dissertation Advising

The admonitory normative orientation of *negligent thesis/dissertation advising* warns graduate faculty members not to neglect their responsibilities in supervising the thesis/dissertation work of their graduate students. Table 3.9 presents seven behaviors that constitute this norm. These improper behaviors delineate various forms of negligence in thesis or dissertation advising and include the thesis/dissertation advisor not giving any substantive feedback on drafts to any of one's graduate students (F9), being routinely unavailable to answer graduate students' questions about their thesis dissertation (F10), routinely taking more

Table 3.9 Factor Loadings of Specific Behaviors of the Admonitory Norm of Negligent Thesis/Dissertation Advising

GTMBI specific behaviors	Factor loadings
F9. The thesis/ssertation advisor does not give any substantive feedback on drafts to any of his/her graduate students.	.699
F10. The thesis/dissertation advisor is routinely unavailable to answer a graduate student's questions about his/her thesis or dissertation.	.682
F8. The thesis/dissertation advisor routinely takes more than a month to give feedback on a student's draft chapter.	.632
F11. The advisor fails to prepare advisees for questioning at the final oral defense.	.623
F12. A thesis/dissertation advisor provides only criticism of his/her graduate student's work during the oral defense of the thesis/dissertation.	.498
F13. The thesis/dissertation advisor fails to hold his/her students' thesis/dissertation work to the same departmental and professional standards expected of all other graduate students.	.450
F4. The thesis/dissertation director refuses to give his/her graduate student guidance in the selection of a thesis/dissertation topic.	.413

Note: Percentage of variance explained = 7.25. Cronbach alpha = 0.88. Extent of consensus: 4.00–5.00 = 37.1%; 3.00–3.99 = 48.1%; 2.00–2.99 = 14.6%.

than a month to give feedback on a student's draft chapter (F8), and failing to prepare advisees for questioning at their final oral defense (F11). The remaining four reproached behaviors that make up this normative pattern delineate additional prohibitions in thesis and dissertation advising.

The mean value calculated for this normative array (3.68) qualifies it for designation as an admonitory norm. Nevertheless, consensus on the admonitory status of this norm fails to exist, given that less than half of faculty respondents (48.1%) view it as admonitory. However, almost half (37.1%) of faculty respondents to the GTMBI accord this normative configuration inviolable status (4.00 or higher on the possible actions scale).

Insufficient Course Structure

This admonitory norm reminds faculty members to provide sufficient structure to the graduate-level courses they teach. It consists of six deprecated profes-

Table 3.10 Factor Loadings of Specific Behaviors of the Admonitory Norm of Insufficient Course Structure

GTMBI specific behaviors	Factor loadings
C4. Assignment or other course requirements are not fully or accurately presented in the course syllabus.	.756
C3. A syllabus does not contain dates when assignments are due.	.750
C2. An outline or syllabus is not prepared for the graduate course.	.713
C5. Objectives for the course are not specified by the professor.	.653
D6. Instructions and requirements for course assignments are not clearly described to students.	.487
C1. Required texts and other reading materials are routinely not ordered by the professor in time to be available at the beginning of the term.	.447

Note: Percentage of variance explained = 6.69. Cronbach alpha = 0.89. Extent of consensus: 4.00–5.00 = 27.3%; 3.00–3.99 = 48.9%; 2.00–2.99 = 23.5%.

sorial behaviors pertaining to course structure and organization, as displayed in Table 3.10.

These behaviors delineate deficiencies in the structure of graduate-level courses. Three of these insufficiencies pertain to course syllabi: not preparing an outline or syllabus for a course (C2), preparing a syllabus that does not contain dates when assignments are due (C3), and not fully or accurately presenting assignments or other course requirements in the course syllabus (C4).

Other shortcomings in the structure of graduate courses rebuked by this particular norm include not specifying the objectives for the course (C5), not clearly describing instructions and requirements for course assignments to students (D6), and routinely not ordering required texts and other reading materials in time to be available at the beginning of the term (C1).

This normative configuration meets the criterion for designation as an admonitory norm, given its mean of 3.44. However, less than half (48.9%) of faculty respondents accord it admonitory norm status. Moreover, about a fourth (23.5%) of faculty regard the behaviors of this pattern as falling between discretionary behavior and mildly inappropriate behavior (2.00 to 2.99 on the possible actions scale), and another fourth (27.3%) express an inviolable level of disdain for these behaviors (4.00 to 5.00 on the possible actions scale).

Table 3.11 Factor Loadings of Specific Behaviors of the Admonitory Norm of Pedagogical Narrowness

GTMBI specific behaviors	Factor loadings
D17. The professor's perspective in every class is U.S.-dominated, without acknowledgment of contributions from other countries.	.674
D18. The professor does not include pertinent scholarly contributions of women and minorities in the content of the seminar.	.662
D20. Memorization of course content is stressed at the expense of analysis and critical thinking.	.494
D24. The professor does not encourage graduate students to ask questions during class time.	.492
G7. A faculty member consistently votes to not admit international students to the graduate program.	.415

Note: Percentage of variance explained = 5.62. Cronbach alpha = 0.83. Extent of consensus: 4.00–5.00 = 28.1%; 3.00–3.99 = 46.0%; 2.00–2.99 = 25.3%.

Pedagogical Narrowness

This normative pattern applies primarily to the content and emphasis of graduate courses. Specifically, this admonitory norm reproves faculty members for choosing a limited pedagogical approach in their graduate courses. Table 3.11 presents the five proscribed behaviors constituting this norm. Narrowness in pedagogy includes such faculty behaviors as espousing a U.S.-dominated perspective in every graduate class without acknowledgment of contributions from other countries (D17), not including pertinent scholarly contributions of women and minorities in the content of a seminar (D18), stressing the memorization of course content at the expense of analysis and critical thinking (D20), and not encouraging graduate students to ask questions during class time (D24).

The mean value (3.42) computed for this normative configuration indicates that it meets the criterion for designation as an admonitory norm. Despite this mean value, consensus fails to obtain, as 46.0% of faculty members completing the GTMBI regard this norm as admonitory (3.00 to 3.99 on the possible actions scale). Approximately equal proportions of faculty view this norm as either inviolable (28.1%) or between discretionary behavior and mildly inappropriate behavior (25.3% rate it between 2.00 and 2.99 on the possible actions scale). This

Table 3.12 Factor Loadings of Specific Behaviors of the Admonitory Norm of Student Assignment Misallocation

GTMBI specific behaviors	Factor loadings
A1. A professor who supervises graduate research assistants requires his/her assigned students to routinely work many extra hours per week beyond the time specified by the institution.	.737
F2. A professor agrees to direct a thesis/dissertation only under the condition that he/she will be a coauthor on all publications based on the work.	.700
E12. The professor assigns a graduate student to grade the work of other graduate students.	.565
A7. A professor regularly cancels research team meetings/appointments that have been scheduled ahead.	.450

Note: Percentage of variance explained = 4.86. Cronbach alpha = 0.69. Extent of consensus: 4.00–5.00 = 35.6%; 3.00–3.99 = 37.6%; 2.00–2.99 = 24.2%.

disparity in the level of disdain for violations of this norm reinforces the ambiguity of the faculty response to such violations.

Student Assignment Misallocation

The admonitory norm of *student assignment misallocation* censures professorial behaviors that put graduate students in awkward positions or misuse their time and efforts. Table 3.12 displays the four proscribed behaviors reflective of this normative array.

These four disdained behaviors provide some clarity to the proscriptions of this particular norm. Of the four behaviors, three pertain to the doctoral apprenticeship: requiring that graduate research assistants routinely work many extra hours beyond the time specified by the institution (A1), regularly canceling research team meetings/appointments that have been scheduled (A7), and assigning a graduate student to grade the work of other graduate students (E12). The fourth behavior pertains to thesis/dissertation supervision: a professor agreeing to direct a thesis/dissertation only under the condition that he or she will be a coauthor on all publications based on the work (F2).

The average degree of disdain for this pattern of proscribed behaviors (mean = 3.47) indicates the admonitory character of this norm. However, consensus does not exist on its admonitory nature, since less than two-fifths (37.6%) of

Table 3.13 Factor Loadings of Specific Behaviors of the Admonitory Norm of Graduate Program Disregard

GTMBI specific behaviors	Factor loadings
G12. A faculty member refuses to serve on the departmental graduate admissions committee.	.745
G11. A faculty member refuses to participate in departmental graduate curricular planning.	.708
G13. A faculty member strongly advocates accepting a graduate student applicant who fails to exhibit minimal skills in speaking or reading English.	.588
G14. A faculty member strongly advocates enrolling a graduate student applicant whose specialized interests for study are not offered by the department.	.520

Note: Percentage of variance explained = 4.76. Cronbach alpha = 0.81. Extent of consensus: 4.00–5.00 = 25.7%; 3.00–3.99 = 43.1%; 2.00–2.99 = 30.2%.

faculty respondents rated this set of behaviors between a 3.00 and 3.99 on the possible actions scale. In contrast, more than a third (35.6%) of faculty view it as inviolable (4.00 to 5.00 on the possible actions scale). In addition, a fourth (24.2%) of respondents to the GTMBI place their response between discretionary behavior and mildly inappropriate behavior (2.00 to 2.99 on the possible actions scale). Such variations accentuate the uncertainty in faculty response to violations of this norm.

Disregard for Graduate Program

This norm rebukes faculty members who exhibit a lack of concern for the welfare of their graduate program. The four prohibited behaviors that constitute this admonitory normative pattern delineate the ways in faculty members express such a disregard. Table 3.13 exhibits these behaviors. Three pertain to graduate student admissions. These behaviors are refusing to serve on the departmental graduate admissions committee (G12), strongly advocating the acceptance of a graduate student applicant who fails to exhibit minimal skills in speaking or reading English (G13), and strongly advocating enrolling a graduate student applicant whose specialized interests for study are not offered by the department (G14). The fourth behavior that defines this normative configuration pertains to graduate curricular planning, as it takes the form of a faculty member who refuses to participate in such planning (G11).

This normative pattern falls short of consensus on its status as admonitory, since 43.1% of faculty respondents perceived it to fall between a 3.00 and a 3.99 on the possible actions scale. This lack of consensus obtains despite a mean of 3.28 computed for this normative array. Evidence for ambiguity in faculty response to violations of this norm emerges from the 30.2% of faculty respondents who place the behaviors of this norm between discretionary and mildly inappropriate, as well as the 25.7% of respondents who accord inviolable status to these behaviors (rated between 4.00 and 5.00 on the possible actions scale) indicative of a disregard for graduate programs.

Conclusion

This chapter describes five inviolable and eight admonitory normative arrays that constitute the normative structure of graduate teaching and mentoring. Violations of the five inviolable norms require severe action. Moreover, considerable consensus exists among faculty respondents to the GTMBI on the inviolability of these norms.

Although faculty respondents view the eight admonitory normative patterns as representing inappropriate forms of behavior, transgressions of them provoke an unfavorable but uncertain response. With the exception of neglectful teaching, consensus among faculty respondents does not exist on the admonitory status of these normative patterns. This lack of consensus occurs despite mean values that meet the designated criterion for admonitory normative status.

CHAPTER FOUR

Norm Espousal by Institutional Type and Academic Discipline

The structure of the academic profession consists of two major differentiating dimensions: institutional type and academic discipline. This chapter describes variations in the espousal of inviolable and admonitory norms of graduate study by institutional type and by academic discipline.

Institutional Type and Norm Espousal

Institutional type functions as a differentiating force in that institutional missions greatly influence institutional structures (Ruscio, 1987). Institutional structures affect the work of college and university faculty members (Blackburn & Lawrence, 1995; Ruscio, 1987). To elaborate, the emphasis placed on teaching and research, attitudes, beliefs, reference groups, and professorial roles differs across different types of colleges and universities. Such differences underscore the differentiating force of institutional type.

In the case of norms of undergraduate college teaching, Braxton and Bayer (1999) found that academics holding faculty appointments in research universities voice less disdain for violations of five of the seven inviolable norms than their colleagues in more teaching-oriented collegiate institutions. Likewise, academic professionals in research universities express lower degrees of indignation for violations of five of the nine admonitory norms for undergraduate college teaching empirically identified by Braxton and Bayer (1999) than their counterparts in institutions embracing institutional missions that emphasize teaching. Thus undergraduate college teaching norms add to the various ways in which institutional type differentiates the structure of the academic profession.

Braxton and Bayer (1999) postulate that faculty in research universities have a lower degree of disdain for undergraduate teaching improprieties because of the high degree of autonomy they hold in such universities (Baldridge, Curtis, Ecker, & Riley, 1978; Birnbaum, 1988). Moreover, the high value placed on autonomy constitutes one of the defining values of the academic profession (Finkelstein, 1984). Because of the high value faculty place on autonomy and the high degree of it they hold in research universities, faculty in such settings tend to hold the view that colleagues or administrators should avoid intervening in the case of teaching norm violations.

This study includes two types of doctorate-granting universities: research universities with a high level of research activity and research universities with a very high level of research activity. These two types of research universities represent two of the three categories of doctorate-granting universities of the Carnegie Foundation for the Advancement of Teaching's Classification of Institutions (2005): RU/H and RU/VH. An index composed of federal funding for research, funding for research from nonfederal sources, and a per capita measure of research activity provides the basis for the classification of universities into these two categories.

The elements that constitute this index suggest that the institutional missions and their accompanying institutional structures may produce some differences between the attitudes, beliefs, and work patterns of faculty in universities with a very high level of research activity and those of their academic counterparts in universities with a high level of research activity. Such subtle distinctions may lead to variations in the degree of disdain faculty members in these two types of research universities voice for violations of the five inviolable and eight admonitory norms of graduate teaching and mentoring.

Moreover, professional status carries with it an obligation for both espousal of and adherence to ethical principles (Abbott, 1983; Carlin, 1966; Handler, 1967). High status increases visibility, which in turn elevates the symbolic significance of professional behavior (Carlin, 1966). As a consequence, individuals with high professional status conduct themselves in ways that are exemplary and beyond reproach (Carlin, 1966). By extension, research universities with a very high level of research activity perceive themselves as holding high status among research universities. This perception of the obligations of high status may influence faculty holding academic appointments in research universities with a very high level of research activity to have a higher degree of disdain for violations of the inviolable and admonitory norms of graduate teaching and mentoring than their faculty counterparts in research universities with high levels of research activity.

These formulations suggest that faculty in these two types of research universities differ on the level of disdain they have for behaviors that violate the five inviolable and eight admonitory norms of graduate study. These formulations do not lead to a directional hypothesis about such differences, but they do give rise to the following questions: *Does faculty espousal of the inviolable and admonitory norms of graduate study vary between research universities of very high and high research intensity? Are there norms whose violations elicit similar levels of disdain from faculty in both types of research universities?*

We used a 2 × 4 analysis of variance to address these two guiding questions. Separate analyses of variance were conducted for each of the five inviolable norms and eight admonitory norms that constitute the normative structure of graduate study. Institutional type and academic discipline form the two factors of these analyses of variance. Institutional type consisted of two levels: research universities of very high levels of research activity and research universities of high levels of research activity. Academic discipline consisted of four groups: biology, chemistry, history, and psychology.

Following statistical significant main effects identified through the analyses of variance executed, the Scheffe method of post hoc mean comparisons was used. The .025 level of statistical significance was used to identify statistically reliable differences. This level of statistical significance was applied because cluster sampling, which was used in this study, increases the probability of committing Type I errors. This increased probability of committing Type I errors occurs because variances of variables of interest in the population may be underestimated because of the homogeneity of the elements of the clusters sampled (Kish, 1957). Thus a more conservative level of statistical significance was used rather than the customary .05 level.

The level of faculty disdain for the behaviors that constitute each of the inviolable and admonitory norms of the normative structure of graduate study are measured using composite scales. Composite scales were computed for each of

Table 4.1 Results of the Analysis of Variance of the Five Inviolable Normative Patterns by Institutional Type—Research Universities with High and Very High Levels of Research Activity

Normative pattern	F-Ratio	Mean RU/H	Mean RU/VH
Disrespect toward student efforts	4.12	4.29	4.22
Misappropriation of student work	0.68	4.46	4.44
Harassment of students	1.97	4.56	4.52
Whistle-blowing suppression	0.05	4.46	4.45
Directed research malfeasance	0.04	4.98	4.98

Note: The F-ratio for institutional type is independent of the F-ratio for academic discipline. RU/H = Research Universities (high research activity); RU/VH = Research Universities (very high research activity).

the five inviolable norms and for each of the eight admonitory norms. These composite scales were computed by summing faculty members' perceptions of the severity of action that they believe should be meted out for each of the specific behaviors that make up a given normative pattern and then by dividing this sum by the number of specific behaviors that constitute a given inviolable or admonitory norm. These specific behaviors are specified in Chapter 3. As described in Chapter 2, faculty respondents used a five-point scale (1 = appropriate behavior, should be encouraged, to 5 = very inappropriate behavior, requiring formal administrative intervention) to register their perceptions of each behavior.

Because this section of the chapter pertains to possible variations in norm espousal between the two types of research universities represented in this study, only the findings for institutional type are presented. These findings are independent of the effects of academic discipline on faculty espousal of the five inviolable and eight admonitory norms.

Institutional Type and Inviolable Norm Espousal

The above-mentioned formulations suggest that faculty in universities with a very high level of research activity will differ from their academic counterparts in universities with high levels of research activity in the level of disdain they voice for violations of the five inviolable norms of graduate study. Despite this expectation, academics in both types of universities register similar levels of indignation for the specific behaviors that make up each of the five inviolable norms. Put differently, the normative patterns of *disrespect toward student efforts*, *misappropriation of student work*, *harassment of students*, *whistle-blowing suppression*, and *directed*

Table 4.2 Results of the Analysis of Variance of the Eight Admonitory Normative Patterns by Institutional Type—Research Universities with High and Very High Levels of Research Activity

Normative pattern	F-Ratio	Mean RU/H	Mean RU/VH
Neglectful teaching	5.66*	3.53	3.42
Inadequate advising/mentoring	0.25	3.43	3.41
Degradation of faculty colleagues	2.09	3.47	3.39
Negligent thesis/dissertation advising	4.03	3.73	3.63
Insufficient course structure	9.42**	3.52	3.36
Pedagogical narrowness	3.79	3.46	3.36
Student assignment misallocation	2.22	3.47	3.40
Graduate program disregard	0.70	3.29	3.25

Note: The F-ratio for institutional type is independent of the F-ratio for academic discipline. RU/H = Research Universities (high research activity); RU/VH = Research Universities (very high research activity).

*$p < .025$; **$p < .01$

research malfeasance act as core norms for these two types of research universities. The findings of the analyses of variance exhibited in Table 4.1 support these observations.

Institutional Type and Admonitory Norm Espousal

In contrast to the consensus found regarding inviolable norms, some institutional variability exists in the level of reproach expressed by individual faculty members for two of the eight admonitory normative orientations of graduate study. Table 4.2 exhibits the findings of the analyses of variance conducted. Specifically, academics in research universities marked by high levels of research activity (mean = 3.53) express a somewhat higher degree of disdain for *neglectful teaching* than do their faculty colleagues in research universities characterized as having a very high level of research activity (mean = 3.42). Put differently, in comparison with their colleagues in universities with very high levels of research activity, faculty members in less intense research universities reprove to a greater extent professorial behaviors that exhibit a lack of commitment and effort in the role of graduate level teaching. Likewise, academics in universities categorized as high in their level of research activity (mean = 3.52) also voice a greater degree of indignation regarding the specific behaviors that constitute the admonitory norm of *insufficient course structure* than do faculty holding appointments in universities with very high levels of research activity (mean = 3.36). In other words, academics in universities with less research activity tend to express a greater degree of disdain for not providing students in graduate-level courses with a sufficient degree of course structure and organization.

For the remaining six admonitory norms of graduate study, faculty members in these two types of research-oriented universities express similar levels of disdain. Thus the normative patterns of *inadequate advising/mentoring, degradation of faculty colleagues, negligent thesis/dissertation advising, pedagogical narrowness, student assignment misallocation*, and *graduate program disregard* serve as core norms for the two types of doctoral-granting universities represented in this study. The results of the analyses of variance reported in Table 4.2 attest to these assertions.

Academic Discipline and Norm Espousal

Like institutional type, academic disciplines differentiate the structure of the academic profession. The paradigmatic development of academic disciplines provides the basis for such differentiation. Paradigmatic development pertains to such matters as agreement on the importance of problems, theoretical orientations, and methodology (Kuhn, 1962, 1970). Disciplines vary in their level of paradigmatic development. Those represented in this study vary in the following way: biology and chemistry are high, whereas history and psychology are low (Biglan, 1973).

From their review of empirical research, Braxton and Hargens (1996) note that disciplines high in their level of paradigmatic development emphasize research more than teaching, whereas disciplines low in their level of paradigmatic development place more emphasis on teaching than on research. Disciplines differ in other ways based on their level of paradigmatic development, including lower journal rejection rates and higher levels of publication productivity for faculty in high paradigmatic disciplines (Braxton & Hargens, 1996). In contrast, faculties in disciplines of low paradigmatic development receive higher course evaluations and evince complementarity between the professorial roles of teaching and research (Braxton & Hargens, 1996). In addition, academics in disciplines having low paradigmatic development demonstrate an affinity for pedagogical practices directed toward the improvement of undergraduate education (Braxton, 1995).

In addition to these patterns of differences, Braxton and Bayer (1999) found that academic biologists voice a greater degree of disdain for violations of five of the seven inviolable norms and eight of nine admonitory norms that constitute the normative structure for undergraduate college teaching.

Taken together, these findings suggest that distinctions between academic disciplines in the level of indignation faculty express for the proscriptive behaviors of the inviolable and admonitory norms of graduate study transpire. This supposition leads to the following questions: *Does faculty espousal of the inviolable and admonitory normative patterns of graduate study vary across the four academic disciplines represented in this volume? Are there norms whose violations elicit similar levels of disdain from faculty in each of the four academic disciplines?*

We used the same 2 × 4 analyses of variances used to identify variations in norm espousal by institutional type to address the two questions posed above. The findings described in the subsections that follow pertain to possible variations in norm espousal across the four academic disciplines of biology, chemistry, history, and psychology. These findings are independent of the effects of institutional type on faculty espousal of the five inviolable and eight admonitory norms that constitute the normative structure of graduate study.

Academic Disciplines and Inviolable Norm Espousal

Our expectation for disciplinary variations in faculty norm espousal arises for only one of the five inviolable norms of graduate study. In this case, academic historians (mean = 4.65) tend to voice a somewhat higher level of contempt for behaviors associated with the norm of *misappropriation of student work* than do academic chemists (mean = 4.34), biologists (mean = 4.39), and psychologists (mean = 4.43). Put differently, in contrast to faculty in the other three academic disciplines, historians tend to scorn to a greater extent the failure of graduate faculty members to give graduate student the credit they deserve for their scholarly efforts.

For the other four inviolable norms that constitute the normative structure of graduate study, faculty members holding appointments in biology, chemistry, history, and psychology share similar levels of disapproval for these proscriptive behaviors. Thus the norms of *disrespect toward students*, *harassment of students*, *whistle-blowing suppression*, and *directed research malfeasance* act as core norms for the four academic disciplines. Table 4.3 shows the results of the analyses of variance conducted that support these assertions.

Academic Disciplines and Admonitory Norm Espousal

Variations in faculty norm espousal across the four academic disciplines obtain for each of the eight admonitory norms of graduate study. With the exception of the norm of *neglectful teaching*, academic historians tend to differ from their

Table 4.3 Results of the Analysis of Variance of the Five Inviolable Normative Patterns by Academic Discipline

Normative pattern	F-Ratio	Biology	Chemistry	History	Psychology	Post hoc mean comparisons
Disrespect toward student efforts	3.67*	4.22	4.22	4.36	4.23	
Misappropriation of student work	25.42**	4.39	4.34	4.65	4.42	mean for history is greater than the means for biology, chemistry, and psychology at the .025 level of statistical significance
Harassment of students	0.70	4.53	4.52	4.56	4.55	
Whistle-blowing suppression	1.72	4.49	4.43	4.51	4.39	
Directed research malfeasance	1.17	4.99	4.97	4.98	4.99	

Note: The F-ratio for academic discipline is independent of the F-Ratio for institutional type.

*$p < .025$; **$p < .01$

counterparts in other disciplines on their level of indignation for violations of the other seven admonitory norms. In the case of *neglectful teaching*, chemists (mean = 3.58) tend to reproach to a greater degree those behaviors reflective of the proscriptive norm of *neglectful teaching* than do academic psychologists (mean = 3.35). However, chemists, biologists, and historians have similar levels of scorn for a lack of commitment and effort in the role of graduate-level teaching by colleagues.

For four of the admonitory normative orientations, academic historians tend to express a somewhat greater degree of contempt for the behaviors reflective of these normative patterns than do psychologists holding academic appointments in research universities. Specifically, historians express more disdain for violations of the behaviors associated with the norms of *inadequate advising/mentoring* (mean = 3.58), *degradation of faculty colleagues* (mean = 3.60), *insufficient course structure* (mean = 3.55) and *pedagogical narrowness* (mean = 3.55) than do psychologists (means = 3.26, 3.29, 3.29, and 3.22, respectively). For each of these four norms, historians, chemists, and biologists exhibit similar levels of disapproval. Moreover, historians also express a somewhat greater degree of indignation for *neglectful thesis/dissertation advising* (mean = 3.84) than do their faculty counterparts in chemistry (mean = 3.61). However, academic biologists, psychologists, and historians share equivalent degrees of disapproval.

In addition to these distinctions, academic historians (mean = 4.29) rebuke to a somewhat greater degree than biologists (mean = 3.13), chemists (mean = 2.96), and psychologists (mean = 3.37) those proscriptive professorial behaviors associated with the norm of *student assignment misallocation*. Furthermore, psychologists (mean = 3.37) tend to convey more disdain for these behaviors than do chemists or biologists. Such behaviors are those that put graduate students in awkward positions or misuse their time and efforts. For historians, their level of contempt for such actions occurs at the level of an inviolable norm. In stark contrast, such behaviors fail to reach admonitory status for chemists.

Academic historians and academic chemists share similar levels of indignation for behaviors reflective of the admonitory norm of *graduate program disregard*. However, faculty members in biology (mean = 3.17) and psychology (mean = 3.15) tend to express less scorn for faculty members who exhibit a lack of concern for the welfare of their graduate program than do historians (mean = 3.45).

These patterns of differences indicate that no core admonitory norms for academic disciplines exist. For each of the eight admonitory normative orientations disciplinary differences transpire. Table 4.4 exhibits the results of the analyses of variance performed that support these observations.

Table 4.4 Results of the Analysis of Variance of the Eight Admonitory Normative Patterns by Academic Discipline

Normative pattern	F-Ratio	Biology	Chemistry	History	Psychology	Post hoc mean comparisons
Neglectful teaching	4.70**	3.47	3.58	3.49	3.35	mean for chemistry is greater than that for psychology at the .025 level of statistical significance
Inadequate advising/mentoring	9.27***	3.44	3.41	3.58	3.26	mean for history is greater than that for psychology at the .025 level of statistical significance
Degradation of faculty colleagues	6.34***	3.36	3.46	3.60	3.29	mean for history is greater than that for psychology at the .025 level of statistical significance
Negligent thesis/dissertation advising	5.25***	3.64	3.61	3.84	3.63	mean for history is greater than that for chemistry at the .025 level of statistical significance
Insufficient course structure	4.56**	3.47	3.45	3.55	3.29	mean for history is greater than that for psychology at the .025 level of statistical significance
Pedagogical narrowness	6.78***	3.42	3.45	3.55	3.22	mean for history is greater than that for psychology at the .025 level of statistical significance
Student assignment misallocation	170.1***	3.13	2.96	4.29	3.37	mean for history is greater than the means for biology, chemistry, and psychology at the .025 level of statistical significance
Graduate program disregard	6.26***	3.17	3.31	3.45	3.15	mean for history is greater than the means for biology and psychology at the .025 level of statistical significance

Note: The F-ratio for academic discipline is independent of the F-ratio for institutional type.
*$p < .025$; **$p < .01$; ***$p < .001$

Core Norms for Institutional Type and Academic Discipline

Differences in the structure of the academic profession owing to institutional type and academic discipline suggest a need for integrating mechanisms that compensate for such fragmentation (Ruscio, 1987)

Core norms for institutional type and for academic disciplines exist. For institutional type, all five of the inviolable norms and six of the eight admonitory norms function as core norms. In addition, four of the five inviolable normative arrays operate as core norms for the four academic disciplines. However, none of the admonitory normative configurations serve this role.

Are there core norms that compensate for the fragmenting forces of institutional type and academic discipline? Given that neither variation by institutional type nor that by academic discipline transpires for four of the five inviolable norms, these four norms act as core norms for both institutional type and academic discipline. *Disrespect toward students*, *harassment of students*, *whistle-blowing suppression*, and *directed research malfeasance* constitute these four core norms. However, none of the eight admonitory norms serve as core norms for institutional type and academic discipline.

In Chapters 5, 6, and 7, we continue to delineate norms that are undifferentiated by various faculty characteristics and indices of professional attainments and involvement in graduate education. Nevertheless, the delineation of core norms requires that their level of espousal is invariant across such factors as institutional type, academic discipline, gender, citizenship, professional age, academic rank, administrative experience, research activity (articles and books), indicators of involvement in graduate study, and tenure. In Chapter 7, we use multiple regression analyses that simultaneously control for these various factors to identify those inviolable and admonitory norms that are core or differentiated normative patterns.

CHAPTER FIVE

Personal Attributes and Norm Espousal

As differentiating dimensions, academic discipline and institutional type fragment the academic profession (Ruscio, 1987). Ruscio points to the need for integrating mechanisms to compensate for such fragmentation. The pattern of findings presented in the previous chapter delineates a set of four inviolable norms that function as core norms for both institutional type and academic discipline. None of the eight admonitory normative patterns serve as core norms. Thus the four inviolable core norms (*disrespect toward student efforts*, *harassment of students*, *whistle-blowing suppression*, and *directed research malfeasance*) function as integrating mechanisms for fragmentation in the structure of the academic profession.

Individual faculty members are embedded within each of the two differentiating dimensions in the structure of the academic profession. Such nesting gives rise to the question: What role do individual faculty members play in furthering fragmentation in the structure of the academic profession, or do they in some ways integrate the structure of the academic profession? Explicitly, is the variation in the level of disdain they express for violations of each of the five inviolable and eight admonitory norms associated with the personal attributes, professional involvements, and professional attainments of individual academics? Alternately, do core norms emerge because of invariance? Personal attributes include gender, citizenship, and professional age, whereas professional involvements and professional attainments include academic rank, administrative experience, participation in the graduate studies, research activity, and tenure status.

This chapter concentrates on the relationship between personal attributes of individual faculty members and the level of indignation they express for violations of the five inviolable and eight admonitory norms of graduate study. The next chapter focuses on the professional involvements and attainments of individual faculty members and the level of disdain they express with regard to these normative orientations of graduate study.

Gender

Female faculty members embrace a greater commitment to teaching than male academics (Bayer & Astin, 1975; Finkelstein, 1984; Tierney & Rhoads, 1993). Male and female academics also differ in their perceptions of the characteristics of good teaching (Goodwin & Stevens, 1993). To elaborate, female faculty perceive that a concern for student self-esteem constitutes a characteristic of good teaching more than do male academics (Goodwin & Stevens, 1993). Beyond these teaching differences, the moral compass used by women emphasizes care and responsibility (Gilligan, 1977, 1982, 1993).[1] Given these gender differences, male and female faculty members may also differ in the degree of disdain they voice for violations of the norms of graduate study.

To further reinforce the need to test for gender, Braxton and Bayer (1999) found gender differences in faculty espousal of two inviolable norms. Female academics reprove behaviors associated with the norms of *condescending negativism* and *personal disregard* to a greater extent than do male academics. Braxton and Bayer also observed gender differences on three of the nine admonitory norms of undergraduate college teaching: *authoritarian classroom*, *inadequate communication*, and *undermining colleagues*. For all three norms, female faculty members voice a greater degree of scorn for the behaviors reflective of these norms than do male academics.

These gender differences in undergraduate teaching norm espousal suggest the possibility of gender differences with respect to the norms of graduate study. We report two sets of findings regarding such possible gender differences in faculty espousal of the five inviolable and eight admonitory norms. The first set of findings focus on bivariate mean differences between female and male faculty members. We used independent *t*-tests to discern such differences. The second set of findings involve the use of multiple linear regression to determine the influence of gender on faculty espousal of these normative arrays while controlling for the effects of institutional type, academic discipline, citizenship, and professional age.[2] Both sets of statistical tests were conducted using a .025 level of statistical significance.[3]

Gender Differences and Similarities in Norm Espousal

We note bivariate gender differences on two of the five inviolable norms. For the norm of *harassment of students*, female academics (mean = 4.62) voice a slightly stronger degree of contempt for the behaviors of this normative pattern than do male faculty members (mean = 4.49). Likewise, female faculty members (mean = 4.51) also express a slightly greater degree of disdain for behaviors reflective of the norm of *misappropriation of student work* than do their male counterparts (mean = 4.43). However, no statistically significant gender differences obtain for the inviolable norms of *disrespect toward student efforts*, *whistle-blowing suppression*, and *directed research malfeasance*. These assertions receive support from the results of the *t*-tests executed for each of the five inviolable norms reported in Table 5.1.

The statistically significant differences on the two inviolable norms of *harassment of students* and *misappropriation of student work* disappear when controls for academic discipline, citizenship, institutional type, and professional age are introduced through the use of multiple linear regression. Moreover, statistically significant gender differences fail to emerge in the multiple regression analyses conducted on the other three inviolable norms. Table 5.4 (later in this chapter) displays the results of these five regression analyses.

For two of the eight admonitory norms, we observe statistically significant mean differences between male and female academics. Specifically, females (mean = 3.58) reprove to a slightly greater degree behaviors reflective of the admonitory normative configuration of *degradation of faculty colleagues* than do their male counterparts (mean = 3.36). Female academics (mean = 3.66) also voice a slightly stronger degree of contempt for behaviors reflective of the norm of *student assignment misallocation* than do male faculty members (mean = 3.36). The results of the *t*-tests exhibited in Table 5.1 support these observations.

With the use of statistical controls for institutional type, academic discipline, citizenship, and professional age by means of multiple linear regression, the gender differences for the norm of *student assignment misallocation* become statis-

Table 5.1 Bivariate Relationship between the Five Inviolable Norms and the Eight Admonitory Norms and Gender

Normative pattern	Mean female	Mean male	*t*-Value
Inviolable norms			
Disrespect toward student efforts	4.31	4.24	2.05
Misappropriation of student work	4.51	4.43	2.73*
Harassment of students	4.62	4.49	4.17**
Whistle-blowing suppression	4.48	4.44	0.75
Directed research malfeasance	4.98	4.98	0.23
Admonitory norms			
Neglectful teaching	3.45	3.49	0.89
Inadequate advising/mentoring	3.44	3.42	0.29
Degradation of faculty colleagues	3.58	3.36	3.99**
Negligent thesis/dissertation advising	3.73	3.67	1.25
Insufficient course structure	3.42	3.46	0.61
Pedagogical narrowness	3.48	3.38	1.82
Student assignment misallocation	3.66	3.36	4.73**
Graduate program disregard	3.28	3.28	0.04

*$p < .01$; **$p < .001$

tically nonsignificant. However, the gender differences found for the normative array of *degradation of faculty colleagues* remain, as being a female academic (beta = .10, $p < .01$) exerts a somewhat stronger degree of influence on the espousal of this norm than does being a male faculty member. Put differently, female academics reprove to a slightly greater degree the making of negative comments about the courses and research methods of colleagues in one's department. Table 5.5 (later in this chapter) provides the results of the regression analyses that support these observations.

Citizenship

Subscriptions to the norms of science delineated by Merton (1942, 1973) differ between graduate students based on their citizenship status (Anderson & Louis, 1994). International graduate students subscribe more to norms counter to the Mertonian norms of science than do graduate students who hold U.S. citizenship. By extension, faculty members may also vary in their level of indignation for the proscriptive behaviors of the inviolable and admonitory norms of graduate study according to their citizenship status.

As with gender, we present two sets of findings regarding such possible differ-

Table 5.2 Bivariate Relationship between the Five Inviolable Norms and the Eight Admonitory Norms and Citizenship Status

Normative pattern	F-Ratio	Mean, U.S. citizen native born	Mean, U.S. citizen naturalized	Mean, Non–U.S. citizen	Post hoc mean
Inviolable norms					
Disrespect toward student efforts	0.006	4.26	4.28	4.25	
Misappropriation of student work	0.28	4.46	4.49	4.44	
Harassment of students	0.08	4.54	4.53	4.52	
Whistle-blowing suppression	2.80	4.47	4.46	4.30	
Directed research malfeasance	3.94	4.99	5.00	4.94	
Admonitory norms					
Neglectful teaching	4.52	3.45	3.67	3.59	
Inadequate advising/mentoring	2.86	3.41	3.59	3.50	
Degradation of faculty colleagues	5.59*	3.39	3.62	3.66	mean for non–U.S. citizen is greater than that for U.S. citizen, native born, at the .025 level of statistical significance
Negligent thesis/dissertation advising	1.00	3.67	3.79	3.74	
Insufficient course structure	0.95	3.43	3.54	3.52	
Pedagogical narrowness	12.15**	3.36	3.62	3.77	mean for non– U.S. citizen is greater than that for U.S. citizen, native born, at the .025 level of statistical significance
Student assignment misallocation	1.44	3.48	3.57	3.33	
Graduate program disregard	2.72	3.25	3.48	3.37	

$^{*}p < .01$; $^{**}p < .001$

ences in faculty espousal of the five inviolable and eight admonitory norms of graduate study based on the citizenship status of individual faculty members. The first set of findings focus on differences between faculty who hold U.S. citizenship, those who are naturalized U.S. citizens, and those who are not U.S. citizens. We used one-factor analyses of variance to identify such possible differences between these three faculty groups.[4] The second set of findings involve the use of multiple linear regression to determine the influence of faculty citizenship status on faculty espousal of these normative arrays while controlling for the effects of institutional type, academic discipline, gender, and professional age. Both sets of statistical tests were conducted using a .025 level of statistical significance.

Differences and Similarities in Norm Espousal by Citizenship Status

From our bivariate analyses, we observe that the citizenship status of individual faculty members makes little or no difference in the degree of indignation they express for violations of each of the five inviolable norms of graduate study. As indicated in Table 5.2, the five analyses of variance conducted failed to yield statistically significant differences across the three groups of faculty based on their citizenship for each of the five inviolable norms.

With the influence of academic discipline, institutional type, gender, and professional age held constant, citizenship status also fails to wield statistically significant effects on the level of disdain individual academics voice for violations of each of the five inviolable norms. Table 5.4 shows the results of the multiple regression analyses conducted that provide support for this assertion.

In the case of admonitory norms, statistically significant variation among faculty transpires along the lines of their citizenship status for two of the eight admonitory normative configurations. Specifically, international faculty members (mean = 3.66) reprove behaviors associated with the norm of *degradation of faculty colleagues* a bit more than do faculty who hold U.S. citizenship (mean = 3.39). International faculty (mean = 3.77) also disdain behaviors indicative of the admonitory norm of *pedagogical narrowness* somewhat more than do their faculty counterparts who are U.S. citizens (mean = 3.36). Expressed differently, international faculty tend to censure members who do not include the pertinent contributions of women and minorities in the content of a seminar, those who do not encourage graduate students to ask questions during class time, and those who do not acknowledge the contributions of scholars from countries other than the United States. Table 5.2 contains the results of the analyses of variance conducted that support these observations.

However, the relationship between faculty citizenship status and faculty espousal of the norm of of *degradation of faculty colleagues* becomes statistically unreliable with the introduction of controls for academic discipline, institutional type, gender, and professional age through the use of multiple linear regression. Nevertheless, faculty members who are native-born U.S. citizens (beta = $-.13$, $p < .025$) continue to voice statistically significant less disdain for behaviors associated with the admonitory norm of pedagogical narrowness than do faculty who are either naturalized U.S. citizens or not U.S. citizens. The supporting multiple regression results appear in Table 5.5.

Professional Age

The formulations of the conceptual framework that underlies the research reported in this volume point to the origin of norms as direct and indirect personal experience with behaviors that detrimentally affect oneself or others (Horne, 2001). With advancing professional age comes a greater likelihood of personal experience with professorial behaviors that negatively affect students. Thus professional age may directly affect the level of disdain faculty express for the behaviors that constitute the five inviolable and eight admonitory normative patterns of graduate study. Put differently, as professional age increases, the level of contempt faculty express for violations of inviolable and admonitory norms also increases. Alternatively, we might expect little or no relationship between professional age and the level of scorn individual faculty members voice for the behaviors that make up the five inviolable and eight admonitory normative arrays. This alternative conjecture stems from the endurance of the outcomes of the graduate school socialization process throughout an academic's career (Mullins, 1973).[5] Thus the internalization of these norms that occurred during the graduate school socialization process changes very little as a function of professional age.

As with gender and citizenship, we present two sets of findings regarding such possible relationships between professional age and faculty espousal of the five inviolable and eight admonitory norms of graduate study. The first set of findings focus on zero-order or bivariate correlations between faculty members' professional age and the level of contempt they voice for violations of the inviolable and admonitory norms. We used Pearson product-moment correlations to test for these zero-order relationships. The second set of findings involve the use of multiple linear regression to determine the influence of faculty professional age

Table 5.3 Bivariate Relationship between the Five Inviolable Norms and the Eight Admonitory Norms and Professional Age

Normative pattern	Correlation coefficient
Inviolable norms	
Disrespect toward student efforts	.09
Misappropriation of student work	.12*
Harassment of students	−.02
Whistle-blowing suppression	.12*
Directed research malfeasance	.06
Admonitory Norms	
Neglectful teaching	.18*
Inadequate advising/mentoring	.19*
Degradation of faculty colleagues	.09
Negligent thesis/dissertation advising	.12*
Insufficient course structure	.10
Pedagogical narrowness	.05
Student assignment misallocation	.10
Graduate program disregard	.14*

*$p < .01$

on faculty espousal of these normative arrays while controlling for the effects of institutional type, academic discipline, gender, and citizenship.[6] Both sets of statistical tests were conducted using a .025 level of statistical significance.

Professional Age and Norm Espousal

For two of the five inviolable norms statistically significant correlations obtain. Specifically, the tendency of faculty members to voice more contempt for the proscribed behaviors associated with the norms of *misappropriation of student work* ($r = .11, p < .01$) and *whistle-blowing suppression* ($r = .12, p < .001$) increases with increments in their professional age. Little or no zero-order relationships exist between professional age and the level of disdain faculty express for violations of the norms of *harassment of students* and *directed research malfeasance.* Table 5.3 displays the Pearson product-moment correlations for professional age and each of the five inviolable normative patterns.

Table 5.4 Regression of the Five Inviolable Normative Patterns on Gender, Citizenship Status, and Professional Age

	Disrespect toward student efforts	Misappropriation of student work	Harassment of students	Whistle-blowing suppression	Directed research malfeasance
Institutional type	−.09*	−.04	−.05	−.01	−.01
	(−.09)	(−.05)	(−.04)	(−.01)	(−.00)
Chemistry	−.001	−.06	−.01	−.04	−.08
	(−.001)	(−.05)	(−.01)	(−.06)	(−.03)
Psychology	.01	.04	.01	−.06	−.02
	(.01)	(.04)	(.01)	(−.08)	(−.01)
History	.13**	.29	.03	.02	−.01
	(.15)	(.27)	(.03)	(.03)	(−.00)
Gender	.01	.05	.05	−.01	−.00
	(.01)	(.03)	(.03)	(−.01)	(−.00)
Non–U.S. citizen	.004	.01	−.03	−.06	−.11
	(.01)	(.02)	(−.04)	(−.12)	(−.05)
U.S. citizen	−.03	−.06	−.03	.01	−.04
	(−.04)	(−.07)	(−.04)	(.02)	(−.02)
Professional age	.11**	.15***	−.01	−.09	.05**
	(.01)	(.01)	(.00)	(.01)	(.00)
Constant	4.21	4.36	4.58	4.40	5.00
Total R squared	.04***	.12***	.02	.03	.02

Note: Unstandardized regression coefficients are in parentheses.
*$p < .025$; **$p < .01$; ***$p < .001$

In addition, bivariate, statistically significant, but small relationships exist between professional age and four of the eight admonitory normative configurations: *neglectful teaching* ($r = 18$, $p < .01$), *inadequate advising/mentoring* ($r = .12$, $p < .01$), *negligent thesis/dissertation advising* ($r = 12$, $p < .01$), and *graduate program disregard* ($r = .14$, $p < .01$). However, statistically chance bivariate relationships exist between professional age and *degradation of faculty colleagues, insufficient course structure, pedagogical narrowness,* and *student assignment misallocation.* Table 5.3 provides the supporting correlation coefficients.

The relationship between professional age and *disrespect toward student efforts* becomes statistically significant (beta = .11, $p < .01$) with the use of statistical controls for academic discipline, gender, institutional type, and citizenship status in multiple linear regression. Moreover, the association between professional age and the level of scorn expressed for *misappropriation of student work* (beta = .15, $p < .001$) remains statistically significant and in the expected direction with academic discipline, institutional type, gender, and citizenship status statistically held constant. Table 5.4 contains the results of the multiple linear regression analyses conducted.

In contrast, all eight of the admonitory normative patterns exhibit statistically significant positive relationships with professional age net of the effects of academic discipline, institutional type, gender, and citizenship status. Thus the introduction of these controls through the multiple regression analyses conducted resulted in four statistically chance bivariate relationships becoming statistically significant. These four normative patterns consist of *degradation of faculty colleagues* (beta =.13, $p < .001$), *insufficient course structure* (beta = .12, $p < .001$), *pedagogical narrowness* (beta = .09, $p < .025$), and *student assignment misallocation* (beta = .15, $p < .001$). As professional age increases, the faculty members' level of disdain for the behaviors reflective of these four admonitory norms also increases. Moreover, professional age wields a statistically significant but small positive influence on the other four admonitory normative patterns. Put differently, as professional age increases, faculty levels of disdain also increase for the behaviors reflective of the admonitory norms of *neglectful teaching* (beta = .19, $p < .001$), *inadequate advising/mentoring* (beta = .21, $p < .001$), *negligent thesis and dissertation advising* (beta = .15, $p < .001$), and *graduate program disregard* (beta = .15, $p < .001$). Table 5.5 shows the results of the multiple linear regression analyses conducted.

Table 5.5 Regression of the Eight Admonitory Normative Patterns on Gender, Citizenship Status, and Professional Age

	Neglectful teaching	Inadequate advising/ mentoring	Degradation of faculty colleagues	Negligent thesis/ dissertation advising	Insufficient course structure	Pedagogical narrowness	Student assignment misallocation	Graduate program disregard
Institutional type	−.12*** (−.15)	−.05 (−.07)	−.08 (−.12)	−.09* (−.12)	−.13*** (−.19)	−.08 (−.12)	−.06 (−.11)	−.05 (−.08)
Chemistry	.05 (.07)	−.05 (−.07)	.03 (.05)	−.04 (−.06)	−.03 (−.05)	−.02 (−.03)	−.11*** (−.20)	.05 (.09)
Psychology	−.05 (−.08)	−.09 (−.14)	−.00# (−.01)	.02 (.02)	−.08 (−.14)	−.09 (−.16)	.14*** (.29)	.01 (.02)
History	.04 (.06)	.12* (.17)	.15*** (.26)	.15** (.22)	.07 (.11)	.09 (.16)	.62*** (1.18)	.17*** (.29)
Gender	−.01 (−.01)	.05 (.04)	.10** (.10)	.01 (.01)	.01 (.01)	.01 (.01)	.05 (.06)	.02 (.02)
Non–U.S. citizen	.01 (.02)	.02 (.05)	.05 (.10)	.03 (.06)	.03 (.08)	.08 (.21)	.00# (.00#)	.00# (.00#)
U.S. citizen	−.11 (−.19)	−.10 (−.17)	−.11 (−.23)	−.07 (−.13)	−.05 (−.09)	−.13* (−.27)	−.08 (−.18)	−.11 (−.23)
Professional age	.19*** (.01)	.21*** (.01)	.13*** (.01)	.15*** (.01)	.12*** (.01)	.09* (.01)	.15*** (.01)	.15*** (.01)
Constant	3.50	3.36	3.40	3.63	3.48	3.57	3.09	3.19
Total R squared	.07***	.09***	.07***	.05***	.05***	.07***	.04***	.05***

Note: Unstandardized regression coefficients are in parentheses.
$^{*}p < .025$; $^{**}p < .01$; $^{***}p < .001$; # coefficient less than .01

Emergent Questions

Two questions emerge from the results of the multiple regression analyses conducted for each of the five inviolable and eight admonitory norms.

1. Gender and citizenship wield little or no independent effect on faculty disdain for behaviors associated with each of the five inviolable norms of graduate study. However, professional age positively affects the level of indignation faculty express for violations of three of the five inviolable norms: *disrespect toward student efforts*, *misappropriation of student work*, and *whistle-blowing suppression*. This pattern of findings give rise to the question: Will the influence of professional age on these three inviolable norms remain when such indicators of professional involvement and professional attainment as academic rank, administrative experience, participation in the graduate studies, research activity, and tenure status are statistically controlled? Chapter 7 addresses this question.

2. Unlike with inviolable norms, gender and citizenship affect faculty levels of contempt for violations of certain admonitory norms of graduate study. Specifically, female faculty members tend to rebuke to a greater extent behaviors associated with the admonitory norm of *degradation of faculty colleagues*, whereas being a U.S. citizen results in a lower degree of scorn for those proscriptive behaviors reflective of the norm of *pedagogical narrowness*. Moreover, professional age positively affects the level of faculty disapproval for each of the eight admonitory norms. The following questions emerges from this set of findings: Will the influence of gender on *degradation of faculty colleagues* and the influence of faculty citizenship on *pedagogical narrowness* remain when such indicators of professional involvement and professional attainment as academic rank, administrative experience, participation in the graduate studies, research activity, and tenure status are statistically controlled? Likewise, will the independent influence of professional age on each of the eight admonitory norms also remain after professional involvement and attainment indicators are held constant? Chapter 7 also attends to these two questions.

Chapter 6 centers attention on the question of whether individual faculty members vary in the level of disdain they express for violations of each of the five inviolable and eight admonitory norms of graduate study as a function of their level of professional involvement and professional attainment independent of the influence of institutional type and academic discipline.

NOTES

1. We wish to thank an anonymous reviewer of this book for this suggestion.

2. Academic discipline, citizenship, gender, and institutional type were measured as dummy variables. The three dummy variables representing academic discipline were chemistry (1 = chemistry, 0 = other), history (1 = history, 0 = other), and psychology (1 = psychology, 0 = other). The dummy variables depicting citizenship were U.S. citizen (1 = U.S. citizen, 0 = other), non–U.S. citizenship (1 = non–U.S. citizenship, 0 = other). In the case of gender, females were coded as 1 and males as 0. The dummy variable representing institutional type was coded as very high research activity = 1 and high research activity as 0.

3. For all 13 multiple regression analyses executed, high multicolinearity was not a problem, as tolerance and VIF (variance inflation factor) indices were within acceptable boundaries.

4. Because of unequal numbers of faculty members in each of the three groups based on citizenship status, we used the general linear model. We also tested for the homogeneity of variance assumption.

5. We wish to thank an anonymous reviewer of this book for this suggestion.

6. Professional age was developed using an item on the GTMBI, "Year highest earned degree received." The year 2006 minus the year indicated on this question was used to compute professional age.

CHAPTER SIX

Norm Espousal and Faculty Professional Attainments and Involvement

This chapter centers attention on the professional attainments and involvements of faculty members and the level of disdain they voice for violations of each of five inviolable norms and each of the admonitory norms of graduate study. Professional attainments include academic rank, tenure, and research activity as indexed in the number of journal articles and books published during the past three years. Administrative experience in the form of being a department head/chair or a dean constitutes one form of professional involvement, whereas another form of involvement consists of participation in graduate studies.

We conducted two types of analyses to ascertain the relationship between the professional attainments and involvements in graduate study of individual faculty members and the level of disdain they espouse for violations of the inviolable and admonitory norms that constitute the normative structure for graduate study. As in the previous chapter, one set focused on bivariate relationships, and the second set entailed the use of multiple linear regression to ascertain the influence of each of the indices of professional attainment and involvement in graduate study on faculty espousal of the five inviolable and the eight admonitory norms above and beyond the influence of institutional type and academic discipline.[1] We used the .025 level of statistical significance to identify statistically reliable relationships.

However, the multiple regression analyses executed did not include controls for the personal attributes of gender, citizenship, and professional age.[2] The next chapter reports the findings of multiple regression analyses that include such controls to address the two emergent questions at the end of Chapter 6, as well as questions that spring from the configuration of findings of this chapter.

Academic Rank

Academic rank provides an indicator of not only professional attainment but also the professional status of an individual faculty member. Higher rank leads to higher professional status. Higher professional status increases the visibility of the individual faculty member. As a consequence, the professional behavior of an individual with high status possesses symbolic significance (Carlin, 1966). As a consequence, the professorial conduct of faculty members with high professional status is more likely exemplary and beyond reproach (Carlin, 1966). Thus higher professional status carries with it an obligation to comply with ethical principles (Abbott, 1983; Carlin, 1966; Handler, 1967). Based on these formulations we might expect that as their academic rank increases, the level of disdain that individual faculty members voice for violations of the inviolable and admonitory norms of graduate study also increases.

In addition to these formulations, Braxton and Bayer (1999) found that full professors expressed a greater level of disdain for such normative orientations of undergraduate college teaching as the inviolable norm of *personal disregard* and the admonitory norms of *advisement negligence*, *inconvenience avoidance*, and *undermining colleagues*. Thus a relationship between academic rank and the level of disdain expressed for violations of the five inviolable and the eight admonitory norms of graduate study may exist.

Academic Rank: Differences and Similarities in Norm Espousal

We observe small, positive bivariate relationships between academic rank and the level of scorn individual faculty members express for behaviors reflective of the inviolable norms of *misappropriation of student effort* ($r = .10, p < .01$) and *whistle-blowing suppression* ($r = .14, p < .01$).[3] However, we failed to identify statistically significant bivariate relationships between the inviolable norms of *disrespect toward*

Table 6.1 Bivariate Relationship between the Five Inviolable Norms and the Eight Admonitory Norms and Academic Rank

Normative pattern	Correlation coefficient
Inviolable norms	
Disrespect toward student efforts	.07
Misappropriation of student work	.10*
Harassment of students	−.02
Whistle-blowing suppression	.14*
Directed research malfeasance	.05
Admonitory norms	
Neglectful teaching	.12*
Inadequate advising/mentoring	.13*
Degradation of faculty colleagues	.03
Negligent thesis/dissertation advising	.04
Insufficient course structure	.08
Pedagogical narrowness	−.03
Student assignment misallocation	.09
Graduate program disregard	.05*

*$p < .01$

student efforts, *harassment of students*, and *directed research malfeasance*. These observations receive support from the correlation coefficients displayed in Table 6.1.

The small, positive relationships between academic rank and the level of disdain for violations of the inviolable norms of *misappropriation of student effort* and *whistle-blowing suppression* disappear when controls for academic discipline, institutional type, administrative experience, the three indices of involvement in graduate study, the two indices of research activity, and tenure are applied through the use of hierarchical, linear regression. In addition, statistically significant effects of academic rank on the other three inviolable norms also fail to emerge. Table 6.6 (later in this chapter) exhibits the results of these five regression analyses.

Between academic rank and the level of contempt individual faculty members voice for behaviors reflective of two of the eight admonitory norms of graduate study, *neglectful teaching* ($r = .12, p < .01$) and *inadequate advising/mentoring* ($r = .13, p < .01$), small, positive bivariate relationships also exist. For the other six admonitory norms of *degradation of faculty colleagues*, *negligent thesis/dissertation advising*, *insufficient course structure*, *pedagogical narrowness*, *student assignment misallocation*, and *graduate program disregard*, we did not delineate statistically significant bivariate relationships between these normative arrays and academic rank. The correlation coefficients exhibited in Table 6.1 empirically bolster these various assertions.

Our multiple regression analyses confirm the continued existence of statistically insignificant relationships between academic rank and the admonitory norms of *degradation of faculty colleagues*, *negligent thesis/dissertation advising*, *insufficient course structure*, *pedagogical narrowness*, *student assignment misallocation*, and *graduate program disregard*. Moreover, the statistically significant bivariate relationships between academic rank and *neglectful teaching* and *inadequate advising mentoring* vanish when statistical controls for academic discipline, institutional type, the three indicators of involvement in graduate study, the indicators of research activity, and tenure are introduced in the multiple regression analyses performed with these two normative patterns as the dependent variables. Table 6.7 (later in this chapter) displays the results of these eight regression analyses.

Administrative Experience

We define administrative experience as whether a faculty member serves or has served as either a departmental chairperson or a dean. Deans and departmental chairpersons hold some degree of formal authority because of their membership in the administrative structure of a university (Leslie, 1973; Tucker, 1993). Their responsibilities include attending to inadequate performance and unethical behavior of faculty (Tucker, 1993). Because of such positional responsibilities, faculty with administrative experience may likely have observed or received reports of wrongdoing with respect to graduate study. Such experiences may lead to the formation of more fully crystallized opinions about the negative consequences of violations of the norms of graduate study than the views of their faculty colleagues who do not have any administrative experience. Accordingly, faculty with administrative experience may rebuke to a greater degree behaviors indicative of the inviolable and admonitory norms of graduate study than their faculty colleagues without administrative experience.

Moreover, research shows that faculty with administrative experience tend to voice a slightly higher degree of contempt for violations of the undergraduate teaching norms of *inconvenience avoidance* and *undermining colleagues* than faculty without such experience (Braxton & Bayer, 1999).

Administrative Experience: Differences and Similarities in Norm Espousal

We conducted independent *t*-tests to determine whether faculty with administrative experience differ from their faculty colleagues without such experience on the level of disdain they have for violations of the five inviolable and the eight admonitory norms of graduate study.[4] Table 6.2 shows the results of the *t*-tests conducted.

For two of the five inviolable norms, we note bivariate mean differences between faculty with administrative experience and their faculty counterparts without administrative experience Specifically, faculty with administrative experience (mean = 4.36) express slightly more disdain for behaviors associated with the normative pattern of *disrespect toward student effort* in contrast to faculty without administrative experience (mean = 4.23). Likewise, faculty with administrative experience (mean = 4.57) also voice a somewhat greater degree of scorn for behaviors that constitute the inviolable normative pattern of *misappropriation of student work* in comparison with those faculty members who have no administrative experience (mean = 4.42). Moreover, faculty with administrative experience and those without such experience express similar levels of disdain for violations of the inviolable norms of *harassment of students*, *whistle-blowing suppression*, and *directed research malfeasance* given the statistically insignificant *t*-test results for these three normative patterns.

A different pattern of findings emerge with the influence of academic discipline, institutional type, academic rank, academic rank, research activity, involvement in graduate study, and tenure held constant through the use of multiple linear regression. With such controls, the influence of administrative experience on the level of disdain expressed for violations of the two inviolable norms of *disrespect towards student effort* and *misappropriation of student work* becomes statistically insignificant. Nevertheless, the role of administrative experience in shaping faculty views on the norms of *harassment of students*, *whistle-blowing suppression*, and *directed research malfeasance* remains statistically unremarkable. Table 6.6 contains the five multiple regression analyses conducted that support these observations.

From the eight independent *t*-tests conducted, we identify statistically signifi-

Table 6.2 Bivariate Relationship between the Five Inviolable Norms and the Eight Admonitory Norms and Administrative Experience

Normative pattern	Mean experience	Mean no experience	*t*-Value
Inviolable norms			
Disrespect toward student efforts	4.36	4.23	2.78**
Misappropriation of student work	4.57	4.42	4.46**
Harassment of students	4.57	4.53	1.06
Whistle-blowing suppression	4.52	4.44	1.56
Directed research malfeasance	4.99	4.98	2.22
Admonitory norms			
Neglectful teaching	3.57	3.45	2.42*
Inadequate advising/mentoring	3.56	3.39	3.29***
Degradation of faculty colleagues	3.54	3.41	1.97
Negligent thesis/dissertation advising	3.77	3.66	1.91
Insufficient course structure	3.50	3.43	1.23
Pedagogical narrowness	3.48	3.39	1.22
Student assignment misallocation	3.69	3.39	4.13***
Graduate program disregard	3.39	3.25	2.22

$^{*}p < .025$; $^{**}p < .01$; $^{***}p < .001$

cant mean differences between faculty with and without administrative experience in the degree of derision they register for violations of three admonitory normative patterns. In each of these three cases, faculty having administrative experience tend to voice a somewhat greater degree of contempt than faculty without any administrative experience. Specifically, faculty with administrative experience (mean = 3.57) express more disdain for *neglectful teaching* than those faculty without administrative experience (mean = 3.45). Likewise, faculty with administrative experience (mean = 3.56) scorn to a greater degree behaviors associated with the admonitory norm of *inadequate advising/mentoring* than faculty with no administrative experience (mean = 3.39). Faculty members with administrative experience (mean = 3.69) also express more contempt for those behaviors reflective of the admonitory norm of *student assignment misallocation* in comparison with faculty having no administrative experience (mean = 3.39).

Faculty with and without administrative experience, however, belittle to a similar extent behaviors that constitute the admonitory norms of *degradation of faculty colleagues*, *negligent thesis/dissertation advising*, *insufficient course structure*, *pedagogical narrowness*, and *graduate program disregard*. Table 6.2 contains the supporting statistical results.

These three bivariate findings vanish with the application of statistical controls for academic discipline, institutional type, academic rank, research activity, involvement in graduate study, and tenure through the multiple regressions conducted with the level of disdain expressed for violations of the admonitory norms of *neglectful teaching*, *inadequate advising/mentoring*, and *student assignment misallocation*. In addition, the similarities observed between faculty with and without administrative experience on the admonitory norms of *degradation of faculty colleagues*, *negligent thesis/dissertation advising*, *insufficient course structure*, *pedagogical narrowness*, and *graduate program disregard* persist with the execution of multiple regression analyses. The results of the regression analyses contained in Table 6.7 support these assertions.

Participation in Graduate Study

Indices of participation in graduate study during the past three years include the number of graduate courses or seminars taught, the number of graduate students served as their major professor, and the number of graduate student committees served on in a capacity other than as the major professor. Through such involvement, individual faculty members may directly experience improprieties of graduate study. Graduate students may also informally or formally report incidents of transgressions to individual faculty members because of their involvement in graduate study. Because of such experiences, individual faculty members may form more fully developed views about the negative consequences of violations of the norms of graduate study for the welfare of graduate students. As a consequence of such views individual faculty members have a greater degree of disdain for those behaviors reflective of the inviolable and admonitory norms of graduate study.

Involvement in Graduate Study: Similarities and Differences in Norm Espousal

We computed Pearson product-moment correlations to identify statistically significant bivariate relationship between the three indices of involvement in graduate study and the level of disdain individual faculty members express for violations of the five inviolable norms and for the eight admonitory norms of graduate study. Table 6.3 exhibits these correlations.

We find that little or no relationship exists between the number of graduate courses or seminars taught during the past three years[5] and the degree of contempt individual faculty members express for violations of each of the five inviolable and eight admonitory norms. The multiple regression analyses conducted with the five inviolable and eight admonitory norms as dependent variables also corroborate this observation. These regression analyses held constant the effects of academic discipline, institutional type, academic rank, administrative experience, research activity, tenure, and the other two forms of involvement in graduate study. Table 6.6 provides empirical support for this contention.

However, a small, negative bivariate association exists between the number of graduate students served as their major professor[6] ($r = -.10$, $p < .01$) and the level of scorn expressed for behaviors indicative of the admonitory norm of *student assignment misallocation* exists. Table 6.3 displays the correlation coefficients that support these statements

This particular relationship becomes statistically unreliable when we hold constant the influence of academic discipline, institutional type, academic rank, administrative experience, research activity, tenure, and the other two indices of involvement in graduate study through the use of multiple regression. The results of the regression analyses conducted exhibited in Table 6.7 provide support for this observation.

We also observe from Table 6.3 that a negative bivariate association between the level of disdain voiced for violations of the admonitory norm of *student assignment misallocation* also obtains for the number of graduate student committees served on in a capacity other than as the major professor[7] ($r = -.19$, $p < .001$).[8] This association, however, becomes statistically insignificant when controls for academic rank, administrative experience, research activity, tenure, and the other two forms of involvement in graduate study are introduced through the use of multiple regression.

These two forms of involvement in graduate study, however, bear little or no relationship to the level of disdain individual faculty voice for violations of the five inviolable norms and the other six admonitory norms of graduate study as evidenced by the correlations displayed in Table 6.3. The multiple regression analyses executed with these normative orientations as the dependent variables sustains this observation of little or no relationship for the five inviolable norms

Table 6.3 Bivariate Relationship between the Five Inviolable Norms and the Eight Admonitory Norms and Participation in Graduate Study

	Correlation coefficients for number of		
Normative pattern	Graduate seminars/ courses taught	Graduate students' major professor	Member student committee
Inviolable norms			
Disrespect toward student efforts	.03	−.02	.01
Misappropriation of student work	.01	−.04	−.02
Harassment of students	−.01	.01	.06
Whistle-blowing suppression	.05	.04	.04
Directed research malfeasance	.02	−.02	−.01
Admonitory Norms			
Neglectful teaching	.08	.01	.05
Inadequate advising/mentoring	.01	−.02	−.05
Degradation of faculty colleagues	.04	.00	.01
Negligent thesis/dissertation advising	.04	−.07	−.05
Insufficient course structure	.05	.01	−.01
Pedagogical narrowness	.04	−.01	.03
Student assignment misallocation	.01	−.10*	−.19**
Graduate program disregard	.01	−.06	−.03

*$p < .01$; **$p < .001$

and the remaining admonitory norms except *graduate program disregard.* The previously statistically insignificant bivariate relationship between the number of graduate student committees served on as the student's major professor and this particular admonitory normative array becomes statistically significant (beta = −.10, $p < .025$) because of the statistical controls used in the multiple regression analyses conducted with the norm of *graduate program disregard* as the dependent variable. The level of disdain expressed for violations of behaviors associated with the norm of *graduate program disregard* tends to decrease as the number of such committees increases. The regression analyses results exhibited in Table 6.7 provide support for these observations.

Research Activity

Faculty members who highly value research tend to place a lower value on teaching (Creamer, 1998; Fox, 1992; Fulton & Trow, 1974; Smart, 1991). As a consequence, faculty members who place a high value on research ascribe less social significance to violations of the norms of graduate study. Thus such faculty may likely voice a lower degree of disdain for violations of the inviolable and admonitory norms of graduate study.

However, research activity may bring with it experiences with conducting research and the process of publishing that resulted in negative consequences. Firsthand experience with such negative consequences may result in stronger levels of contempt for the behaviors reflective of such inviolable norms as *misappropriation of student work*, *whistle-blowing suppression*, and *directed research malfeasance* and the admonitory norm of *student assignment misallocation*. These normative patterns pertain to various aspects of research. We indexed research activity using two forms of publication productivity during the past three years: journal articles, books, and monographs.[9]

Research Activity: Similarities and Differences in Norm Espousal

We calculated Pearson product-moment correlations to identify statistically significant bivariate relationships between article, book, and monograph publication productivity and the level of contempt faculty express for violations of the inviolable and admonitory norms of graduate study. Table 6.4 shows the results of these computations.

We observe a negative bivariate relationship between the number of journal articles published during the past three years and the violable norm of *misappropriation of student work* ($r = -.16, p < .001$). In contrast, little or no relationship exists between journal article publication levels and the other four inviolable norms of *disrespect toward student effort*, *harassment of students*, *whistle-blowing suppression*, and *directed research malfeasance*. Moreover, little or no relationship exists between book and monograph publication productivity and each of the five inviolable norms of graduate study. However, a modest, negative bivariate relationship exists between the number of articles published during the past three years and the admonitory normative array of *student assignment misallocation* ($r = -28, p < .001$). Table 6.4 displays the correlation coefficients that provide support for these assertions.

Table 6.4 Bivariate Relationship between the Five Inviolable Norms and the Eight Admonitory Norms and Research Activity

	Correlation coefficients for number of	
Normative pattern	Journal articles published	Books/monographs published
Inviolable norms		
Disrespect toward student efforts	−.06	.04
Misappropriation of student work	−.16**	.08
Harassment of students	−.04	−.01
Whistle-blowing suppression	−.01	.08
Directed research malfeasance	−.03	−.09
Admonitory norms		
Neglectful teaching	.02	.03
Inadequate advising/mentoring	−.07	.11*
Degradation of faculty colleagues	−.08	.09
Negligent thesis/dissertation advising	−.06	.05
Insufficient course structure	−.02	.06
Pedagogical narrowness	−.06	.07
Student assignment misallocation	−.28**	.22**
Graduate program disregard	−.03	.07

*$p < .01$; **$p < .001$

The multiple regression analyses performed with each of the five inviolable norms of graduate study as dependent variables sustains the bivariate finding of little or no relationship between book and monograph publication productivity and these normative patterns. Moreover, regression analyses with the normative patterns of *disrespect toward student effort*, *harassment of students*, *whistle-blowing suppression*, and *directed research malfeasance* as dependent variables also finds a little or no relationship between journal article publications and the level of disdain voiced for violations of these norms. However, the negative bivariate association between the number of journal articles published during the past three years and the level of contempt registered for behaviors associated with the violable norm of *misappropriation of student work* becomes statistically insignificant when the influence of academic discipline, institutional type, academic rank, book or monograph publications productivity, the three forms of involvement in graduate study, and tenure are held constant through multiple regression. Table 6.6 show the results of these five regression analyses.

Positive bivariate associations occur between book and monograph publication levels and the level of disapproval faculty declare for behaviors associated with the admonitory norms of *inadequate advising/mentoring* ($r = .11, p < .01$) and *student assignment misallocation* ($r = 22, p < .001$). Little or no associations occur between book and monograph publication productivity and the remaining six admonitory norms.

Such statistically insignificant associations between book and monograph publication productivity and the level of disdain expressed for violations of the admonitory norms of *neglectful teaching*, *degradation of faculty colleagues*, *negligent thesis/dissertation advising*, *insufficient course structure*, *pedagogical narrowness*, and *graduate program disregard* persist in the regression analyses conducted with these normative patterns as the dependent variables. However, the two statistically significant bivariate relationships between book and monograph publication productivity and the degree of scorn faculty express for behaviors reflective of the admonitory norms of *inadequate advising/mentoring* and *student assignment misallocation* disappear when controls for academic discipline, institutional type, academic rank, administrative experience, journal article publication levels, the three indices of involvement in graduate study, and tenure are applied through the multiple regression analyses executed with these two norms as the dependent variables. Table 6.7 supports these observations.

Tenure

We might anticipate that faculty holding tenure may voice stronger degrees of disapproval for behaviors associated with proscriptive inviolable and admonitory norms of graduate study than untenured faculty. To elaborate, the passage of time as an academic presents tenured faculty with more possible opportunities to personally observe or learn of incidents of violations of the norms of graduate study than untenured faculty members. Such experience leads to the development of more fully developed opinions of the consequences of such violations for graduate student careers. In addition, allegations of misconduct by tenured faculty are taken more seriously than allegations by untenured faculty (Black, 1976). Furthermore, fear of stigmatization as a whistle-blower may hold less significance for the career of a tenured faculty member than that of an untenured

Table 6.5 Bivariate Relationship between the Five Inviolable Norms and the Eight Admonitory Norms and Tenure Status

Normative pattern	Mean tenured	Mean untenured on tenure track	*t*-Value
Inviolable norms			
Disrespect toward student efforts	4.29	4.19	2.38*
Misappropriation of student work	4.49	4.38	3.29***
Harassment of students	4.54	4.54	−.08
Whistle-blowing suppression	4.50	4.33	3.60***
Directed research malfeasance	4.99	4.96	1.59
Admonitory norms			
Neglectful teaching	3.52	3.36	3.28***
Inadequate advising/mentoring	3.47	3.29	3.43***
Degradation of faculty colleagues	3.45	3.42	0.46
Negligent thesis/dissertation advising	3.69	3.64	1.02
Insufficient course structure	3.49	3.32	2.84**
Pedagogical narrowness	3.41	3.44	−0.57
Student assignment misallocation	3.52	3.31	3.07**
Graduate program disregard	3.29	3.25	0.60

$^{*}p < .025$; $^{**}p < .01$; $^{***}p < .001$

academic. Damage to a career and professional standing results from being labeled as a whistle-blower (Tangney, 1987). However, tenured faculty may feel less vulnerable to the damaging consequences of such labeling.

Tenure Status: Similarities and Differences in Norm Espousal

We executed independent *t*-tests to discern statistically significant mean differences between tenured and untenured faculty on the level of disdain expressed for violations of the five inviolable and the eight admonitory norms pertinent to graduate study.[10] Table 6.5 contains the results of these *t*-tests.

From the findings reported in Table 6.5, we note that tenured faculty and untenured faculty voice similar degrees of scorn for the behaviors associated with the inviolable norms of *student harassment* and *directed research malfeasance.* In contrast, statistically significant mean differences obtain for three of five in-

Table 6.6 Regression of the Five Inviolable Normative Patterns on Academic Rank, Administrative Experience, Participation in Graduate Study, Research Activity, and Tenure Status

	Disrespect toward student efforts	Misappropriation of student work	Harassment of students	Whistle blowing suppression	Directed research malfeasance
Institutional type	−.08	−.04	−.06	−.03	−.00#
	(−.08)	(−.03)	(−.05)	(−.04)	(−.00)#
Chemistry	.01	−.07	−.00#	−.06	−.07
	(.01)	(−.06)	(−.00)#	(−.09)	(−.02)
Psychology	−.00#	.01	.02	−.08	−.02
	(−.00)#	(.01)	(.02)	(−.12)	(−.01)
History	.09	.23*	.04	−.03	−.01
	(.11)	(.22)	(.04)	(−.04)	(−.00)#
Academic rank	−.00#	−.00#	−.09	.09	−.04
	(−.00)#	(−.00)#	(−.05)	(.07)	(−.01)
Administrative experience	.06	.08	.05	−.00#	.06
	(.07)	(.08)	(.05)	(−.01)	(.02)
Graduate seminars/courses taught	.02	.02	−.03	.04	.05
	(.01)	(.01)	(−.01)	(.02)	(.00)#

Graduate students' major professor	−.06	−.03	−.01	−.01	−.02
	(−.01)	(−.00)#	(.00)#	(.00)#	(−.02)
Member student committee	.00#	−.01	.08	.00#	−.05
	(.00)#	(−.01)	(.09)	(−.00)#	(−.02)
Journal articles published	.02	.00#	−.02	.01	.02
	(.01)	(.00)#	(−.01)	(.00)#	(.00)#
Books published	.00#	−.00#	−.00#	.05	−.13
	(.00)#	(−.00)	(−.00)#	(.04)	(−.02)
Tenure status	.05	.07	.02	.04	.13
	(.06)	(.07)	(.02)	(.04)	(.04)
Constant	4.19	4.36	4.62	4.25	4.99
Total R squared	.03	.09**	.02	.01	.03

Note: Unstandardized regression coefficients are in parentheses.
*$p < .001$; # coefficient less than .01

Table 6.7 Regression of the Eight Admonitory Normative Patterns on Academic Rank, Administrative Experience, Participation in Graduate Study, Research Activity, and Tenure Status

	Neglectful teaching	Inadequate advising/ mentoring	Degradation of faculty colleagues	Negligent thesis/ dissertation advising	Insufficient course structure	Pedagogical narrowness	Student assignment misallocation	Graduate program disregard
Institutional type	−.11**	−.03	−.06	−.08	−.13**	−.06	−.06	−.03
	(−.14)	(−.04)	(−.09)	(−.11)	(−.19)	(−.10)	(−.10)	(−.05)
Chemistry	.07	−.03	.06	−.01	−.04	.02	−.09*	.08
	(.10)	(−.04)	(.10)	(−.02)	(−.06)	(.03)	(−.17)	(.14)
Psychology	−.11*	−.13**	−.04	−.03	−.13**	−.13**	.11**	−.04
	(−.16)	(−.20)	(−.07)	(−.05)	(−.22)	(−.23)	(.23)	(−.07)
History	.02	.04	.12	.11	.03	.07	.57***	.15**
	(.02)	(.06)	(.19)	(.17)	(.05)	(.11)	(1.07)	(.25)
Academic rank	.07	.03	.02	.04	.01	−.05	.04	.09
	(.05)	(.03)	(.02)	(.03)	(.00)#	(−.05)	(.04)	(.09)
Administrative experience	.03	.05	.04	.03	−.01	.03	.02	.04
	(.04)	(.07)	(.07)	(.04)	(−.02)	(.05)	(.05)	(.06)
Graduate seminars/ courses taught	.09	.03	.05	.06	.04	.06	.03	.05
	(.04)	(.02)	(.03)	(.03)	(.02)	(.03)	(.02)	(.02)

Graduate students' major professor	−.09 (−.02)	−.03 (−.01)	−.03 (−.01)	−.09 (−.02)	−.03 (−.01)	−.03 (−.01)	−.05 (−.01)	−.10* (−.02)
Member student committee	−.01 (−.01)	−.08 (−.15)	.02 (.05)	−.06 (−.13)	−.05 (−.11)	.04 (.08)	−.04 (.10)	−.04 (.08)
Journal article published	.06 (.03)	.01 (.00)#	−.03 (−.02)	.06 (.03)	.07 (.05)	.00# (.00#)	.00# (.00)#	.06 (.04)
Books published	.00# (.00#)	.07 (.06)	.06 (.06)	.01 (.01)	.03 (.02)	.06 (.06)	.06 (.06)	.03 (.03)
Tenure status	.04 (.05)	.05 (.07)	−.06 (−.10)	−.01 (−.02)	.08 (.14)	−.03 (−.05)	.02 (.03)	−.09 (−.15)
Constant	3.21	3.35	3.29	3.59	3.34	3.38	3.05	2.99
Total R squared	.06***	.06***	.03*	.04**	.05***	.04**	.39***	.04**

Note: Unstandardized regression coefficients are in parentheses.
$^{*}p < .025$; $^{**}p < .01$; $^{***}p < .001$; # coefficient less than .01

violable norms. Specifically, tenured faculty express a slightly higher degree of contempt for behaviors indicative of the norm of *disrespect toward student effort* (mean = 4.49) than do untenured academics (mean = 4.19). In addition, tenured faculty (mean = 4.49) also express a higher degree of disdain for behaviors related to the norm of *misappropriation of student work* than do academics not holding tenure (mean = 4.38). The behaviors pertinent to the norm of *whistle-blowing suppression* also bring forth a stronger degree of ridicule from tenured faculty (mean = 4.50) than from untenured faculty members (mean = 4.33).

The regression analyses we performed with the five inviolable norms as dependent variables maintain the pattern of little or no relationship between tenure status and the level of disdain faculty members voice for behaviors indicative of the norms of *student harassment* and *directed research malfeasance*. However, the statistically significant pattern of mean differences between tenured and untenured faculty on their level of scorn for behaviors related to the norms of *disrespect toward student effort*, *misappropriation of student work*, and *whistle-blowing suppression* vanish when the effects of academic discipline, institutional type, academic rank, the two indices of research activity, and the three indictors of involvement in graduate study are statistically controlled through the multiple regression analyses performed with these norms as the dependent variables. These observations find support in the results of the regression analyses displayed in Table 6.6.

We also observed a similar pattern of tenured faculty voicing greater disdain violations of for four of the eight admonitory norms than do untenured academic professionals. Specifically, tenured faculty (mean = 3.52) express a slightly higher degree of disapproval for behaviors indicative of the norm of *neglectful teaching* than do untenured faculty (mean = 3.36). Likewise, behaviors indicative of the norm of *inadequate advising/mentoring* elicit a higher degree of contempt from tenured faculty members (mean = 3.47) than from faculty not holding tenure (mean = 3.29). Untenured faculty (mean = 3.32) also express less disdain for behaviors reflective of the norm of *insufficient course structure* than do their tenured counterparts (mean = 3.49). Behaviors associated with the admonitory norm of *student assignment misallocation* also spark a slightly higher level of disapproval from tenured faculty members (mean = 3.52) than from untenured academics (mean = 3.31). Similar levels of disdain between tenured and untenured faculty obtain for the other four admonitory norms of *degradation of faculty colleagues*, *negligent thesis/dissertation advising*, *pedagogical narrowness*, and *graduate program disregard*. Table 6.5 displays the results of the *t*-tests described herein.

The similar levels of disdain between tenured and untenured faculty members for violations of the admonitory norms of *degradation of faculty colleagues*, *negligent thesis/dissertation advising*, *pedagogical narrowness*, and *graduate program disregard* persist when the influence of academic discipline, institutional type, academic rank, administrative experience, research activity, and involvement in graduate study are statistically controlled through multiple regression analyses with these four norms as the dependent variables. Moreover, the pattern of tenured faculty expressing greater levels of disapproval for violations of the admonitory norms of *neglectful teaching*, *inadequate advising/mentoring*, *insufficient course structure*, and *student assignment misallocation* than untenured faculty reported above disappears as a consequence of the regression analyses performed with these four admonitory norms as the dependent variables. Table 6.7 contains the results of these four regression analyses that provide support for these assertions.

An Emergent Question

The results of these multiple regression analyses indicate that our indictors of faculty professional attainments and involvement in graduate study wield little or no independent influence on the espousal of the seven inviolable and the eight admonitory norms that constitute the normative structure of graduate study. This pattern of findings raises the question: Will this configuration of findings persist with statistical controls introduced for the personal attributes of gender, citizenship status, and professional age in multiple regression analyses? Chapter 7 addresses this question as well as the two emergent questions posed at the end of Chapter 5.

NOTES

1. Academic discipline and institutional type were measured as dummy variables. The three dummy variables representing academic discipline were chemistry (1 = chemistry, 0 = other), history (1=history, 0=other), and psychology (1 = psychology, 0 = other). The dummy variable representing institutional type was coded as very high research activity = 1 and high research activity = 0.

2. For all 13 multiple regression analyses executed, high multicollinearity was not a problem, as tolerance and VIF (variance inflation factor) indices were within acceptable boundaries.

3. Academic rank is measured as an ordinal variable with 3 = full professor, 2 = associate professor, and 1 = assistant professor. This measurement was used in both the correlations computed and the multiple regression analyses conducted.

4. Administrative experience is measured as a dummy variable with 1 = currently or have served as a department head/chair or a dean, 0 = no such service.

5. The question "In the past three years, how many graduate courses/seminars have you taught?" was used to measure this index of involvement in graduate study. Responses to this question were measured using the following scale: none = 1, 1 = 2, 2 = 3, 3 = 4, 4 = 5, 5 or more = 6.

6. This index of involvement in graduate study was measured using responses to the question "In the past three years, how many graduate students have you served as their major professor?" The actual number of times provided the numerical scale for this variable.

7. This index of involvement in graduate study was measured using responses to the question "In the past three years, how many graduate student committees have you served on for which you were not the student's major professor?' The actual of times indicated is used for the numerical scale for this variable.

8. The skewnesss of this variable was greater than 2.00. We transformed this variable using logbase10. This transformation substantially reduced the level of skewness well below the 2.00 level.

9. The following question was used to measure publication productivity: "During the past three years, how many of each of the following have you published?"

A. Journal articles. Respondents used the following scale: none = 1, 1–2 = 1, 3–4 = 3, 5–10 = 4, and 11 or more = 5.

B. Books and monographs. Respondents used the following scale: none = 1, 1 = 2, 2 = 3, 3 or more = 4.

10. This variable was measured as a dummy variable with 1 = tenured and 0 = untenured.

CHAPTER SEVEN

Core Norms, Differentiated Norms, and Key Differentiating Factors

In Chapter 4, we delineated four core norms, or norms undifferentiated by either academic discipline or institutional type. However, none of the eight admonitory norms emerged as core norms. In Chapter 5, we noted that three inviolable norms are core norms, as these norms are undifferentiated by faculty personal attributes of gender, citizenship, and professional age. Moreover, none of the eight admonitory norms are core norms, as each of the eight norms are influenced by gender, citizenship, or professional age. Five core norms and eight core admonitory norms emerged from Chapter 6, as the professional attainments and involvements in graduate study of individual faculty members exert little or no influence on the espousal of these norms that constitute the normative structure of graduate study.

However, these assertions remain tentative pending the results of multiple regression analyses that simultaneously control for the net influence of academic discipline, institutional type, faculty personal attributes (gender, citizenship, professional age), and the professional attainments and involvements of faculty members (e.g., academic rank, administrative experience, involvement in graduate study, research activity, and tenure). From these regression analyses, we can identify both core and differentiated norms that surface from robust statistical controls. For those norms that spring forth as differentiated, we center attention on the array of factors that influence the level of disdain expressed for the behaviors that constitute these normative patterns with particular attention to the percentage of variance explained by the identified factors as well as the magnitude of their weight.

Inviolable Norms: Core and Differentiated

Table 7.1 exhibits the results of the multiple regression analyses conducted to discern core and differentiated inviolable norms. In these regression analyses, each of the five inviolable norms were regressed on institutional type, academic discipline, gender, citizenship, professional age, academic rank, administrative experience, research activity (articles and books), the three indicators of involvement in graduate study, and tenure. Put differently, five regression analyses resulted, one for each inviolable norm.[1] As in previous regression analyses, we used the .025 level of statistical significance to identify statistically significant equations and coefficients of specific variables.

Disrespect toward Student Efforts

The regression equation derived for *disrespect toward student efforts* failed to attain statistical significance. As a consequence, this normative pattern constitutes a core, inviolable norm of graduate study. The results of the regression analysis shown in Table 7.1 support this assertion.

Misappropriation of Student Work

This particular normative pattern constitutes a differentiated norm. Academic historians (beta = .25, $p < .001$) and female academics (beta = .09, $p < .025$) voice greater degrees of contempt for the behaviors reflective of the norm of *misappropriation of student work* than do male faculty members or faculty in the other three disciplines included in this study. We discuss these factors further in a later section titled "Array of Factors Influencing Norm Espousal." These assertions receive support through the results of the regression analysis displayed in Table 7.1.

Harassment of Students

The regression equation for this norm failed to reach the .025 level of statistical significance as indicated by the results of the regression analysis exhibited in Table 7.1. Accordingly, the proscribed norm of *harassment of students* stands as a core, inviolable norm of graduate study.

Whistle-Blowing Suppression

This normative pattern arises as a core, inviolable norm. The assignment of this status receives backing from the failure of the regression equation for this norm to attain statistical significance as indicated in Table 7.1.

Directed Research Malfeasance

The regression analysis shown in Table 7.1 indicates that the regression equation for this normative orientation fails to attain statistical significance. Hence, the inviolable norm of *directed research malfeasance* attains the status of a core, inviolable norm of graduate study.

Admonitory Norms: Core and Differentiated

Table 7.2 displays the results of the multiple regression analyses conducted to discern core and differentiated admonitory norms. Each of the eight admonitory norms were regressed on institutional type, academic discipline, gender, citizenship, professional age, academic rank, administrative experience, research activity (articles and books), the three indicators of involvement in graduate study, and tenure. A total of eight regression analyses were executed, one for each admonitory norm.[2] As in previous regression analyses, we applied the .025 level of statistical significance to identify statistically significant equations and coefficients of specific variables.

Neglectful Teaching

The admonitory normative orientation of *neglectful teaching* achieves the status of a differentiated norm. Professional age (beta = 17, $p < .01$) acts as the agent of differentiation of this proscribed norm. As the professional age of faculty members increases, their level of disregard for the behaviors reflective of this normative pattern also increases. Moreover, institutional type also functions to differ-

Table 7.1 Regression of the Five Inviolable Normative Patterns on Faculty Personal Attributes and Their Professional Involvement and Attainments

	Disrespect toward students	Misappropriation of student work	Harassment of students	Whistle-blowing suppression	Directed research malfeasance
Institutional type	−.08 (−.09)	−.05 (−.04)	−.05 (−.05)	−.02 (−.02)	−.00# (.00)
Chemistry	.03 (.03)	−.06 (−.06)	.02 (.02)	−.04 (−.06)	−.08 (−.03)
Psychology	−.01 (−.01)	.02 (.02)	.00# (.00)#	−.08 (−.12)	−.02 (−.01)
History	.10 (.12)	.25*** (.23)	.02 (.02)	−.02 (−.03)	.02 (.01)
Gender	.09 (.10)	.09* (.08)	.13 (.12)	.06 (.07)	−.02 (−.01)
Non–U.S. citizen	.02 (.04)	.02 (.03)	−.00# (−.00)#	−.06 (−.12)	−.08 (−.04)
U.S. citizen	−.01 (−.01)	−.06 (−.07)	−.01 (−.01)	.00# (−.00#)	−.05 (−.02)
Professional age	.09 (.00)#	.13 (.01)	.00 (.00)	.03 (.00#)	.02 (.00)

Academic rank	−.07 (.04)	−.08 (−.04)	−.09 (−.05)	.03 (.02)	−.08 (−.01)
Administrative experience	.06 (.07)	.07 (.07)	.08 (.08)	−.01 (−.01)	.06 (.02)
Graduate seminars/courses taught	.02 (.01)	.02 (.00)#	−.02 (−.0)	.05 (.02)	.06 (.01)
Graduate students' major professor	−.06 (−.01)	−.03 (−.00)#	−.02 (−.01)	.05 (.02)	−.03 (−.00)#
Member student committee	.01 (.01)	−.01 (−.01)	.07 (.09)	−.00# (−.01)	−.04 (−.02)
Journal article published	.04 (.02)	.02 (.01)	−.01 (−.01)	.00# (.00)#	.04 (.01)
Books published	.02 (.01)	.00# (.00)#	.01 (.00)#	.06 (.05)	−.12 (−.02)
Tenure status	.06 (.07)	.08 (.08)	.02 (.02)	.05 (.07)	.13 (.05)
Constant	4.13	4.36	4.56	4.24	5.01
Total R squared	.04	.11***	.03*	.03	.04

Note: Unstandardized regression coefficients are in parentheses.
$^{*}p < .025$; $^{**}p < .01$; $^{***}p < .001$; # coefficient less than .01

entiate this normative array (beta = $-.13$, $p < .001$). Table 7.2 exhibits the regression analysis results that support this contention.

Inadequate Advising/Mentoring

Academic discipline and professional age act as mechanisms of differentiation for the admonitory norm of *inadequate advising/mentoring*. Specifically, faculty members in the discipline of psychology (beta = $-.11$, $p < .025$) tend to voice less scorn for this normative pattern than their colleagues in the other three academic disciplines, whereas professional age (beta = .19, $p < .01$) wields a positive influence on the level of disdain expressed for the behavior indicative of this norm. Table 7.2 shows the results of the regression analysis that provide empirical backing for these statements.

Degradation of Faculty Colleagues

Three factors contribute to the designation of this normative pattern as a differentiated norm. To elaborate, female academics (beta = 19, $p < .001$) voice more contempt for behaviors reflective of the norm of *degradation of faculty colleagues* than their male colleagues. However, academic historians (beta = .13, $p < .025$) tend to express a higher degree of disdain for such behaviors than their colleagues in the other three academic disciplines. Likewise, professional age (beta = .20, $p < .001$) positively affects the level of scorn directed toward this normative orientation. The results of the regression analysis conducted for this particular norm shown in Table 7.2 provide backing for these contentions.

Negligent Thesis/Dissertation Advising

Institutional type, academic discipline, and professional age also act as forces of differentiation for the norm of *negligent thesis/dissertation advising*. Specifically, faculty in universities with very high levels of research activity (beta = $-.10$, $p < .025$) tend to have less contempt for the behaviors of this normative orientation than faculty in universities of high levels of research activity. Faculty members in the discipline of history (beta = .14, $p < .025$) tend to express a greater level of disdain than faculty in the other three disciplines. As the professional age of the faculty member increases (beta = .23, $p < .000$), their level of disregard for the behaviors expressive of *negligent thesis/dissertation advising* also increases. Table 7.2 exhibits the regression results that support these assertions.

Insufficient Course Structure

Faculty members in universities with very high levels of research activity (beta = −.15, $p < .001$) tend to express a lower degree of disdain for the behaviors indicative of this norm than their faculty counterparts in universities with high levels of research activity. In contrast to faculty members in the other three academic disciplines, academic psychologists (beta = −.12, $p < .025$) express a lower degree of contempt for the proscribed behaviors of this norm. Thus, the norm of *insufficient course structure* stands as a differentiated admonitory norm. These observations find support in the results of the regression analysis shown in Table 7.2.

Pedagogical Narrowness

This norm emerges as a differentiated norm. Professional age and academic discipline acts as agents of this differentiation. Faculty members in the discipline of psychology (beta= −.11, p.025) tend to espouse a lower degree of disdain for behaviors reflective of the norm of *pedagogical narrowness* than do faculty members in the other three disciplines included in this study. Moreover, professional age (beta = .15, $p < .025$) exerts a positive influence on the level of contempt expressed for this normative pattern. The results of the regression analysis for this particular norm shown in Table 7.2 support these observations.

Student Assignment Misallocation

Institutional type, academic discipline, gender, and professional age function as mechanisms of differentiation for this particular norm. Specifically, faculty members holding academic appointments in universities with very high levels of research activity (beta = −.07, $p < .025$) tend to voice a slightly lower degree of scorn for the behaviors reflective of the norm of *student assignment misallocation* than do faculty members in universities with high levels of research activity. Academic chemists (beta = −.09, $p < .025$) tend to espouse less contempt, whereas faculty in the disciplines of psychology (beta = .12, $p < .001$) and history (beta = .58, $p < .000$) express higher degrees of contempt for the behaviors that constitute this norm. In contrast to male faculty members, female academics (beta = .10, $p < .001$) also express more scorn for the proscribed behaviors of this norm. Furthermore, as the professional age of faculty members (beta = .16, $p < .001$) advances, their level of disdain for the behaviors of this normative pattern also increases. Table 7.2 supports these assertions.

Table 7.2 Regression of the Eight Admonitory Normative Patterns on Faculty Personal Attributes and Their Professional Involvement and Attainments

	Neglectful teaching	Inadequate advising/ mentoring	Degradation of faculty colleagues	Negligent thesis/ dissertation advising	Insufficient course structure	Pedagogical narrowness	Student assignment misallocation	Graduate program disregard
Institutional type	−.13**	−.05	−.08	−.10*	−.15***	−.08	−.07*	−.05
	(−.17)	(−.06)	(−.13)	(−.14)	(−.22)	(−.12)	(−.12)	(−.08)
Chemistry	.06	−.04	.06	−.01	−.04	−.01	−.09*	.06
	(.08)	(−.05)	(.10)	(−.02)	(−.06)	(−.01)	(−.17)	(.11)
Psychology	−.10	−.11*	−.02	−.02	−.12*	−.11*	.12***	−.02
	(−.14)	(−.17)	(−.04)	(−.03)	(−.20)	(−.20)	(.2$4)	(−.04)
History	.05	.07	.13*	.14*	.06	.07	.58***	.18**
	(.06)	(.11)	(.23)	(.21)	(.09)	(.12)	(1.12)	(.31)
Gender	.05	.06	.19***	.08	.02	.09	.10***	.03
	(.07)	(.09)	(.30)	(.11)	(.03)	(.14)	(.18)	(.05)
Non–U.S. citizen	.03	.04	.05	.03	.06	.11	−.01	.02
	(.06)	(.09)	(.13)	(.07)	(.14)	(.29)	(−.03)	(.04)
U.S. citizen	−.09	−.09	−.11	−.07	−.02	−.09	−.08	−.07
	(−.15)	(−.15)	(−.23)	(−.12)	(−.03)	(−.19)	(−.19)	(−.15)
Professional age	.17**	.19**	.20***	.23***	.08	.15*	.16***	.24***
	(.01)	(.01)	(.01)	(.01)	(.01)	(.01)	(.01)	(.02)

Academic rank	−.04 (−.03)	−.09 (−.07)	−.09 (−.09)	−.11 (−.09)	−.05 (−.04)	−.13 (−.12)	−.05 (−.05)	−.07 (−.07)
Administrative experience	.01 (.02)	.03 (.05)	.04 (.07)	.01 (.02)	−.02 (−.03)	.02 (.04)	.01 (.02)	.01 (.02)
Graduate seminars/courses taught	.08 (.03)	.02 (.01)	.04 (.02)	.05 (.02)	.03 (.01)	.04 (.02)	.02 (.01)	.03 (.02)
Graduate students' major professor	−.09 (−.02)	−.04 (−.01)	−.03 (−.01)	−.09 (−.02)	−.05 (−.01)	−.03 (−.01)	−.05 (−.01)	−.10 (−.02)
Member student committee	.01 (.02)	−.06 (−.12)	.03 (.07)	−.05 (−.10)	−.04 (−.09)	.05 (.12)	−.02 (−.06)	−.01 (−.02)
Journal article published	.07 (.05)	.03 (.02)	.01 (.01)	.09 (.05)	.10 (.06)	.02 (.01)	.04 (.03)	.09 (.06)
Books published	.01 (.01)	.07 (.06)	.06 (.06)	.02 (.02)	.03 (.0FIX	.06 (.06)	.06 (.07)	.04 (.04)
Tenure status	.05 (.07)	.06 (.08)	−.04 (−.08)	−.02 (−.03)	.09 (.1 FIX	−.01 (−.01)	.02 (.04)	−.09 (−.17)
Constant	3.25	3.39	3.24	3.57	3.29	3.37	3.01	3.04
Total R squared	.08***	.09***	.10***	.07***	.06***	.08***	.43***	.07***

Note: Unstandardized regression coefficients are in parentheses.
*$p < .025$; **$p < .01$; ***$p < .001$; # coefficient less than .01

Disregard for Program

This particular normative pattern stands as a differentiated admonitory norm. Academic discipline and professional age serve to differentiate the level of disdain faculty members express for behaviors associated with this particular norm. In comparison with faculty members in the other three academic disciplines, historians (beta = .18, $p < .001$) tend to express a greater degree of contempt for the behaviors reflective of the norm of *disregard for program.* Likewise, professional age (beta = .24, $p < .001$) wields a positive influence on the level of scorn expressed. Table 7.2 contains the results of the regression analysis that support these observations.

The inviolable norms of *disrespect toward student efforts*, *harassment of students*, *whistle-blowing suppression*, and *directed research malfeasance* emerge from robust multivariate statistical analyses as core inviolable norms. The robustness of the core nature of these four inviolable norms springs from the findings that none of the array of factors included in the four regression analyses yielded statistically significant results.[3] However, the inviolable norm of *misappropriation of student work* arises as a differentiated inviolable norm of graduate study.

In stark contrast to inviolable norms, none of the eight admonitory norms receive designation as a core norm. These eight admonitory norms stand as differentiated normative patterns. Thus differentiated admonitory norms include *neglectful teaching*, *inadequate advising/mentoring*, *degradation of faculty colleagues*, *negligent thesis/dissertation advising*, *insufficient course structure*, *pedagogical narrowness*, *student assignment misallocation*, and *disregard for program.*

Arraying the Factors Influencing Norm Espousal

In this section of the chapter, we center attention on the various factors described above that differentiate espousal of the inviolable norm of *misappropriation of student work* and each of the eight admonitory norms. We seek to determine which of these factors contributes the most to the explained variance in the espousal of these norms. Academic discipline—history—and gender constitute the differentiating factors for the inviolable norm of *misappropriation of student work.* These same two factors as well as institutional type, the academic disciplines of chemistry and psychology, and professional age also play a differentiating role that varies from admonitory norm to admonitory norm. Thus we include these six factors—institutional type, chemistry, psychology, history, gender, and professional age—in stepwise multiple regression analyses we conducted to delineate the factor that contributes the most to the percentage of explained variance in these normative patterns. Put differently, we seek to determine which factor plays the principal role in the differentiation in the level of disdain expressed for violations of these differentiated norms. With a few exceptions that we note, we present statistically significant contributions to explained variance using the .025 level of statistical significance. Table 7.3 displays the results of these stepwise regression analyses.

Differentiated Inviolable Norm

Misappropriation of Student Work

As indicated above, history, gender, and professional age function as the statistically significant differentiating factors for this inviolable norm. From the stepwise regression executed, history emerges as the factor that explains the most variance in the espousal of this inviolable normative pattern (7.4% of the variance). Although professional age (1.5% of the explained variance) and being a female academic (0.9%) contribute statistically significant changes in explained variance, these changes pale in comparison with history. Table 7.3A shows the stepwise regression results that support these assertions.

Differentiated Admonitory Norms

Neglectful Teaching

Professional age (3.1% of the variance) continues to serve as the principal agent of differentiation in faculty espousal of *neglectful teaching* given the results of the stepwise regression analyses. However, holding an academic appointment in a university with very high research activity contributes an additional 1.1% of the variance and being an academic psychologist adds another 1.0%. Table 7.3B exhibits the stepwise regression results that support these observations.

Inadequate Advising/Mentoring

As previously indicated, psychology and professional age play a stastically significant role in the differentiation of this particular normative orientation. Professional age (3.5% of the variance) emerges from the stepwise regression as the factor that contributes the most to the variability in faculty levels of disdain

Table 7.3 Stepwise Regression Analyses

	R Square Change	Statistical significance of the R Square Change
A. Stepwise Regression Analysis for the Inviolable Norm of Misappropriation of Student Work		
Institutional type	failed to enter	
Chemistry	failed to enter	
Psychology	failed to enter	
History	8.4%	$p < .001$
Gender	0.9%	$p < .01$
Professional age	1.5%	$p < .001$
B. Stepwise Regression Analysis for the Admonitory Norm of Neglectful Teaching		
Institutional type	1.1%	$p < .01$
Chemistry	failed to enter	
Psychology	1.0%	$p < .01$
History	failed to enter	
Gender	failed to enter	
Professional age	3.1%	$p < .001$
C. Stepwise Regression Analysis for the Admonitory Norm of Inadequate Advising/Mentoring		
Institutional type	failed to enter	
Chemistry	failed to enter	
Psychology	failed to enter	
History	2.7%	$p < .001$
Gender	failed to enter	
Professional age	3.5%	$p < .001$
D. Stepwise Regression Analysis for the Admonitory Norm of Degradation of Faculty Colleagues		
Institutional type	failed to enter	
Chemistry	failed to enter	
Psychology	failed to enter	
History	1.3%	$p < .001$
Gender	2.1%	$p < .001$
Professional age	1.7%	$p < .001$
E. Stepwise Regression Analysis for the Admonitory Norm of Negligent Thesis/Dissertation Advising		
Institutional type	0.7%	$p < .025$
Chemistry	failed to enter	
Psychology	failed to enter	

Table 7.3 (Continued)

	R Square Change	Statistical significance of the R Square Change
History	2.1%	$p < .001$
Gender	failed to enter	
Professional age	1.5%	$p < .001$
F. Stepwise Regression Analysis for the Admonitory Norm of Insufficient Course Structure		
Institutional type	1.37%	$p < .01$
Chemistry	failed to enter	
Psychology	1.3%	$p < .01$
History	failed to enter	
Gender	failed to enter	
Professional age	1.1%	$p < .01$
G. Stepwise Regression Analysis for the Admonitory Norm of Pedagogical Narrowness		
Institutional type	failed to enter	
Chemistry	failed to enter	
Psychology	1.9%	$p < .001$
History	failed to enter	
Gender	failed to enter	
Professional age	failed to enter	
H. Stepwise Regression Analysis for the Admonitory Norm of Student Assignment Misallocation		
Institutional type	failed to enter	
Chemistry	failed to enter	
Psychology	2.7%	$p < .001$
History	36.5%	$p < .001$
Gender	0.8%	$p < .001$
Professional age	1.6%	$p < .001$
I. Stepwise Regression Analysis for the Admonitory Norm of Disregard for Program		
Institutional type	failed to enter	
Chemistry	failed to enter	
Psychology	failed to enter	
History	1.85%	$p < .001$
Gender	failed to enter	
Professional age	1.9%	$p < .001$

expressed for behaviors indicative of *inadequate advising/mentoring*. In addition, history contributes 2.7% to the explained variance in the espousal of this normative pattern. Table 7.3C exhibits the result of the stepwise regression analysis.

Degradation of Faculty Colleagues

Previously, we noted three factors—gender, history, and professional age—that play a role in the differentiation of this normative pattern. Our stepwise regression analysis identifies gender (2.1%) as the factor that contributes the most to the percentage of explained variance in faculty levels of scorn for behaviors reflective of the norm of *degradation of faculty colleagues*. Professional age also contributes 1.7% to the explained variability in faculty espousal of this norm, whereas history contributes the smallest degree (1.3%). Table 7.3D shows the stepwise regression analyses that provide empirical support for these statements.

Negligent Thesis/Dissertation Advising

Institutional type, academic discipline, and professional age were previously identified as factors that differentiate faculty espousal of this norm. History emerges (2.1) as contributing the most to the percentage of variance explained in the level of disdain faculty voice for behaviors reflective of *negligent thesis/ dissertation advising*. Professional age contributes 1.5% followed by holding an academic appointment in a university with a very high level of research activity (0.7%). Table 7.3E displays the supporting stepwise regression results.

Insufficient Course Structure

We previously pointed to being in a university with very high research activity and being an academic psychologist as factors that differentiate the level of faculty derision of the behaviors that constitute this particular normative configuration. Our stepwise regression analysis indicates that these two factors contribute equal proportions (1.3%) to the percentage of explained variability in faculty espousal of the norm *insufficient course structure*. Moreover, professional age contributes an additional 1.1%. The results of the stepwise regression analysis reported in Table 7.3F corroborate these statements.

Pedagogical Narrowness

Being an academic psychologist and professional age were described above as factors that differentiate this particular admonitory norm. According to our stepwise regression analysis, being an academic psychologist (1.9%) contributes the most to the percentage of explained variance in faculty espousal of *pedagogical narrowness*. However, professional age fails to enter this stepwise regression. Table 7.3G provides the supporting stepwise regression results.

Student Assignment Misallocation

As described previously in this chapter, four factors play a role in the differentiation of faculty response to the behaviors indicative of this normative pattern. However, our stepwise regression analysis clearly demarcates these four factors. Specifically, membership in the discipline of history contributes the most to the percentage of variance explained, a quite large contribution of 36.5%. Being an academic psychologists contributes the next largest percentage (2.7%), followed by professional age (1.6%) and being a female academic (0.8%). Table 7.3H displays the stepwise regression results that provide empirical backing for these observations.

Disregard for Program

We previously delineated history and professional age as factors that differentiate faculty espousal for this normative orientation. Our stepwise regression analysis indicates that both of these factors contribute nearly equally to the percentage of variance explained in the level of scorn faculty voice for behaviors reflective of the norm of *disregard for program*. Specifically, history contributes 1.8% and professional age contributes 1.9%. Table 7.3I contains the results of the stepwise regression analysis that provide support for these statements.

A Key Question

From these stepwise regression analyses, a key question emerges: Do structural dimensions of the academic profession—academic discipline and institutional type—or do faculty personal attributes play the larger role in norm differentiation? If we apply a criterion of 2% or more of the variance explained, academic discipline (being an academic historian), a structural dimension of the academic profession, differentiates the largest number of normative orientations: the violable norm of *misappropriation of student work* (8.4%) and the three admonitory norms of *inadequate advising/mentoring* (2.7%) negligent *thesis/dissertation advising* (2.1%), and *student assignment misallocation* (36.5%). The faculty personal attribute of professional age follows academic discipline, as it differentiates three admonitory norms: the norm of *neglectful teaching* (2.9%), the norm of *inade-*

quate advising/mentoring (3.5%), and the norm of *student assignment misallocation* (2.7%). Gender, a faculty personal attribute, plays such a role in one admonitory norm, as being female contributes 5.7% of the explained variance in the level of disapproval expressed for behaviors indicative of degradation *of faculty colleagues.*

Conclusion

The principal findings of this chapter center on four matters:

1. The various indices of professional attainment and involvement in graduate studies play little or no role in influencing the level of faculty disapproval expressed for behaviors reflective of the five inviolable norms and the eight admonitory norms of graduate study above and beyond the influence of academic discipline, institutional type, and the personal attributes of gender, citizenship, and professional age.
2. As a result of robust statistical analyses, we delineated four core inviolable norms: *disrespect toward student efforts*, *harassment of students*, *whistle-blowing suppression*, and *directed research malfeasance*. However, no core admonitory norms emerged.
3. The structural dimension of academic discipline contributes to the explained variance of more differentiated norms than do the personal attributes of professional age and gender. In particular, the discipline of history contributes 2% or more of the explained variance of one inviolable norm and three of the eight admonitory normative orientations.
4. Considerable unexplained variance exists across the various regression analyses reported in this chapter. See Tables 7.1 and 7.2 for the percentage of variance explained by the full set of personal attributes and the professional involvement and attainments of faculty members.

In Chapter 11, we present explanations to account for the important role the discipline of history plays in the differentiation of one inviolable norm and three admonitory norms.

NOTES

1. High multicollinearity does not pose a problem for each of these five regression analyses, as tolerance and variance inflation factor indices are within acceptable bounda-

ries (Ethington, Thomas, & Pike, 2002). The measurement of the various variables included in these regression analyses were previously described in notes in Chapters 5 and 6.

2. High multicollinearity does not pose a problem for each of these eight regression analyses, as tolerance and variance inflation factor indices are within acceptable boundaries (Ethington, Thomas, & Pike, 2002). The measurement of the various variables included in these regression analyses were previously described in notes in Chapters 5 and 6.

3. For this assertion, we acknowledge the suggestion of an anonymous reviewer of this book.

CHAPTER EIGHT

Graduate School Socialization and the Internalization of the Norms of Graduate Study

This chapter focuses on the role of the graduate school socialization process in the internalization of the inviolable and admonitory norms of graduate study empirically delineated in this volume. Such norms provide moral boundaries for the professional choices faculty make in their performance of the various aspects of the role of graduate teaching and mentoring. The internalization of these normative patterns takes place in varying degrees. The following conceptual framework provides a set of formulations for the internalization of these norms and the aspects of the role of graduate teaching and mentoring associated with them. The consequences of graduate student experience with norm violations by their graduate faculty are also presented.

Conceptual Framework

Through graduate study, graduate students acquire the attitudes, values, norms, and disciplinary knowledge and skill required for faculty research and teaching role performance (Austin & Wulff, 2004; Merton, Reader, & Kendall, 1957).

This powerful socialization process also influences the impression graduate students hold of the professorial role, styles of work, and standards of performance that will guide their subsequent career as a member of the professoriate (Fox, 1985; Zuckerman, 1977). They also acquire a sense of professional commitment and identity (Bucher & Stelling, 1977).

This socialization process takes place through such formal dimensions as course requirements, qualifying examinations, and the dissertation (Braxton & Bayer, 1999). Such role-taking behaviors as serving as a graduate research assistant or a teaching assistant also play a key part in the graduate school socialization process by shaping the professional identity and commitment of graduate students (Bucher & Stelling, 1977). Other critical dimensions of the socialization process include formal and informal relationships between faculty and students (Cole & Cole, 1973). Mentoring constitutes an important form of the relationships between faculty and graduate students.

Through these formal and informal dimensions of the graduate school socialization process graduate students acquire different degrees of familiarity with various aspects of the role of graduate teaching and mentoring. These aspects include advising and mentoring, course design and course planning, treatment of course content, treatment of students in class, and grading of student assignments and examinations (Braxton & Bayer, 1999). Graduate students who serve as teaching assistants acquire a greater degree of familiarity with these aspects of graduate teaching and mentoring than do other graduate students. The supervision of graduate research assistants and directing dissertations or theses constitute additional roles associated primarily with graduate teaching and mentoring. Graduate students also acquire varying degrees of familiarity with these two aspects. Graduate students who serve as graduate research assistants acquire a greater familiarity with the supervision of graduate assistants than do teaching assistants or other graduate students.

These various dimensions of the socialization process provide graduate students with numerous opportunities to observe and listen to faculty who teach graduate courses, supervise graduate research assistants, and supervise dissertation or thesis committees. Graduate students who aspire to become members of the professoriate are perceptive observers and listeners (Austin, 2002). Austin (2002) states that graduate students listen carefully to formal and informal conversations with supervisors and advisors. They also pay close attention to offhanded comments faculty and advance graduate students casually make about professorial roles (Austin, 2002). Thus graduate students receive messages about the conduct of various aspects of the role of graduate teaching and mentoring through listening and observing.

As a consequence, graduate students internalize to varying degrees the inviolable and admonitory normative orientations associated with the various aspects of the role of graduate teaching and mentoring delineated above. The higher the level of disdain individual faculty members espouse for the proscribed behaviors associated with such normative configurations, the greater the likelihood of their adherence to such norms. This assertion finds empirical support in research that indicates that the strength of faculty endorsement of a particular norm positively influences the extent of observance of that norm (Braxton, 1990). Thus graduate students who observe and listen to graduate faculty members who adhere to the inviolable and admonitory norms related to the various aspects of the role of graduate teaching and mentoring tend to internalize these normative patterns.

In the ensuing sections of this chapter, the above-mentioned formulations provide a basis for the discussion of specific aspects of the role of graduate teaching and mentoring and the normative orientations that provide parameters for the conduct of these specific aspects. In particular, such discussions focus on the internalization of the focal norms by graduate students. Findings reported in Chapters 3, 4, 5, and 6 concerning such matters as the level of consensus on the inviolable or admonitory status of a given norm and variation in the level of espousal of a given norm across institutional type, academic discipline, gender, citizenship status, and profession age of faculty members provide an empirical basis for formulations concerning graduate faculty adherence to a given norm as well as the internalization of a given norm by graduate students. Zero-order findings are used because they depict observations that can be made by the naked eye. The outcomes for graduate students of personal experience with faculty observance or violations of the focal norm are also discussed.

Aspects of Graduate Teaching and Mentoring and Internalization of Normative Orientations

In this section of the chapter, the inviolable and admonitory normative patterns are arrayed according to the aspect of graduate teaching and mentoring for which these norms provide moral boundaries for their performance. In some instances, a given norm is placed in more than one aspect of graduate teaching and mentoring. The aspects of graduate teaching and mentoring fit into two broader categories: the community of the classroom, and the apprenticeship. The community of the classroom includes course design and course planning, the treatment of course content, interactions with students in and out of class, and the grading of student assignments and examinations. The apprenticeship includes advising and mentoring, the supervision of graduate research assistant supervision, and thesis or dissertation supervision. For these aspects of graduate teaching and mentoring, the conceptual framework stated above provides a basis for a discussion of internalization of the focal norms by graduate students. All five of the inviolable normative patterns and six of the eight admonitory normative orientations fit into one or more of these categories and their specific aspects. The admonitory norms of *degradation of faculty colleagues* and *graduate program disregard* were not arrayed because their proscriptions fall outside the parameters of the community of the classroom and the apprenticeship.

The Community of the Classroom

The classroom of graduate courses and seminars constitutes a community. Small communities develop around specific courses and seminars (Hirschy & Wilson, 2002). The relationships between graduate faculty members and graduate students shape the learning environment of such classroom communities. Moreover, the professional choices made by graduate faculty members in the conduct of their courses provide opportunities for graduate students to become familiar with such choices. In this case, professional choices involve either adhering to or violating the focal norms of graduate teaching and mentoring. These choices involve such dimensions of conducting a course as course design and planning, the treatment of course content, interactions with students in and out of class, and the grading of student assignments and examinations.

However, the commitment graduate faculty have to graduate-level teaching underlies these various dimensions of the community of the classroom. The admonitory norm of *neglectful teaching* rebukes graduate faculty members who neglect their graduate-level teaching.

Uncertain internalization by graduate students of the norm of *neglectful teaching* seems likely. Graduate students will likely observe a range of graduate faculty behavior regarding conformity to this norm. This assertion emanates from the moderate degree of consensus (57.1%) that exits on the admonitory status of this norm. As indicated in Chapter 4, less than a fifth of respondents view this normative pattern as inviolable and another fifth view its associated behaviors as falling between discretionary behavior and mildly inappropriate behavior, generally to be ignored. Accordingly, some graduate students will experience faculty who adhere to this norm either because they view it as admonitory or because they view it as inviolable. Those faculty who regard it as discretionary behavior or mildly inappropriate but ignorable behavior may occasionally violate this norm. Graduate students harmed by faculty who violate the proscriptions of *neglectful teaching* may internalize the proscriptions of this norm (Horne, 2001). In contrast, unharmed graduate students may come to view the behaviors as discretionary or somewhat inappropriate but not as admonished or inviolable behaviors.

Nevertheless, graduate students enrolled in research universities marked by high levels of research activity will more likely internalize this norm than graduate students in universities characterized as having a very high level of research activity. This assertion springs from the finding reported in Chapter 5 that faculty in research universities with a high level of research activity voice a somewhat greater degree of contempt for behaviors associated with this norm than faculty in universities with very high levels of research activity. The gender and citizenship of graduate faculty members observed make little difference to the internalization of this norm.

As indicated in Chapter 5, academic chemists, biologists, and historians voice comparable levels of disdain for the proscriptions of this norm. However, chemists tend to express a greater degree of scorn than psychologists. Thus graduate students in chemistry will more likely internalize this norm than graduate students in psychology.

Graduate students who frequently observe more senior faculty may internalize the norm of *neglectful teaching*. The positive relationship between professional age and the level of disdain expressed for the behaviors of this norm provides justification for this assertion. Chapter 5 describes this relationship.

Course Design and Course Planning

The admonitory norm of *insufficient course structure* provides parameters for designing and planning graduate courses and seminars. This normative array admonishes graduate faculty members to provide sufficient structure to their graduate-level courses by developing an outline or syllabus for their courses.

For this particular norm, graduate students may experience a range of faculty behavior given the lack of consensus on the admonitory status of this normative pattern noted in Chapter 3. To elaborate, faculty that express an inviolable level of disdain or an admonitory level of disdain will likely adhere to this particular norm. In contrast, those graduate faculty members who view the behaviors associated with this norm as falling between discretionary behaviors and mildly inappropriate but ignorable behavior may occasionally violate this norm. Thus uncertainty characterizes the internalization of the norm of *insufficient course structure* by graduate students.

Students studying in graduate programs in universities with high levels of research activity are more likely to internalize this particular admonitory norm than students enrolled in graduate programs in universities of depicted as having a very high level of research activity. This proposition emanates from the pattern of findings reported in Chapter 4. Specifically, faculty members in universities categorized as high in their level of research activity are more likely to follow the proscriptions of the norm of *insufficient course structure* than their faculty counterparts in universities characterized as having very high levels of research activity. Such likelihood stems from the tendency of academics in universities with less research activity to express a greater degree of disapproval for not designing graduate-level courses than their colleagues in universities with very high levels of research activity.

Graduate students in history departments are also more likely to internalize the norm of *insufficient course structure* than students in departments of psychology. However, graduate students in chemistry and biology departments are also more likely to internalize this particular norm. Such tendencies flow from the findings reported in Chapter 4. As described in this chapter, academic historians tend to express a somewhat greater degree of contempt for the behaviors reflective of these normative patterns than do psychologists holding academic appointments in research universities. However, historians, chemists, and biologists voice similar levels of disapproval; these levels of norm espousal lead to the likelihood of historians, chemists, and biologist adhering to the proscriptions of the norm of *insufficient course structure* to a greater degree than academic psychologists.

As noted in Chapter 5, gender and citizenship status make little difference in the degree of contempt faculty members voice for behaviors reflective of the norm of *insufficient course structure.* As a consequence, these two personal characteristics bear little or no relationship to the probability of faculty adherence to this particular norm. In turn, graduate students taking courses from male and female faculty as well as faculty who are U.S. citizens or non–U.S. citizens will internalize this normative array to a similar degree.

In contrast, graduate students who take a course from faculty of advancing professional age will internalize the norm of *insufficient course structure.* This contention springs from the positive correlation between professional age and the level of contempt expressed for behaviors associated with this particular normative array. This positive relationship suggests that as professional age increases, faculty adherence to this norm likewise increases. See Chapter 5 for particulars.

This particular normative pattern of graduate study also parallels such norms of undergraduate college teaching as the inviolable norm of *inattentive planning* and the admonitory norm of *insufficient syllabus*. The Introduction describes the proscriptions of these two norms. Thus the internalization of the norm of *insufficient course structure* by graduate students also translates into the likely internalization of the proscriptions of the undergraduate college teaching norms of *inattentive planning* and *insufficient syllabus*.

Treatment of Course Content

An inviolable norm and an admonitory norm of graduate study impart boundaries that define unacceptable behavior in the treatment of course content by faculty offering graduate-level courses and seminars. The inviolable norm of *disrespect toward student efforts* is the inviolable normative pattern, and *pedagogical narrowness* stands as an admonitory norm.

Disrespect toward student efforts also provides guidelines for graduate faculty choice in the community-of-the-classroom dimension of in-class and out-of-class interactions with students, the grading of assignments and examinations, and two aspects of the research apprenticeships: research assistant supervision and thesis/dissertation advisement. In the case of the treatment of course content, this particular normative orientation proscribes not permitting students to express viewpoints different from those of the professor. See Chapter 3 for more specificity.

Graduate students are likely to observe little variation in graduate faculty behavior pertaining to the proscriptions of the norm of *disrespect toward student efforts* because of the considerable degree of consensus (72.7% of faculty respondents) among faculty on the inviolable status of this normative array. Thus graduate students will likely experience high levels of graduate faculty adherence to this norm in their treatment of course content in graduate courses and graduate seminars. As a consequence, graduate students will likely internalize this particular norm. Moreover, the institutional type, the academic discipline, and the gender, citizenship status, and professional age of graduate faculty members observed will not alter the internalization of the norm of *disrespect toward student efforts* by graduate students.

The undergraduate college teaching norm of *authoritarian classroom* parallels this particular inviolable norm of graduate study. However, the norm of authoritarian classroom occupies status as an admonitory norm in the normative structure of undergraduate college teaching. *Authoritarian classroom* rebukes faculty behavior that displays a rigid and closed approach to course content and to different points of view expressed by students (Braxton & Bayer, 1999). Thus internalization of the norm of *disrespect toward student efforts* likewise results in some degree of internalization of the norm of *authoritarian classroom.*

As previously indicated, the admonitory norm of *pedagogical narrowness* also pertains to the treatment of course content. It focuses on the content and emphases of graduate courses, as it rebukes narrowness in the content covered in a course. Specifically, such proscribed behaviors include endorsing U.S.-dominated content without acknowledging the contributions of scholars from other countries and not including pertinent scholarly contributions of women and minorities in the content of a seminar.

In Chapter 3, it was noted that considerable disparity exists in the level of contempt faculty members express for the behaviors of this particular norm. This disparity finds expression in the 28.1% of faculty who view these behaviors as inviolable in their level of scorn and the 25.3% of faculty who view them as between discretionary behavior and mildly inappropriate but ignorable behavior. Moreover, 46.0% of faculty members judge this norm as admonitory. This disparity suggests the likelihood that graduate students will observe a range of faculty behaviors reflective of this normative pattern. Some graduate faculty will adhere to the proscriptions of this normative pattern, whereas other graduate faculty will violate them. As a consequence, the internalization of the norm of *pedagogical narrowness* seems uncertain.

The institutional type and the gender and professional age of graduate faculty members observed by graduate students will wield little influence on the internalization of this normative array. However, the academic discipline and the citizenship of observed graduate faculty members make some difference. As indicated in Chapter 4, academic historians tend to voice more disdain for the behaviors reflective of this normative pattern than do academic psychologists; historians, biologists, and chemists display little or no differences. Thus graduate students observing graduate faculty in history, biology, and chemistry will likely experience more adherence to this norm than graduate students in departments of psychology. In addition, graduate students observing international graduate faculty will more likely encounter adherence to the norm of *pedagogical narrowness* than those graduate students taking a seminar or a course from a graduate faculty member with U.S. citizenship.

In-Class and Out-of-Class Interactions with Students

Two inviolable normative orientations present parameters for the conduct of graduate faculty interaction with graduate students in and out of class: *disrespect toward student efforts* and *harassment of students*. The norm of *disrespect toward student efforts* reproves the making of condescending remarks to students in class and routinely ignoring comments or questions from international graduate students. The same formulations previously posited under treatment of course content pertain to interactions between graduate faculty and graduate students. Thus graduate students will likely internalize this norm. Moreover, graduate students studying in departments of biology, chemistry, and history will also internalize this norm to a greater degree than graduate students in departments of psychology. Likewise, graduate students taking courses or seminars from international faculty will also tend to internalize this norm to a greater degree than graduate students enrolled in courses and seminars of faculty with U.S. citizenship.

The inviolable norm of *harassment of students* relates to graduate faculty behaviors that occur within and outside the classroom. As described in Chapter 3, contemptible in-class behaviors include making suggestive sexual comments to students, making racist or sexist remarks in class, and conducting class while obviously intoxicated. Out-of-class graduate faculty behaviors indicative of this normative pattern include having sexual relationships with a graduate student in one's program, a male professor telling a graduate student who is a woman to avoid his specialty because only men can excel in it, and criticizing the academic performance of a graduate student in front of other graduate students.

Graduate students will encounter very little variation in graduate faculty member adherence to this normative array given the considerable degree of consensus among faculty members (89.7%) on its inviolability (see Chapter 3 for details) Accordingly, graduate students will firmly internalize the norm of *harassment of students*. Moreover, the moderation of such internalization will be unlikely to occur because of institutional type, the discipline, and the citizenship status and professional age of graduate faculty members observed by graduate students.

However, graduate students taking graduate courses or seminars from female faculty may experience greater degrees of internalization of this norm given that women tend to voice a somewhat higher degree of contempt for the behaviors indicative of this norm than do their male counterparts.

The norm of *harassment of students* matches the proscriptions of *moral turpitude*, an inviolable norm of undergraduate college teaching (Braxton & Bayer, 1999). Likewise, *disrespect toward student efforts* resembles the inviolable norm of *condescending negativism*, a norm of undergraduate college teaching (Braxton & Bayer, 1999). Hence, the internalization of the norms of *student harassment* and *disrespect toward student efforts* beget the internalization of the norms of *moral turpitude* and *condescending negativism*.

Grading of Student Assignments and Examinations

Behaviors prohibited by the inviolable norm of *disrespect toward student efforts* offer boundaries for the grading of student assignments and examinations by graduate faculty members. These proscribed behaviors include allowing personal friendships with a graduate student to intrude on the objective grading of his or her work; using no term papers, tests, lab reports, or other criteria to assign the final grades for a course; awarding A's to all graduate students enrolled in a seminar regardless of whether the students do any assignments or attend class; and taking social, personal, or other nonacademic characteristics into account in the assigning of grades.

Internalization of this norm by graduate students likely occurs. Furthermore, graduate students in departments of biology, chemistry, and history will tend to internalize this normative pattern to a greater extent than graduate students studying in psychology departments. Graduate students taking courses or seminars from international faculty will also likely internalize this norm to a greater degree than graduate students enrolled in courses and seminars of faculty with U.S. citizenship. Previously developed formulations in this chapter discussed in the section "Treatment of Course Content" support these assertions.

Those behaviors of the norm of *disrespect toward student efforts* that pertain to the grading of student work correspond to the proscriptions of the norm of *particularistic grading*, an inviolable norm of the normative structure of undergraduate college teaching (Braxton & Bayer, 1999). Graduate students who internalize the norm of *disrespect toward student efforts* also internalize the norm of *particularistic grading*.

The Apprenticeship

The apprenticeship constitutes one of the defining aspects of graduate study (Walker, Golde, Jones, Bueschel, and Hutchings, 2008). It takes the form of a one-to-one relationship between a faculty member and a student through which much teaching and learning transpires (Walker et al., 2008). Close work between a master and an apprentice in graduate seminars, laboratories, and research projects shapes this distinctive feature of graduate study.

The graduate faculty member's role in the apprenticeship includes advising and mentoring, supervising graduate research assistants, and supervising the thesis or dissertation of a graduate student. These dimensions of the apprenticeship entail "making visible and explicit those aspects of scholarly and professional expertise that are typically taken for granted and thus unarticulated" (Walker et al., 2008, p. 91). Put differently, graduate students learn the ropes of research and career advancement in academia. Additional outcomes of the apprenticeship include coauthored publications with one's advisor or mentor, the formulation of a program of research, and the identification of a thesis or dissertation topic.

Individual graduate faculty members make choices in their advising and mentoring, their supervision of graduate research assistants, and their supervision of dissertations or theses. Norms also present guidelines for appropriate and inappropriate behavior in making these choices.

Advising and Mentoring

The admonitory norm of *inadequate advising/mentoring* directly pertains to advising and mentoring graduate students. As described in Chapter 3, this norm rebukes graduate faculty members who insufficiently advise or counsel their advisees about degree requirements and preparation for academic careers.

The internalization of this normative pattern by graduate students appears uncertain given that graduate faculty will likely exhibit a range of behaviors regarding the proscriptions indicative of this norm. Although slight majorities (53.9%) of faculty members view this norm as admonitory, other proportions of faculty view it as being either inviolable or somewhere between discretionary and mildly inappropriate but ignorable behavior. Consequently, graduate students will observe a range of behaviors by their mentors, behaviors that include violating this norm or adhering to this norm.

Moreover, graduate students studying in departments of biology, chemistry, and history will likely observe similar degrees of faculty adherence to this normative array. However, students in history will tend to observe their faculty mentors adhering to this norm to a greater degree than graduate students in psychology. Likewise, students with more senior mentors will also encounter more compliance with this norm. Similar patterns of faculty behaviors regarding this normative pattern, however, occur by gender and citizenship status of the graduate faculty member acting as a mentor.

Receiving reports of personally known incidents of research misconduct constitutes one possible situation an advisor or mentor might encounter. The inviolable norm of *whistle-blowing suppression* offers parameters for handling such incidents. Specifically, this normative pattern reproves such behaviors as advising a graduate student to ignore a personally witnessed incident of research misconduct by either another graduate student or by a faculty member.

The internalization of the norm of *whistle-blowing suppression* by graduate students seems very likely, as they will experience little deviance from this normative pattern by graduate faculty. This assertion stems from the high degree of consensus that exists on the inviolability of this normative orientation. Moreover, similar levels of norm internalization by graduate students will transpire across the four academic disciplines represented in this study. In addition, similar levels of internalization will occur regardless of the gender or the citizenship status of the graduate faculty member observed by graduate students. However, the professional age of the graduate faculty member makes a slight difference, as professional age has a positive correlation with the level of disdain expressed for the behaviors that constitute this normative orientation. Thus graduate students who observe their older mentors may internalize the norm of whistle-blowing suppression to a somewhat greater extent.

Supervision of Graduate Research Assistants

Four inviolable norms provide boundaries for faculty professional choices in their supervision of graduate research assistants. Such choices pertain to the research apprenticeship. The four normative patterns are *disrespect toward student efforts*, *misappropriation of student work*, *whistle-blowing suppression*, and *directed research malfeasance*.

The norm of *disrespect toward student efforts* rebukes such behaviors relevant to the research apprenticeship as routinely blaming one's graduate students when the professor's own research work is called into question. As indicated in the section "Treatment of Course Content," graduate students will internalize this particular norm, as they will likely observe high levels of graduate faculty adherence to this norm. These contentions spring from the high degree of consensus (72.7%) among faculty on the inviolable status of the norm of *disrespect toward student efforts*. Moreover, graduate faculty conformity to this norm is unattenuated by institutional type, academic discipline, faculty members' gender, their citizenship status, or their professional age.

Research conducted as part of the research apprenticeship frequently creates opportunities for graduate students to demonstrate their research promise and to publish with their mentor. The norm of *misappropriation of student work* delineates inappropriate behaviors of graduate faculty involving such opportunities. Specifically, such behaviors as routinely removing graduate students from research projects when they begin to show innovative results and publishing an article without offering coauthorship to a graduate assistant who has made a substantial conceptual or methodological contribution to the article evokes high degrees of disdain from faculty members.

Internalization of this inviolable norm by graduate students appears highly likely. In observing their mentor in conducting the research apprenticeship, graduate students will likely experience high degrees of adherence to the proscriptions of the normative pattern of *misappropriation of student work*. Such likelihood stems from the strikingly high level of consensus that exists on the inviolability of this normative array (87.1% of faculty). However, graduate students studying in history departments tend to internalize this normative pattern to a greater extent than graduate students in departments of biology, chemistry, and psychology. This assertion finds support in the finding that academic historians tend to espouse a somewhat higher level of scorn for behaviors associated with this particular norm than their faculty colleagues in the other three academic disciplines represented in this volume.

Moreover, graduate students mentored by female graduate faculty also tend to internalize this normative orientation to greater degree than graduate students mentored by men. This supposition finds support in the finding that female faculty members espouse a slightly greater degree of disdain for behaviors indicative of this norm than do their male counterparts.

Graduate students mentored by more senior (professional age) faculty also tend to internalize the norm of *misappropriation of student work* a bit more than graduate students mentored by more junior faculty given the finding that professional age of faculty is positively related to the level of disdain expressed for violations of this particular norm.

The proscriptions of the norm of *whistle-blowing suppression* also pertain to the supervision of graduate research assistants. In particular, the failure of a faculty member to report a graduate research assistant who has engaged in research or scholarly misconduct constitutes the relevant prohibited behavior.

As posited in the section "Advising and Mentoring," graduate students will likely internalize this normative pattern. The high degree of consensus that exists on the inviolability of this normative orientation among faculty suggests that graduate faculty will mostly follow the proscriptions of this norm. Furthermore, comparable degrees of norm internalization by graduate students will occur across the four academic disciplines represented in this study. Likewise, similar levels of norm internalization will take place regardless of the gender or the citizenship status of the graduate faculty member who supervises the research apprenticeship of graduate students. However, graduate students supervised by more senior graduate faculty members will likely internalize this norm to a slightly higher degree than graduate students supervised by more junior graduate faculty members.

The inviolable norm of *directed research malfeasance* also supplies parameters for handling incidents of research misconduct that might occur in the context of the supervision of graduate research assistants by graduate faculty members. Specifically, this normative array reproves such behaviors as instructing a graduate assistant to alter databooks or lab notes to support a study's hypothesis or instructing a graduate research assistant to fabricate citations for a publication.

The likelihood of internalization of this normative configuration by graduate students appears very high. This assertion finds support in the almost unanimous degree (99.6%) of consensus among faculty on the inviolability of this particular normative pattern. Moreover, comparable levels of norm internalization seem probable for graduate students in each of the four disciplines represented in this volume. In addition, the gender, citizenship status, and professional age of the graduate faculty member supervising graduate research assistants attenuate the strength of the internalization of this norm by graduate students to little or no extent.

In addition to four inviolable norms, the admonitory norm of *student assignment misallocation* offers guidelines of appropriate and inappropriate behavior involving the supervision of graduate research assistants. As stated in Chapter 3, this normative configuration censures graduate faculty behaviors such as requiring that graduate research assistants routinely work many extra hours beyond the time specified by the institution, regularly canceling research team meeting/ appointments that have been scheduled, and assigning a graduate student to grade the work of other graduate students

Uncertain internalization of the norm of *student assignment misallocation* by graduate students appears likely. Graduate students will likely observe a range of graduate faculty behavior regarding adherence to the proscriptions of this norm given the clear lack of consensus on the admonitory status of this norm. See Chapter 3 for specifics on the level of consensus surrounding the level of disdain voiced for the behaviors of this particular norm.

However, internalization of the norm of *student assignment misallocation* seems likely for graduate students in history departments given that academic historians tend to express greater contempt for the behaviors reflective of this norm than faculty in biology, chemistry, and psychology departments. As stated in Chapter 4, historians accord inviolable status to this normative pattern.

Graduate students who are supervised by female academics also tend to internalize the norm of *student assignment misallocation* to a slightly higher degree than graduate students supervised by male graduate faculty members. This contention emanates from the finding, reported in Chapter 5, that female academics express a slightly stronger degree of contempt for behaviors reflective of this norm than do male faculty members. In addition, slightly stronger norm internalization will also occur for graduate students supervised by more senior faculty given the positive relationship between professional age and the level of scorn expressed for this norm described in Chapter 5.

Supervision of Theses or Dissertations

One inviolable and two admonitory norms apply to the supervision of theses or dissertations. As described in Chapter 3, the admonitory norm of *negligent thesis/dissertation advising* rebukes graduate faculty members who neglect their responsibilities in directing theses or dissertations of graduate students.

Uncertainty best characterizes the internalization of the norm of *negligent thesis/dissertation advising* by graduate students. Graduate students will likely experience a wide range of graduate faculty behavior regarding this norm given the lack of consensus (48.1%) that exists on the admonitory status of this norm. Uncertain internalization applies regardless of the gender or citizenship status of a graduate student's thesis or dissertation advisor. However, graduate students supervised by more senior graduate faculty members appear more likely to internalize this norm than graduate students with thesis or dissertation advisors who are more junior. This contention springs from the positive relationship between professional age and the level of contempt expressed for the behaviors that constitute this norm reported in Chapter 5.

A dimension of the admonitory norm of *student assignment misallocation* also pertains to the supervision of theses and dissertations. This particular dimension rebukes thesis or dissertation advisors who agree to direct a thesis/dissertation only under the condition that he or she will be a coauthor on all publications based on the work.

As stated in the section "Supervision of Graduate Research Assistants," internalization of the norm of *student assignment misallocation* by graduate students is uncertain. Because of the lack of clear consensus on the admonitory status of this norm, considerable variability in experiences graduate students have with their thesis or dissertation advisors adhering or violating this normative pattern seems probable. As previously stated, graduate students in history departments, however, will more likely internalize this norm than graduate students engaged in their thesis or dissertation work in biology, chemistry, and psychology departments.

The inviolable normative pattern of *disrespect toward student efforts* also provides parameters for the supervision of a thesis or a dissertation by graduate faculty members. Germane proscribed behaviors that constitute this norm include a student consistently being unable to get an appointment with his or her thesis/dissertation advisor within three of four weeks to discuss issues concerning the thesis/dissertation and a professor delaying the graduation of his or her best graduate students in order to keep the student around longer.

Internalization by graduate students of the norm of *disrespect toward student efforts* seems very likely. The substantial amount (72.7%) of consensus that exists on the inviolability of this normative array suggests that graduate faculty will likely adhere to its proscriptions. Moreover, institutional type; academic discipline; and the gender, citizenship status, or professional age of the graduate faculty member fail to attenuate the internalization of this norm.

Further Outcomes of Graduate School Socialization

Other outcomes emerge from graduate student observations of norm adherence or norm violations by graduate faculty members in their classroom teaching and in the various aspects of the apprenticeship. In particular, departure from graduate study and detrimental effects on aspirations for becoming a member of the professorate may result from graduate student experience with violations of the inviolable and admonitory norms associated with the various aspects of graduate teaching and mentoring outlined above.

Departure from Graduate Study

Graduate student departure constitutes an important problem of graduate education (Austin & Wulff, 2004). Austin and Wulff (2004) point to Lovitts's (2001) contention that a consistent departure rate of 50% from doctoral programs has occurred since the early 1960s.

Lovitts (2004), Golde and Dore (2004), and Ehrenberg, Jakubson, Groen, So, and Price (2007) empirically identify factors that account for student departure from graduate study. Lovitts (2004) delineates cognitive maps and integration as key factors. Integration also receives support from the research of Golde and Dore (2004) as well as the formulations of Tinto (1993).

Lovitts (2004) defines cognitive maps as mental models that help people make sense of their experiences. In this case, formal requirements and informal expectations define the cognitive maps of graduate students. Graduate students may form faulty cognitive maps because of their experiences with graduate faculty members who violate the proscriptions of the admonitory norms of *insufficient course structure*, *inadequate advising/mentoring*, and *negligent thesis/dissertation advising*. Violations of the norm of *insufficient course structure* entails failing to provide course syllabus. Graduate students who experience violations of this norm may develop poor cognitive maps of course requirements or expectations. If graduate students experience violations of this norm during the first year of graduate study or in core courses, their departure from graduate study may transpire. Research by Ehrenberg and colleagues (2007) also supports this contention.

Poor cognitive maps of degree requirements and the process of preparing for an academic career may result from graduate students' experiences with violations of the norm of *inadequate advising/mentoring* by their graduate faculty advisor or mentor. Such experiences may also result in departure from graduate study.

As described in Chapter 3, the proscribed behaviors embedded in the norm of *negligent thesis/dissertation advising* include the advisor not giving any substantive feedback on drafts to any of his or her graduate students, being routinely unavailable to answer graduate students' questions about their thesis dissertation, routinely taking more than a month to give feedback on a student's draft chapter, and failing to prepare advisees for questioning at their final oral defense. Violations of this normative array by thesis or dissertation advisors may result in ill-formed cognitive maps of expectations for the dissertation and its defense. Graduate students who experience violations of this norm by thesis or dissertation advisor may result in either their departure from graduate study or their failure to complete their thesis or dissertation.

The research of Golde and Dore (2004) and Lovitts (2004) delineates graduate students' perception of their fit or congruence with the learning environment of their graduate department as influential in student departure from graduate study. In particular, Tinto (1993) points to the behaviors of graduate faculty members as key determinants of the student's sense of congruence or ill fit.

Some graduate students enter their graduate programs with considerable interest in teaching. Golde and Dore (2004) assert that "teaching is one of the most appealing aspects of faculty life" (p. 23). As a consequence, some sense of mismatch may spring from graduate student encounters with graduate faculty members who violate the admonitory norm of *neglectful teaching*. This normative pattern rebukes graduate faculty members who neglect their graduate-level teaching by being routinely late for class meetings, meeting the class without having reviewed pertinent materials for the day, not promptly returning graded tests and papers to students, and not following the course outline or syllabus for most of the seminar. Such a perception of academic incongruence may result in departure from graduate study.

Graduate students who experience violations of such inviolable norms as *disrespect toward student efforts*, *harassment of students*, *whistle-blowing suppression*, and *directed research malfeasance* by graduate faculty members may also come to view themselves as academically incongruent. Because "norms and behavior are never perfectly correlated" (Zuckerman, 1988, p. 516), an occasional violation of these inviolable norms is possible.

Violations of *disrespect toward student efforts* shape student perceptions of their fit in several ways. First, this normative pattern rebukes not permitting students to express viewpoints different from those of a graduate faculty member. If the viewpoint of the graduate faculty member conflicts with that of the graduate student, a sense of ill fit may occur. Second, this norm scorns such faculty behaviors as making condescending remarks to students in class or routinely ignoring the comments or questions of international graduate students. Graduate students who experience such proscribe behaviors by graduate faculty members may also view themselves as a poor academic fit for their graduate program.

Third, disdain for such graduate faculty behaviors as allowing personal friendships with graduate students to intrude on the objective grading of their work and taking social, personal, or other nonacademic characteristics into account in the assigning of grades also make up the proscriptions of this particular normative array. A sense of academic incongruence may also result from graduate student experiences with graduate faculty behavior of this sort. These various forms of academic incongruence may result in departure from graduate study.

Graduate students who experience violations of the norm of *harassment of students* may also develop a sense of mismatch with the academic environment of their graduate program. As previously described, this inviolable norm finds contemptible such behaviors as making suggestive sexual comments to students, making racist or sexist remarks in class, conducting class while obviously intoxicated, having sexual relationships with a graduate student in one's program, a male professor telling a graduate student who is a woman to avoid his specialty because only men can excel in it, and criticizing the academic performance of a graduate student in front of other graduate students. Clearly, graduate students' experience with graduate faculty members who engage in such behaviors may result in their departure from graduate study because of their perception of their incongruence that develops from such experiences.

Graduate students with internalized norms and values regarding the responsible conduct of research would also view themselves as highly incongruent if they experience violations of the norms of *whistle-blowing suppression* and *directed research malfeasance* by those graduate faculty members who supervise their research assistantships. Their departure from graduate study is possible.

A sense of academic incongruence may also develop from graduate student experiences with violations of the admonitory norm of *pedagogical narrowness*. Given the wide range of possible graduate faculty behavior regarding the proscribed behaviors of this normative pattern, graduate students may encounter violations of this norm by some graduate faculty members. As previously described, the proscribed behaviors of this norm include endorsing U.S.-dominated content without acknowledging the contributions of scholars from other countries and not including pertinent scholarly contributions of women and minorities in the content of a seminar. International students, female students, and students of color may experience a sense of academic incongruence because of their experience with violations of this particular norm by graduate faculty members. Because of such perceptions of incongruence, their departure from graduate study seems plausible.

Aspirations for an Academic Career

The graduate school socialization process shapes graduate students' perceptions of the professorial role, styles of work, and standards of performance that will guide their subsequent career as a member of the professoriate (Fox, 1985; Zuckerman, 1977) Moreover, a sense of professional commitment and identity emerge (Bucher & Stelling, 1977).

Graduate students learn the importance of publications, as they provide the primary basis for rewards and recognition in the academic profession (Cole & Cole, 1973; Fox, 1985; Gaston, 1978). As a consequence, opportunities for publishing with one's sponsor or mentor during graduate study mold student aspirations for an academic career, as predoctoral publications constitute role-taking behaviors of the academic profession. As previously stated, role-taking behaviors shape professional identify and commitment (Bucker & Stelling, 1977). Predoctoral publications likewise influence subsequent publication productivity (Reskin, 1979) Nettles and Millett (2006) surmise that "the resumes of doctoral students who enter the labor market with doctoral student research accomplishments may well stand out in a pile of applications" (p. 104).

Graduate faculty violations of the norm of *disrespect toward student efforts* may dampen graduate student aspirations for entering the academic profession. As indicated elsewhere in this chapter, this inviolable normative pattern rebukes graduate faculty who, in their supervision of graduate research assistants, routinely remove them from research projects when they begin to show innovative results, or publish an article without offering them coauthorship when they have made a substantial conceptual or methodological contribution to the article. Because of their negative experiences with such role-taking activities as participating in research projects, the professional identity and commitment of graduate students may also suffer (Bucher & Stelling, 1977). However, the high degree of consensus on the violability of this normative pattern suggests that faculty adherence to this norm seems likely. Nevertheless, violations can occur because of Zuckerman's (1988) observation that "norms and behavior are never perfectly correlated" (p. 516).

Conclusion

This chapter advances formulations regarding the internalization of the inviolable and admonitory norms that constitute the normative structure of graduate study. These norms are also arrayed according to the aspects of the role of graduate teaching and mentoring for which these norms function as boundaries for appropriate and inappropriate faculty choices in carrying out these role aspects. These formulations posit internalization of the five inviolable norms of graduate study by graduate students, whereas uncertainty characterizes the internalization of six admonitory normative patterns. This chapter also presents assertions regarding variability in norm internalization as a function of the institutional type, academic discipline, and the gender, citizenship status, and professional age of the graduate faculty member observed.

The formulations of this chapter also discuss the likelihood of norm violations by graduate faculty members. The outcomes of graduate student experience with norm violations include departure from graduate study and dampening of aspirations for an academic career and professional identify and commitment.

CHAPTER NINE

The Support of Graduate Teaching Norms by Supporting Organizations

Norms serve to regulate group behavior, but norms are frequently informal (Durkheim, 1982). Where do faculty members turn when they seek formal guidance on professional ethics? Codes of professional conduct or ethics are a rare example of formal norms. However, statements of norms embedded in codes of professional conduct may not align well with actual informal norms. In the realm of graduate teaching, where faculty tend to adopt a laissez-faire approach toward their colleagues, it is plausible that formal normative statements tend to be weak or limited. In this chapter, we examine formal codes of conduct as they address the teaching of graduate students promulgated by the American Association of University Professors (AAUP) and disciplinary scholarly societies. The AAUP, which is designed to protect the interests of all faculty members, and most scholarly societies, designed to serve the interests of particular disciplines, have codes of conduct for their members. Some have multiple statements covering different topics. These vary considerably in length and breadth and cover both rights and responsibilities.

American Association of University Professors

Our first source of data was policy documents and reports of the American Association of University Professors. The AAUP is both a union and a professional association cutting across academic disciplines. Its guidance on the rights and responsibilities of faculty is accepted by many institutions and faculty members, even those without collective bargaining.

The 10th edition of *AAUP Policy Documents and Reports*, or "Redbook," was examined for statements referring to faculty relations with graduate students, including statements that simply referred to "students" without specifying level (American Association of University Professors, 2006). The presence of the word "student" alone was insufficient; the context needed to refer to a student right or faculty responsibility. Thus, for example, portions of the policy report "The Assignment of Course Grades and Student Appeals" were omitted because they referred to institutional policies dealing with student grade appeals. Most statements in the Redbook were not limited to graduate students. The exceptions included

- the statement "In dealing with graduate students, professors must demonstrate by precept and example the necessity of rigorous honesty in the use of sources and of utter respect for the work of others" (p. 176); and
- the "Statement on Graduate Students," which covers academic freedom, program requirements, intellectual property, institutional governance, rights as employees, physical and environmental support and training, access to records, collective bargaining, limitations on assistantship hours, and fringe benefits.

The remaining statements, despite their lack of references to graduate students, are unlikely to deliberately exclude them. A typical example is "Sexual relations between students and faculty members with whom they also have an academic or evaluative relationship are fraught with potential for exploitation" (p. 247).

Most of the Redbook either agrees with the norms described in Chapters 3 and 4 or covers topics the GTMBI does not address (i.e., access to student records). An exception is in the sections covering sexual relations with students, which is worth quoting in full. The section on sexual harassment states, "The applicability of [the statement that forbids "exploitation of students for private advantage"] to a faculty member's use of institutional position to seek unwanted sexual relations with students . . . is clear" (p. 244). In the section "Consensual Relations between Faculty and Students," it says:

> Sexual relations between students and faculty members with whom they also have an academic or evaluative relationship are fraught with potential for exploitation. The respect and trust accorded a professor by a student, as well as the power exercised by the professor in an academic or evaluative role, make voluntary consent by the student suspect. Even when both parties initially have consented, the development of a sexual relationship renders both the faculty member and the institution vulnerable to possible later allegations of sexual harassment in light of the significant power differential that exists between faculty members and students.
>
> In their relationships with students, members of the faculty are expected to be aware of their professional responsibilities and to avoid apparent or actual conflict of interest, favoritism, or bias. When a sexual relationship exists, effective steps should be taken to ensure unbiased evaluation or supervision of the student (American Association of University Professors, 2006, p. 247).

What is forbidden by this statement is exploitative sexual relationships between faculty members and students for whom they have responsibilities. While suggesting such relationships are fraught with danger, it does not go so far as to entirely rule them out. This contrasts with the norm *harassment of students*, particularly the item "A professor has a sexual relationship with a graduate student in their program." In this instance, the formal statement of the norm appears to be less strong than the actual norm itself.

Three of the inviolable norms we empirically identified were extensively covered by the AAUP Redbook: *disrespect toward student efforts*, *harassment of students*, and *misappropriation of student work*. Examples of *disrespect toward student efforts* include "Graduate students have the right to academic freedom. Like other students, they should be free to take reasoned exception to the data or views offered in any course of study and to reserve judgment about matters of opinion, but they are responsible for learning the content of any course of study for which they are enrolled" (p. 280). *Harassment of students* includes "They avoid any exploitation, harassment, or discriminatory treatment of students" (p. 171). *Misappropriation of student work* include "Graduate students are entitled to the protection of their intellectual-property rights, including recognition of their participation in supervised research and their research with faculty, consistent with generally accepted standards of attribution and acknowledgment in collaborative settings" (p. 281). Additionally, *inadequate advising* was addressed with material relevant to the item "A graduate advisor fails to inform his/her advisees of the requirements for the completion of their degrees" (p. 281). The inviolable norms of *whistle-blowing suppression* and *directed research malfeasance* are not addressed.

Several additional items are covered. Two statements, "[Professors] hold before [students] the best scholarly and ethical standards of their discipline" and "They protect their academic freedom," are very general (p. 171). Other topics addressed by the AAUP but not by the inviolable and admonitory norms that constitute the normative structure of graduate study include

- a willingness to consider student requests for grade changes (p. 127);
- the lack of right to refuse to teach students based on disagreements in belief or potential action (p. 173);
- the responsibilities of remaining professors if a student's dissertation chair leaves (p. 281);
- the lack of right to retaliate against students who file grievances or who participate in collective bargaining (p. 281);
- the requirement that students be able to see their files and the coterminous right of faculty to redact some information therein (p. 281);
- a prohibition on working students excessively in assistantships, typically 20 hours a week (p. 281); and
- faculty provision of training, supervision, a safe working environment, familiarity with academic norms, information about professional opportunities and supporting for pursuing them, and conference funding (p. 281).

Only one admonitory norm is addressed, *neglectful teaching*. "It is improper for an instructor persistently to intrude material that has no relationship to the subject, or to fail to present the subject matter of the course as announced to the students and as approved by the faculty in their collective responsibility for the curriculum" is similar to the item "The professor frequently introduces opinions on religious, political, and social issues clearly outside the realm of seminar content" (p. 174).

In addressing the responsibilities of individual faculty members, the AAUP's documents focus on the faculty's teaching and supervisory roles, although *misappropriation of student work* does address research-related issues. Other statements about research tend to focus on a broader institutional responsibility, such as a safe working environment. Many others address processes that the individual faculty member ought to respect but is not responsible for creating, such as grade change requests or graduate student union formation. This is not surprising given that that Redbook is a manual for faculty-institution relations. Perhaps, too, being promulgated by faculty members with respect to institutions, the responsibilities of faculty members are less likely to be emphasized than are obligations of the institutions and the creation of a stable system.

Disciplinary Codes of Ethics

The second data source was the codes of ethics for scholarly associations in the same four disciplines represented in this volume: biology, chemistry, history, and psychology. A list of associations was created from umbrella organizations such as the American Council of Learned Societies, the Consortium of Social Science Associations, and the affiliate organizations of the American Academy of Arts and Sciences. Honor societies and associations for the teachers of a subject were excluded. Codes of ethics were then downloaded from the Web sites of these organizations. Codes of ethics were not available for many institutions. In a very few instances, the codes were available only in printed materials, or the organization stated that its members were expected to follow the code established by another organization. In some cases in which codes of ethics were not mentioned, it is likely that most members of a rather specialized association are also members of a more general one and thus the specialized organization has felt no need for its own code. Some organizations are dominated by practitioners or amateurs, and these were less likely to have professional codes of ethics. Finally, some simply had no code of conduct available online, whatever the reason.

There are more societies in some disciplines than in others. In biology there were four codes; in chemistry and psychology, one each; and in history, three. To broaden the pool of codes, societies for all pure disciplines were used, categorized according to high (9) or low (19) paradigmatic development. The particular societies used are listed in Table 9.1. The size of the cell does not necessarily reflect the size of the disciplines but simply their organization. The organizational codes used came from the societies listed in Table 9.1.

The codes of ethics were then analyzed for statements that referenced graduate students or could logically be seen as including them. All codes had statements that were presumably applicable to students, but the statements were too broad to map onto the norms. For example, the American Mathematical Society code states, "Mathematical ability must be respected wherever it is found, without regard to race, gender, ethnicity, age, sexual orientation, religious belief,

Table 9.1 Scholarly Societies Categorized along Biglan's Dimensions of High/Low and Life/Nonlife

High/Life	**Low/Life**
American Institute of Biological Sciences[a] American Society for Microbiology[a] Botanical Society of America[a] Society for In Vitro Biology[a]	African Studies Association American Anthropological Association American Association of Physical Anthropologists American Political Science Association American Psychological Association[a] American Sociological Association American Studies Association Archaeological Institute of America Society of American Archaeologists
High/Nonlife	**Low/Nonlife**
American Chemical Society[a] American Geological Institution American Mathematical Society American Physical Society American Statistical Association	American Historical Association[a] American Musicological Society American Philology Association American Philosophical Association Association of American Geographers International Center of Medieval Art Modern Language Association National Council on Public History[a] Organization of American Historians[a] Society of Biblical Literature

[a]Society is in a discipline examined in the larger study.

political belief, or disability" (Ethical Guidelines, section II). Others had more specific statements that did not refer directly to students but might be presumed to include them. When statements did not include students directly, the decision to use them was based on how broad the statement was. Thus "American Society for Microbiology members shall not commit scientific misconduct, defined as fabrication, falsification, or plagiarism" (Code of Ethics, Rules of Conduct) was not included because it does not refer to the behavior of others, but "Expose fraud and professional misconduct whenever found" (American Institute of Biological Sciences, Ethics Statement) was. The relevant portions of each code were then mapped onto the items constituting the norms. A few statements mapped onto multiple items or were so general as to map onto none.

Seven of the codes of ethics had no references at all to either teaching or working with students at any level. The remainder varied greatly in their depth and attention paid not only to faculty/student roles but to all subjects addressed.

There were 17 statements in the high codes and 126 in the low codes. Even given the differing number of codes in each category, the soft disciplines still addressed significantly more items — 6.6 statements per code versus only 1.9 statements per code for the hard disciplines.

Many ethical codes had references to working with collaborators that could be assumed to include graduate students. Of those that did in some way include teaching, mentoring, or advising, most referred to "students" and did not distinguish between undergraduate and graduate students. There are similarities between the relationships, of course. For example, "The professor has a sexual relationship with a graduate student in their program" constitutes part of the inviolable norm *harassment of students* from the GTMBI, while "A faculty member has a sexual relationship with a student enrolled in the course" is one factor in *moral turpitude* from Braxton and Bayer's earlier work on undergraduates (Braxton & Bayer, 1999; Braxton, Proper, & Bayer, 2011). However, the intense mentorship and research supervision of graduate programs are only rarely found at the undergraduate level. Not only do mentors and graduate students spend more time together, but these relationships tend to involve activities, such as publishing together, that are much less prevalent with undergraduates. It is somewhat surprising that so few of the codes distinguished between levels of students.

Some codes contained statements referring to students that were too broad to be mapped onto a specific norm. A typical example of this comes from the National Council on Public History code, which states, "A public historian should contribute time and information to the professional development of students, interns, beginning professionals, and other colleagues" (NCPH Code of Ethics and Professional Conduct, The "Public Historian's Responsibility to the Profession and to Colleagues"). There were 14 instances of similarly broad statements. While these suggest a disciplinary concern with ethics, none of these statements provide explicit guidance for scholars.

Other codes contained items that were not included in any of the inviolable and admonitory normative arrays described in this volume, a total of 25 items. We cannot conclude whether faculty members do or do not regard these as reflective of norms, since we did not include them in the GTMBI. These includes statements about admissions policies ("All classicists should also be aware that it is a national policy, agreed on by the Council of Graduate Schools, that no institution may expect a student to respond to an offer before April 15. There should be no attempt, direct or subtle, to compel or urge such response before the applicants have all the information they need, which may be only shortly before that date" [American Philology Association, APA Statement on Professional Ethics, Section II, Students]); confidentiality ("Teachers should keep confidential what they know about students' academic standing, personal lives, and political or religious views and should not exploit such personal knowledge" [Modern Language Association, Statement of Professional Ethics, "Ethical Conduct in Teaching and Learning"]); the teaching of ethics ("While learning how to apply statistical theory to problems, students should be encouraged to use these guidelines, regardless of whether their target professional specialty will be 'statistician' " [American Statistical Association, Ethical Guidelines for Statistical Practice, section IA); financial well-being ("Teachers/mentors should . . . compensate students/trainees justly for their participation in all professional activities" [American Anthropological Association, Code of Ethics of the American Anthropological Association, section IV-4]); assessment ("Graduate students should be assisted with the progress of their degrees through periodic assessments" [American Studies Association, Statement on Standards in Graduate Education, "Standards Pertaining to Program and Institutional Support"]); placement ("The American Philosophical Association discourages the nomination by graduate departments of job seekers for positions in philosophy, and the submission of their dossiers in response to announcements of positions, without their knowledge or interest" [Code of Ethics of the American Anthropological Association]); sharing knowledge ("Members of the Association are committed to open and full disclosure of their work to all cooperating African Studies Association colleagues and institutions, all graduate and field assistants" [African Studies Association, Guidelines of the African Studies Association for Members: Ethical Conduct in Research and Other Professional Undertakings in Africa]); students as research subjects ("Teachers whose research in any way includes students as subjects must make clear the obligations, rewards, and consequences of participation" [Modern Language Association, Statement of Professional Ethics, "Ethical Conduct in Teaching and Learning"]); and the supervision of teaching ("Teachers working with teaching assistants have a special responsibility to provide them with adequate preparation, continuing guidance, and informed evaluation" (Modern Language Association, Statement of Professional Ethics, Ethical Conduct in Teaching and Learning]).

However, there were a few statements that referred to behaviors included in the GTMBI but that either were not censured or failed to load on any of the inviolable and normative arrays. For example, the American Sociological Association code states, "Sociologists make decisions concerning textbooks, course content, course requirements, and grading solely on the basis of educational criteria without regard for financial or other incentives" (Code of Ethics, section 19.02c). This is similar to the GTMBI item "A seminar professor requires students to purchase a book on which he/she will earn and retain royalties." This suggests either that while a discipline may strive to create a norm, it may not yet be one, or that it is a norm in that particular discipline but not in the larger world of academia.

The inviolable norm of *disrespect toward student efforts* was supported by 19 statements. For example, the American Historical Association code says, "Teachers should judge students' work on merit alone" (Statement on Standards of Professional Conduct, section 5), which maps onto the items "The professor allows personal friendships with a graduate student to intrude on the objective grading of their work" and "Social, personal, or other non-academic characteristics of graduate students are taken into account in the assigning of grades."

Misappropriation of student work was supported by 24 statements in various codes. For example, the Botanical Society of America's "They will not present as their own the work of others, and will credit earlier published studies and individuals whose results they are confirming" (Guidelines for Professional Ethics, section 4B) maps onto "A faculty member publishes an article using innovative ideas derived from a graduate student's term paper without acknowledging the student's contribution."

Harassment of students was supported by 15 statements. Statements ranged from the general ("Beyond specific legal dictates, geographers should strive to create a collegial environment that never tolerates harassment of any kind" [Association of American Geographers, Statement on Professional Ethics, section IIA]) to the specific ("Psychologists do not engage in sexual relationships with students" [American Psychological Association, Ethical Standards, section 3.02]). The expression of this norm was unusual in that most statements were at the very general level and did not match any particular GTMBI item; the major exception was the four statements that explicitly prohibited sexual relationships between students and faculty members.

Whistle-blowing suppression was found in only four cases. For example, "Expose scientific fraud and other forms of professional misconduct whenever it is found" is from the Ethics Code of the American Institute of Biological Sciences. None of the four statements refer directly to students, but the statements are phrased such as to suggest their applicability to all colleagues.

Finally, *directed research malfeasance* appears only twice. Presumably, statements directing members not to engage in research malfeasance themselves could be construed to mean not to direct others to engage in it either; however, unlike the statements for *whistle-blowing suppression,* they did not refer to tolerating or preventing malfeasance in others. Because of this, the lack of specific statements does not suggest that associations' codes are at odds with professional norms.

The admonitory norms received lesser support, with the exceptions of *neglectful teaching* and *inadequate advising/mentoring. Neglectful teaching* was included only in codes from soft disciples, such as this statement from American Philology Association: "Teachers should make explicit at the outset of a course the material to be covered and the standards and procedures for evaluation of students. Every reasonable effort should be made to adhere to this plan" (Section II-Students). *Inadequate advising/mentoring* received nine mentions, all from soft disciplines except this one from the American Mathematical Society: "Mathematicians and organizations involved in advising graduate students should fully inform them about the employment prospects they may face upon completion of their degrees" (Ethical Guidelines, Section III).

Negligent thesis/dissertation advising also was well represented, with four statements. One statement, from American Political Science Association, was "After submitting a proposal for a thesis or dissertation, a student should be informed by the chairperson of his or her committee of its action with regard to the acceptability of the proposal. Action on a proposal should be taken within a reasonable time and communicated to the student in writing" (A Guide to Professional Ethics in Political Science, 11.3). It mapped onto two specific proscribed behaviors that make up this particular normative orientation: "The thesis/dissertation advisor does not give any substantive feedback on drafts to any of their students" and "The thesis/dissertation advisor routinely takes more than a month to give feedback on the student's draft chapter."

Only one rather general statement regarding *degradation of faculty colleagues* appeared: "Sociologists do not permit personal animosities or intellectual differences with colleagues to foreclose students' or supervisees' access to these colleagues or to interfere with student or supervisee learning, academic progress, or professional development" (American Sociological Association, Code of Ethics, 18.02.a). *Pedagogical narrowness* was supported by only two statements, both from history. *Insufficient course structure* was supported by two statements, both in soft disciplines and both in reference to syllabi—for example, "At the outset of each course, teachers should provide students with a statement on approaches to the course materials, on the goals of the course, and on the standards by which students will be evaluated" (Modern Language Association, Statement of Professional Ethics, Ethical Conduct in Teaching and Learning, 2). *Graduate program disregard* was supported twice.

Student assignment misallocation was not supported by any statements. Yet a lack of direct support cannot be taken as a sign that the scholarly societies reject these norms; as Wagner (1966) says, "The point of a code of ethics is not to tell the professional what to do in each and every instance, but to draw his or her attention generally to the most important moral considerations" (p. 10).

Several of the codes contained statements that pertained to behaviors not included in any of the inviolable or admonitory norms or in the GTMBI. Some of these occurred in psychology and were specific to that discipline: "Faculty who are or are likely to be responsible for evaluating students' academic performance do not themselves provide that therapy" is part of the American Psychological Association code (Ethical Principles of Psychologists and Code of Conduct, section 7.04b). Other statements in history and psychology addressed truthfulness or confidentiality. In the American Historical Association code, for example, we find "All who participate in the community of inquiry, as amateurs or as professionals, as students or as established historians, have an obligation to oppose deception. This obligation bears with special weight on teachers of graduate seminars. They are critical in shaping a young historian's perception of the ethics of scholarship. It is therefore incumbent on graduate teachers to seek opportunities for making the seminar also a workshop in scholarly integrity" (Statement on Standards of Professional Conduct, "Plagiarism").

Many specific items included in any of the inviolable or admonitory norms or more generally in the GTMBI did not map onto any statements in codes, which we suggest should not be taken as a lack of support for them. Many of these items are highly specific violations of norms that more general precepts can be presumed to include. For example, no code warned specifically against frequently borrowing money from students, but this can be easily subsumed under general statements such as "Do not exploit students." While strong support for a few individual items is worth examining, for the most part the codes are best examined at the norm level rather than the item level.

The particular GTMBI item that was most frequently mapped to was "A faculty member publishes an article without offering co-authorship to a graduate assistant who has made a substantial conceptual or methodological contribution to the article" from *misappropriation of student work* for the all disciplines. In the soft disciplines, other high counts were found for "Students are not permitted to express viewpoints different from those of the professor" from *disrespect toward student efforts* and "A faculty member publishes an article using innovative ideas derived from a graduate student's term paper without acknowledging the student's contribution" from *misappropriation of student work.*

In addition to examining the data by norms, we examined it by discipline. The four disciplines were chosen because they varied on the high/low dimension in Biglan's typology of disciplines; all were pure rather than applied. (Biglan, 1973). Societies in the high disciplines addressed four inviolable norms, excluding *directed research malfeasance*, and three of the admonitory norms: *inadequate advising/mentoring, negligent thesis supervision*, and *graduate program disregard*. Societies in the low disciplines addressed all inviolable norms and all admonitory norms except for *student assignment misallocation*. The only norms to receive higher support among the hard disciplines were *whistle-blowing suppression* and *graduate program disregard*, but given the small number of statements, it is impossible to conclude these differences are significant.

What is more disturbing is that some societies' codes contained no references to students at all. These include the American Society for Microbiology from the hard disciplines and the American Association of Physical Anthropologists, Archaeological Institute of America, Society of American Archaeologists, National Council on Public History, Organization of American Historians, and Society of Biblical Literature from the soft disciplines. In some cases this may be due to a discipline or subdiscipline that contained a greater mix of practitioners, such as the National Council of Public Historians. In other cases, such as the American Society of Mathematics, this explanation seems less likely.

Scholarly societies' codes of conduct are rarely used to censure members, except in the medical professions. Thus it is likely that these codes serve less as a guide to members who are experiencing genuine ethical confusion than as a public statement of professionalization. Broad statements about teaching that amount to "be respectful" may also serve Wagner's purpose of broadly covering a wide ethical swath instead of providing dos and don'ts. Additionally, teaching may be seen as a concern of the professoriate as a whole rather than of any particular discipline, leading to spartan or general treatment of it by the disciplines. Most of the codes examined were more concerned with research behavior than with teaching behavior, which is unsurprising given the relative emphases these activities are given at most universities. Further, many codes contained statements that could reasonably be applied to students, but no direct mention of students or teaching was included. Many codes urged that members be respectful toward all members of their discipline, for example.

Conclusion

Despite the inviolable status of *whistle-blowing suppression* and *directed research malfeasance*, both of these norms were addressed minimally or not at all by both the AAUP and scholarly society documents on ethics. One possible explanation for this is that the norm is never violated, but even a slight familiarity with academic scandals shows otherwise. Whether it is a historian plagiarizing from a colleague or a laboratory scientist fabricating results, instances of research misconduct even make the major news. Our null finding was not entirely surprising, given complaints that these organizations, when faced with evidence of misconduct that transgresses their ethical statements, decline to enforce sanctions or even investigate (Bartlett, 2003).

Another finding of interest is that hard disciplines are less likely to address the issue of faculty-student relations at all. Nor are they replete with statements about colleagues and laboratory employees that are readily applicable to graduate students.

Both of these findings suggest that these the ethical statements of scholarly societies are intended to signal professionalization rather than be used as a guide for behavior. But what of the AAUP statements, which are in fact frequently used by faculty and institutions alike to guide relationships? It is likely that these parties see the document as more relevant to their relations with each other than with the third party of graduate students. It is likely that the statement on graduate students focuses on the unique aspects of the faculty-student relationship—teaching and mentorship—rather than on aspects shared with postdoctoral research technicians and faculty colleagues that include research.

CHAPTER TEN

Further Perspectives on the Internalization of the Norms of Graduate Teaching and Mentoring

Where do faculty members learn the norms of their profession? To some extent, they learn about them during their own graduate school experience and, later, through their peers and mentors within their institutions. Moreover, the formulations of this volume's underlying the conceptual perspective described in the Introduction posit that graduate faculty members learn norms through the detrimental consequences of norm violations to either themselves or others (Becker, 1968; Horne, 2001) The graduate school experience, discussed in Chapter 9, is probably the most powerful force for teaching norms. Yet faculty members also learn about them through their larger discipline, one aspect of which, disciplinary codes of conduct, is discussed in Chapter 9. Finally, they read about them through the nondisciplinary academic press, including publications such as the *Chronicle of Higher Education* and books that discuss higher education as it is or ought to be. In this chapter, we examine how graduate faculty norms are portrayed in books about the professoriate as it is and ought to be.

Norms, when presented in print, can be stated straightforwardly and unambiguously, rather than tacitly embedded in interactions and activities of academe.

Yet learning about norms only from the press is insufficient. First, moralistic statements probably make less of an impression than actual observation and experience. Second, advice writers may exclude norms because they consider them so obvious as to be unnecessary to speak of or because they wish to change them. For this reason, the picture of norms we draw in this chapter may exclude certain behaviors that authors have omitted but still espouse. Third, while norms may be best observed in their violation, most reform and advice is stated in a positive way, not as thou-shalt-nots. (There are exceptions to this; in particular, statements about sexual harassment are usually stated negatively.) Thus, the picture we draw here is incomplete in many ways, and we must remember that these books are only one influence among many, and not all academics read them.

There are three types of literature from which faculty may learn about academic norms. The first is works like this volume—that is, books and articles that attempt to document faculty values and/or norms. These types of works are fairly rare; when they do appear, they tend to be presented as the result of experience or thought experiments rather than as empirical research. The exceptions to this rule are not discussed separately in this chapter, however, but are cited throughout this book as relevant.

The second type of literature is monographs on doctoral and graduate education reform. Most of these are the fruits of ambitious programs sponsored by foundations such as the Carnegie Foundation for the Advancement of Teaching. "Reform" may suggest adopting new norms instead of carrying on existing ones, but the reforms suggested are typically not so radical as to suggest overhauling academia wholesale. Rather, would-be reformers propose to take the norms academia currently possesses and to remold graduate education so as to better fulfill them. A common refrain, for example, is that programs profess to prepare students for both academic and nonacademic careers but that in reality they emphasize research at the expense of teaching and service and tend to devalue extra-academic careers.

It is likely, however, that the audiences of both of these types of literature are self-selecting and do not include the entire professoriate. The third source of literature has a much wider audience—that is, books of advice for faculty members. Most of these are aimed at new (or would-be) professors, and many have an emphasis on obtaining tenure. A few address faculty members at all stages of their careers. These books, naturally, vary widely in quality. Some lay out nuts-and-bolts plans for achieving tenure; others aim to inspire. Some are heavy on remedial details, while others are quite vague. Yet all include statements about what academic jobs entail, advice on how to achieve common academic goals such as tenure, and advice of a moral or legal nature.

In this chapter, we examine norms surrounding graduate education as portrayed in both monographs advocating reform and books of advice for faculty members. One point worth noting, which we will return to later, is that the role of the individual faculty member with respect to graduate students plays a small part in most of these works. Other actors (both specific, such as department chairs, and reified, such as "programs") and other aspects of the faculty role (such as teaching undergraduates or publishing) receive the lion's share of attention.

Norms as Portrayed in Works on Reforming Graduate Education

This analysis was limited to books and reports, as those tend to be the vehicles for advocating reform across disciplines. In many disciplines, journals and professional association newsletters run articles suggesting improvements in graduate education specific to that particular discipline. This literature is too rich to do justice to in this small space. There are even more columns, blog posts, and the like that advocate changes. In order to keep the analysis manageable and applicable to a variety of disciplines, only cross-disciplinary works were examined. Because our interest was in proposals for reform, this section does not include works that are primarily intended to be descriptive or those that are empirical unless they have a substantive normative component. It thus does not include, for example, the substantial body of work intended to model the graduate student socialization or departure process (e.g., see Aguinis, Nesler, Quigley, Lee, & Tedesch, 1996; Austin & McDaniels, 2006; Givres & Wemmerus, 1988; Weidman, Twale, & Stein, 2001). In other words, we focus on works with normative claims, whether these are statements of current best practices, incremental improvements, or radical change. Because our interest is in faculty, we excluded normative works explicitly aimed at other groups (e.g., recommendations for disciplinary societies or institutions). Books on reforming graduate education are rarely explicitly moral or normative in their suggestions but instead are focused on practical effectiveness. There is a degree of utopianism in their suggestions even though they aim for plausible reforms, however. Reforms come, roughly speaking, in two flavors. The first tinkers at the edges of our current system, with little revolutionary change; the second is more radical, requiring systematic overhaul to academia. Many in the first category of ideas suggest reforms that are not actually novel but that are currently considered best practices, even if not yet widespread. Suggestions to increase graduate student funding, for example, are unlikely to raise eyebrows, and arguments against their implementation are more often practical than philosophical. The more radical category includes ideas that may be controversial and are unlikely to gain traction. For example, calls to drastically reduce the number of admitted students or eliminate the traditional dissertation are likely to invite controversy.

The other characteristic of these reforms is that they are aimed at a variety of actors and audiences, of which individual faculty members are only one. The bulk of recommendations are at the departmental or programmatic level, with a smattering of university-wide suggestions. While many of them involve faculty members, few can be achieved by an individual professor working on his or her own. A typical example of this involves the official assignment of advisors or mentors and their subsequent involvement with students. But many more of these reform proposals are addressed at the graduate program level or even the institutional level. These have to do with admissions policies, course requirements, program funding, and the format of exercises such as qualifying exams and the dissertation. Because of this emphasis, most reforms suggested cannot be carried out by individual faculty members. Professors may come away from these monographs feeling that there is little they can do unless they are deans or directors of graduate studies.

The reform literature shows that the norms are either ignored or, more likely, taken for granted as a starting point. For example, no behaviors that loaded onto the five inviolable norms, except for *misappropriation of student work*, were mentioned in any of the books we examined. The sole exception was one reference to *misappropriation of student work;* the author stated that departments should not tolerate abuse or exploitation (Cronon, 2006).

The admonitory norms fared similarly, with the exception of *inadequate advising/mentoring*. Many of these references were vague or high level rather than specific. A typical example is "Being a good Ph.D. adviser is more than having legions of students help do the things that will make you famous, or even just get a lot of work done. A good Ph.D. adviser is deeply invested in mentoring each students as an individual who, in turn, will someday be a great researcher and adviser, and so on" (Stacy, 2006, p. 200) In two cases, specific behaviors that mapped onto GTMBI items were mentioned:

- "It is frankly troubling to hear of faculty members who take on dozens of student advisees" (Walker, Golde, Jones, Bueschel, & Hutchings, 2008, p. 107)
- "Faculty should supply the neophyte with a consistent and clear process that facilitates socialization" (Weidman et al., 2001, p. 60)

To some extent, the norm *degradation of faculty colleagues* was supported, but only because it is a necessary precondition for students to be able to feasibly have multiple mentors. Several authors speak of the importance of students having more than one advisor/mentor (Bender, 2006; Chan, 2006; Cronon, 2006; Stacy, 2006). Perhaps not coincidentally, all four of these chapters are part of Golde, Walker, and Associates (2006), *Envisioning the Future of Doctoral Education.*

So what do reformers advocate for faculty members? Some of the advice is perfectly in line with our findings, if too vague to be mapped: "Good mentoring involves teaching, advising, criticizing, coaching, cheerleading, challenging, hand-holding, questioning, advocating, nurturing, and, not least, learning and inspiring in both directions" (Cronon, 2006, p. 346). The rest goes beyond the norms to advocate teaching students about professional ethics, pedagogy (especially for teaching assistants) (Association of American Universities, 1998; Cronon, 2006), and the history of and general information about higher education (Bender, 2006; Nyquist, Woodword, & Rogers, 2004). Faculty are encouraged to value nonacademic careers for their students (Chan, 2006), to support their gradual independence (Wulff & Nerad, 2006), to provide them with necessary information to succeed in graduate school and as faculty members (Bender, 2006; Chan, 2006; Stacy, 2006; Weidman et al., 2001), and to offer them opportunities for service and professional development (Austin & McDaniels, 2006). They should foster and support diversity (Stacy, 2006) and strive to develop nurturing skills (Austin & McDaniels, 2006). Some of these suggestions are not in line with faculty norms. For example, the attention to pedagogical development is unlikely to be supported, given that "A faculty member requires their graduate teaching assistant to grade all essay exams from their undergraduate classes without providing any guidelines to the graduate assistant or reviewing any grades assigned by the teaching assistant" did not score high on the GMTBI. Other suggestions may not conflict with norms but go beyond them; the GMTBI, for example, asks no questions that would evaluate graduate faculty's advocacy of teaching the history of higher education.

Norms as Portrayed in Self-Help Books for Faculty

There are almost no books in print devoted to teaching and mentoring graduate students. Most books on teaching are explicitly or implicitly focused on undergraduate teaching. Much of what they suggest, whether for fostering course discussion or creating syllabi, is applicable to teaching graduate students as well. Yet this neglects the unique aspects of teaching at the graduate level, such as chairing dissertations, as well as the differences in maturity and intellectual development of students that typically exist. Some works that neglect graduate students do so for very good reasons, such as Lang's memoir of his first year on the tenure track as an English professor at a liberal arts college with no graduate programs in the liberal arts (Lang, 2005). More often graduate teaching is simply invisible in the text. Many books do not claim to limit themselves to undergraduate teaching but in fact do so (Cahn, 2008; Filene, 2005). Other books spend little time on faculty-student relationships of any type (Rockquemore & Laszloffy, 2008; Whicker, Kronenfeld, & Strickland, 1993). In a few cases, the attention devoted is very brief; one chapter suggests only that research infrastructure should be in place before inviting students to work in your lab and that graduate students ought to be supervised (Zacks & Roediger, 2004). Only one volume is devoted specifically to working with graduate students—*Working Effectively with Graduate Assistants* (Nyquist & Wulff, 1996). As the title suggests, the book is a comprehensive overview on supervising graduate teaching and research assistants; it does not include the teaching of graduate courses or advising outside the supervisory relationship (e.g., advice on the job search). The lack of attention to graduate teaching in most academic advice books, therefore, is a lacuna ripe for a motivated authority to fill.

The advice in a typical volume is a mix of statements of what is typical and of suggestions for maximizing effectiveness. Advice ranges from statements that doing something is either morally or legally wrong or that it is mandatory, to observations of what is typical, to advice that doing X will result in more career success than doing Y. An example of the first is the assertion that plagiarism is "unethical" (Vesilind, 2007). Observations of typical faculty life include discussions such as one in Goldsmith, Komlos, & Gold (2001) on the likelihood of a new professor teaching graduate students. Finally, effectiveness advice includes statements such as this one from Miss Mentor: "The ideal [thesis] director treats all of his or her charges equally—doling out research ideas and grant opportunities, warning against unreliable sources or immense projects that will take a lifetime" (Toth, 2009, p. 13). While perhaps the majority of advice is effectiveness-related, most of it cannot meaningfully be extrapolated to norms around faculty-graduate student relationships. For example, Boice's (2000) excellent book for new faculty discusses at length how to be a more effective teacher, but it focuses on issues such as reducing excessive preparation time. *Neglectful teaching* may be discouraged, but only in a very broad sense.

The inviolable norms of *disrespect toward student efforts*, *misappropriation of student work*, and *harassment of students* were very evident in the books examined. *Harassment of students*, however, was confined almost exclusively to the issue of relationships with students; sexism, public criticism, and teaching while intoxicated were rarely mentioned. Two notable examples include advice not to be sexist (Bernstein & Lucas, 2004) and the only example of advice that failed to align with the norms: "It has been accepted that professors and their graduate students sometimes got together romantically, but that could be changing, particularly in a situation where the professor has evaluative or supervisory authority over the student, as in a course or with an RA" (Schoenfeld & Magnan, 1992, pp. 97–98). Most other statements about professor-student sexual relationships were more strongly worded and encompassed more students, such as the claim that certain relationships are "immoral," "institutionally prohibited," and a "breach of professional ethics" (Deneef, 2007, p. 234). Some examples of *misappropriation of student work* advise setting ground rules for coauthorship in advance (Strain, 2007; Vesilind, 2007), although leaving what those rules ought to be to the reader's imagination. Another slightly less vague statement directs professors to "be generous with sharing authorship when they make contributions to your research" (Gray & Drew, 2008, p. 61).

Moreover, variants of the norms of *whistle-blowing suppression* and *directed research malfeasance* receive some attention by Braxton and Baird (2001), as they urge that graduate education embrace preparation for professional self-regulation. Such preparation for self-regulation should entail an awareness of the types of actions professors may take for personally known incidents of research malfeasance as well as the importance of confidentiality to protect both the accused and the whistle-blower (Braxton & Baird, 2001). In addition, ethical issues of research with students were discussed in terms of authorship, which falls under *misappropriation of student work.* Deneef (2007) includes a rare statement on the professor's own behavior: "You must not only model ethical modes of research and publication but you must be open and explicit with your students about why the entire academic community depends upon its ability to trust the academic integrity of its [members]" (p. 233). Overall, advice on research focuses on effectiveness and publication success rather than appropriate behavior.

As for the admonitory norms, here we also found uneven coverage. *Neglectful teaching* and *inadequate advising/mentoring* were well represented. Half of the advice about *neglectful teaching* consisted of statements that professors ought to adhere to their syllabi (Bernstein & Lucas, 2004; Caplan, 1993; Goldsmith et al., 2001). Most of the *inadequate advising/mentoring* statements were quite general. Typical examples include "Your goal ought to be to provide graduate teaching assistants with as much direction, support, and counsel as they require" (Lucas & Murray, 2007, p. 125) and advice that faculty members should be a "reliable information source," "departmental socializer," "advocate," "role model," and "occupational socializer" (Winston & Polkosnik, 1984, pp. 291–299). *Degradation of faculty colleagues* and *graduate program disregard* were not discussed at all. The other four norms received one to three mentions each, and in the case of *insufficient course structure* the mention was tepid: a syllabus is a "good idea" for students, although "essential" for tenure and review packets (Schoenfeld & Magnan, 1992, p. 137). (Notably, this is the same book that allows for faculty-student romantic attachments within the department.)

Some advice covers topics not included in the GTMBI. Miss Mentor advises readers to document interactions with mentally unstable students and to refer them to counseling (Toth, 1997); Winston and Polkosnik (1994) advise being honest with students whom one believes are unable to satisfactorily complete their program or become practitioners. Mixed advice is given on whether faculty should befriend their graduate students, and the GTMBI itself refers only to unequal treatment among students. Miss Mentor advises that friendship can lead to a "fulfilling camaraderie" (Toth, 2009, p. 76), while Zanna and Darley (2004) say faculty should not befriend students. In one case, items that did not load on the factor analysis were stressed: "It is imperative that you provide TAs who assist you with clear instructions about what you would like them to do" (Nyquist & Wulff, 1996, p. 47) is broader than the GTMBI item "A faculty member requires their graduate teaching assistant to grade all essay exams from their undergraduate classes without providing any guidelines to the graduate assistant or reviewing any grades assigned by the teaching assistant," but similar in spirit.

Nyquist and Wulff (1996) also address "important aspects of ethics and safety" —"Supervisors must ensure not only that their graduate student researchers develop technical research skills, but also that they confront squarely issues of ethical conduct: the careful handling of research data, replication of study information, validity and reliability tests, patents, and so on" (pp. 80–81). They also address social sciences human subjects research. However, they do not explicitly address *whistle-blowing suppression* or *directed research malfeasance.*

In sum, we found that norms around research misconduct, departmental citizenship (such as the graduate program or degradation of colleagues), and respect for students of all genders, races, and national origins were conspicuously absent from books of advice for faculty. Advice about race and gender was aimed almost exclusively at women and minorities. They were advised that they would encounter sexism and racism and given advice on combating them; yet there was little parallel advice not to be sexist or racist, aside from the more specific issue of sexual harassment.

Conclusion

Advocates for reform have little to say about the inviolable norms and speak only to the admonitory norms of *inadequate advising/mentoring* and *degradation of faculty colleagues,* but only in the most general of terms. The reforms, at least those aimed specifically at individual faculty members, are unlikely to gain traction unless the values they are premised on achieve normative status.

The advice for faculty members emphasizes classroom management and formal teaching issues, often in very general formulations, and cautions against harassment and sexual relationships. Less attention is paid to research with students, aside from issues of publication credits, pedagogy and course structure, and diversity. While issues of research are covered in books on "how to achieve tenure" and how to succeed at publishing, graduate students are nearly invisible in these conversations.

It is discouraging to see how little attention is paid to graduate teaching and mentoring in the literature. Advocates for graduate reform focus their attention on programs, rather than on individual faculty members and their relationships with students, and advice on how to succeed as a faculty member almost ignores the presence of graduate students. Even though graduate students may be the minority of students in most fields, techniques for their development are not interchangeable with techniques for the development of undergraduate students. The lack of discussion in this area is worrisome for the future of the professoriate.

CHAPTER ELEVEN

Conclusions and Recommendations for Research, Policy, and Practice

This chapter provides a summary of the findings of this volume, advances a set of conclusions, provides a discussion of selected findings, offers recommendations for further research on the normative structure of graduate study, and concludes with recommendations for policy and practice. However, it begins with limitations to the research underlying this volume that temper the conclusions advanced and the various recommendations made. These limitations are as follows:

1. The 124 behaviors included in Graduate Teaching and Mentoring Behaviors Inventory (GTMBI) are not exhaustive of possible behaviors that might meet normative criteria. For example, those aspects of graduate training and mentoring that center on preparation for college teaching are not reflected in the GTMBI.
2. This research is limited to those disciplines classified by Biglan (1973) as pure life and pure nonlife that are of high and low paradigmatic development. Specifically, biology and psychology are life, whereas chemistry and history are nonlife subject matter areas. Biology and chemistry constitute fields having high paradigmatic development, whereas history

and psychology are disciplines of low paradigmatic development. Hence, the normative preferences of faculty members in applied academic disciplines are not included in this research.

3. This research included two of the three levels of the Doctorate-Granting Universities category of the 2005 Carnegie Classification of Institutions: Research Universities (very high research activity) and Research Universities (high research activity). Thus, the normative preferences of faculty members in the Doctoral/Research Universities level are not included. This level is the lowest level of research activity.
4. The relatively low response rate of 22.6% to the GTMBI by the sample of faculty members receiving this inventory constitutes another limitation to this research. However, we assert that the obtained sample is generally representative of the population of inference of this study on four of the five inviolable normative patterns, all eight of the admonitory normative arrays, gender, institutional type, and academic discipline. Nevertheless, respondents to the initial mailing tend to voice a somewhat greater level of disdain for the normative pattern of whistle blowing suppression than do later respondents. Moreover, a lower percentage of individuals without administrative experience responded to the initial GTMBI mailing wave.
5. Although we asked faculty respondents to the GTMBI to indicate their citizenship status, we did not ask them to specify their racial or ethnic identity As a consequence, the normative preferences of faculty members of different racial and ethnic groups cannot be delineated in this research.
6. The normative structure of graduate study—inviolable and admonitory norms—empirically delineated in this volume are solely reflective of the perceptions of individual faculty members and their individual normative preferences for various behaviors associated with graduate teaching and mentoring. The experience of individual faculty members with deviance from these inviolable and admonitory normative patterns by their colleagues was not ascertained.

Summary of Findings

We use the six research questions delineated in the Introduction to organize this summary of findings.

1. *What is the normative structure for graduate teaching and mentoring?*

We empirically identified a set of five inviolable and a set of eight admonitory normative patterns. Inviolable norms involve behaviors that faculty respondents to the GTMBI believe warrant severe sanctions, whereas those behaviors that faculty respondents believe should be avoided but less severely sanctioned constitute admonitory norms.

In Chapter 3, we describe each of the following five empirically derived inviolable norms that make up the normative structure of graduate study: *disrespect toward student efforts*, *misappropriation of student work*, *harassment of students*, *whistle-blowing suppression*, and *directed research malfeasance*. A substantial degree of consensus on the inviolability of these five normative patterns exists among faculty respondents to the GTMBI.

We describe the eight empirically obtained admonitory normative patterns also in Chapter 3. These eight admonitory norms are *neglectful teaching*, *inadequate advising/mentoring*, *degradation of faculty colleagues*, *negligent thesis/dissertation advising*, *insufficient course structure*, *pedagogical narrowness*, *student assignment misallocation*, and *graduate program disregard*. Unlike with inviolable norms, a lack of consensus on the admonitory status obtains on six of these eight norms: *degradation of faculty colleagues*, *negligent thesis/dissertation advising*, *insufficient course structure*, *pedagogical narrowness*, *student assignment misallocation*, and *disregard for graduate programs*.

2. *Does faculty espousal of the empirically identified inviolable and admonitory normative patterns vary between faculty holding academic appointments in universities with high and very high research intensity?*

The findings reported in Chapter 4 indicate that faculty members in both types of universities register similar levels of indignation for the specific behaviors that make up each of the five inviolable norms. Moreover, faculty members in the two types of research universities similarly rebuke the specific behaviors that constitute the following six admonitory norms: *inadequate advising/mentoring*, *degradation of faculty colleagues*, *negligent thesis/dissertation advising*, *pedagogical narrowness*, *student assignment misallocation*, and *graduate program disregard*. However, academics holding their appointment in universities with lower levels of research reprove to a somewhat greater degree the behaviors reflective of the admonitory norms *of neglectful teaching* and *insufficient course structure* than do their faculty colleagues in universities with higher levels of research activity.

The robust multiple regression analyses described in Chapter 7 sustain this pattern of findings.

3. Does faculty espousal of the empirically identified inviolable and admonitory normative patterns vary across different academic disciplines?

We indicated in Chapter 4 that academic historians, in contrast to their colleagues in biology, chemistry, and psychology, tend to express a greater degree of disdain for behaviors reflective of the inviolable norm of *misappropriation of student work*. This finding persists after the robust multiple regression analyses described in Chapter 8. However, the level of disdain expressed for behaviors associated with the other four inviolable norms—*disrespect toward students, student harassment, whistle-blowing suppression*, and *directed research malfeasance*—stands as invariant across these four academic disciplines.

In contrast, such invariance fails to transpire for any of the eight admonitory norms. Disciplinary differences occur for all eight admonitory norms. Moreover, historians tend to voice greater degrees of scorn for the behaviors associated with the following seven admonitory norms: *inadequate advising/mentoring, degradation of faculty colleagues, insufficient course structure, pedagogical narrowness, neglectful thesis/dissertation advising, student assignment misallocation*, and *graduate program disregard*. The robust multiple regression analyses described in Chapter 7 indicate that this pattern of findings regarding academic historians endures for four of the seven admonitory normative orientations: *degradation of faculty colleagues, neglectful thesis/dissertation advising, student assignment misallocation*, and *graduate program disregard*. Chemists voice greater degrees of indignation for the behaviors associated with the normative array of *neglectful teaching* than do academic psychologists, while historians and biologists differ little from chemists. These findings, however, disappear as a consequence of the robust multiple regression analyses discussed in Chapter 7.

Instead, these robust multiple regression analyses point to the lower degrees of disdain expressed by academic psychologists for violations of the admonitory norms of *inadequate advising/mentoring, insufficient course structure*, and *pedagogical narrowness*. For the admonitory norm of *student assignment misallocation*, psychologists tend to reprove more stridently the behaviors associated with this norm, whereas chemists tend to voice lower degrees of disdain for this same set of behaviors. This configuration of findings emerges from the robust multiple regression analyses reported in Chapter 7.

4. Do the personal attributes of individual faculty such as gender, citizenship, and professional age influence the espousal of the empirically identified inviolable and admonitory normative patterns?

The following configuration of findings emerges from the regression analyses reported in Chapter 7. Net of the influence of these personal attributes as well as the indices of professional attainments and participation on graduate study, we found that female academics voice a greater degree of disdain for behaviors associated with the inviolable normative pattern of *misappropriation of student work*. For the other four inviolable norms, gender wields little or no influence on the espousal of these normative arrays. Nevertheless, gender affects faculty espousal of the admonitory norms of *degradation of faculty colleagues* and *student assignment misallocation*. Female academics voice more contempt for behaviors associated with these two admonitory norms than do male academics.

Faculty citizenship status exerts little or no influence on the espousal of any of the five inviolable norms or on any of the eight admonitory normative orientations. Although professional age fails to influence the espousal of each of the five inviolable norms, this faculty personal attribute exerts an influence on the espousal of seven of the eight admonitory normative arrays. Specifically, the professional age of faculty members affects the degree of disdain they voice for violations of the admonitory norms of *neglectful teaching*, *inadequate advising/mentoring*, *degradation of faculty colleagues*, *negligent thesis/dissertation advising*, *pedagogical narrowness*, *student assignment misallocation*, and *disregard for program*. The greater faculty members' professional age, the greater their degree of disdain expressed for the behaviors associated with these seven admonitory norms; this configuration of finding emerges from the robust regression analyses described in Chapter 7.

5. Do the professional attainments and involvements of individual faculty members such as academic rank, tenure, research activity, administrative experience, and various types of participation in graduate studies influence the espousal of the empirically identified inviolable and admonitory normative patterns?

Both the findings reported in Chapter 6 and the robust multiple regression analyses presented in Chapter 7 indicate that none of the indices of faculty professional attainments and participation in graduate study influence faculty espousal of the five inviolable norms and eight admonitory norms that make up the normative structure of graduate student described in this volume.

> *6. Are there core inviolable norms and core admonitory norms? This general question gives rise to the more explicit question: Are there inviolable and admonitory normative patterns that are invariant across institutional type, academic discipline, personal attributes, and professional attainments and types of involvement in graduate studies?*

The inviolable norms of *disrespect toward student efforts*, *harassment of students*, *whistle-blowing suppression*, and *directed research malfeasance* constitute core inviolable norms. However, the inviolable normative orientation of *misappropriation of student work* arises as differentiated norm. In stark contrast, none of the eight admonitory norms stand as core norms. All eight prevail as differentiated norms. This configuration of findings emerges from the multiple regression analyses described in Chapter 7.

Additional Questions Pursued

Additional questions emerged as we engaged more fully in our study of the normative structure of graduate study. The existence of differentiated norms gives rise to one such question: Which factors play the principal role in the differentiation of these norms?

We indicated in Chapter 4 that institutional type and academic discipline form the two major forces of differentiation in the structure of the academic profession, and in Chapter 7 we demonstrated that academic discipline differentiates the largest number of normative patterns. Specifically, being an academic historian contributes the most to the differentiation of the inviolable norm of *misappropriation of student work* as well as to the admonitory norms of *inadequate advising/mentoring*, *negligent thesis/dissertation advising*, and *student assignment misallocation*.

The personal attribute of professional age also plays a major role in norm differentiation. Like the discipline of history, professional age also differentiates the admonitory norms of *inadequate advising/mentoring* and *student assignment misallocation*. However, professional age emerges as the primary source of differentiation of the admonitory norm of *neglectful teaching*. Moreover, the personal attribute of gender functions as the principal force of differentiation for the admonitory norm of *degradation of faculty colleagues.* In a subsequent section of this chapter, we offer explanations for why history, professional age, and gender act as such differentiating factors.

The empirically derived normative structure for graduate study stimulates the following questions pursued in this book: What is the role of the graduate school socialization process in the internalization of the inviolable and admonitory normative arrays that constitute this normative structure (Chapter 8)? Do the formal codes of conduct promulgated by the American Association of University Professors and disciplinary scholarly societies address the teaching and mentoring of graduate students (Chapter 9)? How are normative expectations for graduate study portrayed in descriptive and proscriptive books on the professoriate (Chapter 10)?

The formulations of Chapter 8 seek to ascertain the role of the graduate school socialization process in the internalization of the inviolable and admonitory norms that make up the normative structure of graduate study. These formulations suggest that graduate students internalize the five inviolable norms. However, "uncertain" best describes the internalization of all of the admonitory norms except *degradation of faculty colleagues* and *graduate program disregard.* These two norms fall outside the parameters of the community of the classroom and the apprenticeship. Uncertain internalization stems from the probabilities of faculty violations of the six admonitory norms. Departure from graduate study, the dampening of aspirations for an academic career, and a diminution of professional identity and commitment are likely outcomes for graduate students who experience violations of these admonitory norms by graduate faculty members.

Norm internalization concerns such dimensions of graduate teaching and mentoring as the treatment of course content (*disrespect toward student efforts*), in-class and out-of-class interactions with students (*disrespect toward student efforts* and *harassment of students*), grading of student assignments and examinations (*disrespect toward student efforts*), supervision of graduate research assistants (*disrespect toward student efforts, misappropriation of student work, whistle-blowing suppression,* and *directed research malfeasance*), and supervision of theses or dissertations (*disrespect toward student efforts*). Uncertain norm internalization pertains to such aspects of graduate teaching and mentoring as the level of commitment graduate faculty members hold for graduate-level teaching (*neglectful teaching*), course design and course planning (*insufficient course structure*), treatment of course content (*pedagogical narrowness*), advising and mentoring (*inadequate advising/mentoring*), and supervision of theses or dissertations (*negligent thesis/dissertation advising* and *student assignment misallocation*).

We focused on the following question in Chapter 9: Do the formal codes of conduct promulgated by the American Association of University Professors and disciplinary scholarly societies address the teaching and mentoring of graduate students? This review of codes of conduct suggests that the instillation of norms is not occurring comprehensively at the disciplinary level. Few norms pertaining to teaching and mentoring are codified by either the AAUP or most disciplinary societies, leaving students unsure as to whether certain behaviors are acceptable or not. Academic apprentices are left to learn academic norms through experience and the informal socialization process. Moreover, the new faculty member—or the experienced faculty member striving to improve teaching and mentoring—can find few guides to dealing with graduate students; almost all the advice books focus on the somewhat different faculty-undergraduate relationship. (One rare exception is the recently published *The Routledge Doctoral Supervisor's Companion*, although it focused on the European doctorate, which differs considerably in form from its American counterpart [Walker & Thomson, 2010].) Long term, this may lead to a vicious cycle; students in dysfunctional departments may come to accept inappropriate behaviors as "normal" and pass them on to their students—if they even persist in their graduate programs.

We centered attention in Chapter 10 on the following question: How are normative expectations for graduate study portrayed in descriptive and proscriptive book on the professoriate? We found that books on the professoriate tend to ignore ethical norms and focus on best practices. Books advocating reform skip straight over the step of ensuring that faculty live up to norms such as misappropriation of student work and go straight into reforming what type of work students do. It is taken for granted, perhaps, that individual faculty members know what the norms are and are striving not to violate them. Advice books tend to focus on the practical rather than the ethical. This seems like a wise choice for harried faculty readers, but we should be careful that norm violations do not occur in the quest for faculty efficiency. Moreover, these books heavily emphasize undergraduate teaching, rendering graduate students nearly invisible. Faculty members could benefit, however, from a more straightforward treatment of graduate faculty norms, not only to avoid norm violations themselves but in consideration of what to do when they see others violate them.

Conclusions

We derived seven conclusions from the pattern of findings and formulations described in this book.

1. The five inviolable norms and the eight admonitory norms constitute a normative structure for graduate study that safeguard the welfare of the clients of graduate study. The five inviolable norms are *disrespect towards student efforts*, *misappropriation of student work*, *harassment of students*, *whistle-blowing suppression*, and *directed research malfeasance*. The eight admonitory norms consist of *neglectful teaching*, *inadequate advising/mentoring*, *degradation of faculty colleagues*, *negligent thesis/dissertation advising*, *insufficient course structure*, *pedagogical narrowness*, *student assignment misallocation*, and *graduate program disregard*.

These norms safeguard the welfare of the clients of graduate study by forming moral boundaries around the professional choices faculty make regarding various dimensions of graduate teaching and mentoring such as course design and course planning (*insufficient course structure*), the treatment of course content (*disrespect toward student efforts* and *pedagogical narrowness)*, in-class and out-of-class interactions with students (*disrespect toward student efforts* and *harassment of students*), the grading of student assignments and examinations (*disrespect toward student efforts*), advising and mentoring (*inadequate advising/mentoring* and *whistle-blowing suppression*), supervision of graduate research assistants (*disrespect toward student efforts, misappropriation of student work, whistle-blowing suppression, directed research malfeasance*, and *student assignment misallocation*), and supervision of theses or dissertations (*disrespect toward student efforts, negligent thesis/dissertation advising*, and *student assignment misallocation*). Put differently, these inviolable and admonitory norms provide guidelines of appropriate and inappropriate behavior regarding the enactment of these various dimensions of graduate teaching and mentoring. Violations of these norms constitute professorial misconduct in graduate study.

The existence of this normative structure strikes a balance between preserving the professional autonomy graduate faculty need in graduate education and safeguarding the needs and welfare of the various clients of graduate study. These clients include the academic discipline (Schein, 1972), the knowledge base of an academic discipline (Braxton, 1990), students in groups (Schein, 1972), students as individuals (Blau, 1973), and colleagues (Braxton & Bayer, 1999).

2. Given that inviolable norms involve behaviors that faculty believe warrant severe sanctions, well-defined and robust moral boundaries result. In contrast, admonitory norms form less sharply defined and weaker moral boundaries given that admonitory norms entail behaviors that faculty believe should be avoided but less severely sanctioned. Additionally, the lack of consensus on the admonitory status of the following six of these norms attenuates the strength of the boundaries for these norms: *degradation of faculty colleagues, negligent thesis/dissertation advising, insufficient course structure, pedagogical narrowness, student assignment misallocation,* and *disregard for graduate programs.*

As a consequence, well-defined and robust moral boundaries form around such dimensions of graduate teaching and mentoring as in-class and out-of-class interactions with students (*disrespect toward student efforts* and *harassment of students*), the grading of student assignments and examinations (*disrespect toward student efforts*), and the supervision of graduate research assistants (*disrespect toward student efforts, misappropriation of student work, whistle-blowing suppression,* and *directed research malfeasance*) given that the inviolable norms pertain to these dimensions. The characteristics of these moral boundaries suggest that graduate faculty violations of pertinent norms may occur infrequently. Because norms and behaviors are never perfectly correlated (Gibbs, 1981; Merton, 1976; Zuckerman, 1988), some norm violations may nevertheless transpire.

The definition and strength of the moral boundaries around dimensions of graduate teaching and mentoring such as the treatment of course content (*disrespect toward student efforts* and *pedagogical narrowness*) advising and mentoring (*inadequate advising/mentoring* and *whistle-blowing suppression*), and the supervision of theses or dissertations (*disrespect toward student efforts, negligent thesis/dissertation advising,* and *student assignment misallocation)* depend on which applicable norm is in play. An inviolable and an admonitory norm apply to each of these three dimensions. If an inviolable norm pertains, well-defined and robust moral boundaries exist. If an admonitory norm pertains, less well-defined and weaker moral boundaries apply. However, weaker and less well-defined moral boundaries take shape around course design and course planning (*insufficient course structure*), as insufficient course structure is an admonitory norm. The existence of weaker and less well-defined moral boundaries may result in graduate faculty violations of these admonitory norms. The lack of consensus on six of these admonitory norms (*degradation of faculty colleagues, negligent thesis/ dissertation advising, insufficient course structure, pedagogical narrowness, student assignment misallocation,* and *disregard for graduate programs*) reinforces such a possibility.

3. In addition to the possibility of graduate faculty violations of the admonitory normative patterns that pertain to course design and planning, the treatment of course content, advising and mentoring, and the supervision of theses or dissertations, the uncertainty of the internalization of these admonitory norms through the graduate socialization process by graduate students is problematic. The failure to internalize these norms may result in the faulty socialization of graduate students; they may fail to enact these dimensions of graduate teaching and mentoring when members of the professoriate do not act in a way that safeguards the welfare of their graduate students as clients. Such faulty socialization also extends to course design and planning in undergraduate teaching. Specifically, uncertain internalization of the proscriptive norm of *insufficient course structure* may also lead to uncertain internalization of the undergraduate teaching norms of *inattentive planning* and *insufficient syllabus*, which pertain to course design and course planning (Braxton & Bayer, 1999).

4. Graduate education should prepare future members of the academic profession for stewardship of one's academic discipline asserts Golde (2006). Stewardship involves the acquisition of disciplinary competence in the generation, conservation, and transformation of knowledge (Golde, 2006). Serving as a moral compass for one's discipline constitutes another aspect of the notion of stewardship of academic disciplines (Golde, 2006). Given that being a moral compass involves the embracement of principles of integrity (Golde, 2006), the five inviolable and eight admonitory norms provide a firm foundation for the role of being a moral compass in exercising stewardship of the academic disciplines. In this case, the most germane disciplines consist of biology, chemistry, history, and psychology.

5. The various clients of graduate study, which are listed in the first conclusion, are protected by the norms discussed in this volume. The welfare of graduate students as clients is safeguarded by such inviolable norms as *disrespect toward student efforts*, *misappropriation of student work*, and *harassment of students* and such admonitory norms as *inadequate advising/mentoring*, *negligent thesis/dissertation advising*, and *student assignment misallocation*.

Moreover, such inviolable norms as *whistle-blowing suppression* and *directed research malfeasance* safeguard the academic discipline and its knowledge base as clients because violations of the proscriptions of these two normative patterns constitute research misconduct. Research misconduct harms the knowledge base of an academic discipline (Braxton, 1999) by misleading researchers, as incidents of misconduct lead to blind alleys of research and scholarship (Braxton, 1993;

Chubin, 1983). The admonitory norm of *pedagogical narrowness* also serves the academic discipline and its knowledge base, as the proscriptions of this norm pertain to the content and emphases of graduate courses.

The interests of professorial colleagues receive consideration by the proscriptions of the admonitory norm of *degradation of colleagues.* Such interests as well as those of the graduate program are protected by the admonitory norm of *disregard for graduate programs.*

Unlike the normative structure of undergraduate college teaching (Braxton & Bayer, 1999), the knowledge base of the academic discipline as client is safeguarded by two inviolable norms: *whistle-blowing suppression* and *directed research malfeasance.* In contrast, the undergraduate teaching norms of *authoritarian classroom* and *instructional narrowness* serve the client of disciplinary knowledge. Admonitory normative status accrues to both of these norms. Thus transgressions involving disciplinary knowledge as client elicit more condemnation at the graduate level than at the undergraduate level.

6. The inviolable norms of *disrespect toward student efforts, harassment of students, whistle-blowing suppression,* and *directed research malfeasance* constitute core norms in graduate study. These four core norms of graduate study function as compensatory integrating mechanisms for fragmentation in the structure of the academic profession. Such fragmentation obtains because of the powerful differentiating roles of institutional type and academic discipline in the structure of the academic profession (Ruscio, 1987). Such differentiation takes place along the lines of the emphasis placed on teaching and research as well as attitudes, values, beliefs, reference groups, and professorial roles (Blackburn & Lawrence, 1995; Braxton & Hargens, 1996; Fulton & Trow, 1974; Ruscio, 1987). The inviolable norm of *misappropriation of student work* as well as the eight admonitory norms of *neglectful teaching, inadequate advising/mentoring, degradation of faculty colleagues, negligent thesis/dissertation advising, insufficient course structure, pedagogical narrowness, student assignment misallocation,* and *graduate program disregard* further fragment the structure of the academic profession. However, such fragmentation assumes a less severe form at the graduate level than at the undergraduate level. In contrast, six inviolable norms of undergraduate teaching function as further forces of fragmentation (Braxton & Bayer, 1999), whereas only one inviolable norm plays such a role at the graduate level. Moreover, only one inviolable norm—*moral turpitude*—of undergraduate college teaching acts as a core proscriptive norm in contrast to the four inviolable core proscriptive norms at the graduate level.

7. The five inviolable and eight admonitory norms empirically delineated in this volume offer parameters for reform in graduate education. Norms impede or facilitate the enactment of reforms in graduate education that involve actions by graduate faculty members. Without the existence of supportive norms, uncertainty in the reliability of faculty enactment of policies and practices formulated to reform graduate education threatens. Such uncertainty stems from the latitude offered to faculty members to follow their own preferences in the enactment of such polices and practices that results from the absence of supportive norms (Braxton, Eimers, & Bayer, 1996). This set of assertions stems from Durkheim's 1895 contention that nonconformity rather than conformity is the natural social condition (1982).

Discussion of Selected Findings

In Chapter 6, we presented rationales for such factors as research activity indexed in the number of journal articles and books published during the past three years, administrative experience, and participation in graduate studies (number of graduate-level courses taught, number of dissertations chaired, and number of student committees served as a member during the past three years) that might influence the espousal of inviolable and admonitory norms. Although we observed some bivariate relationships between these forms of professional attainments and involvements and norm espousal (see Chapter 6), such relationships disappeared with statistical controls introduced through the use of multiple regression analyses. We noted this occurrence elsewhere in this chapter. The failure to detect statistical significant independent effects of these factors invites discussion.

We presented the following formulations regarding the influence of research activity on norm espousal in Chapter 6. To elaborate, research activity in the form of articles and books published reflects a value placed on research and scholarship. Faculty members who highly value research tend to value teaching less (Creamer, 1998; Fox, 1992; Fulton & Trow, 1974; Smart, 1991). Thus we might expect that as research activity increases, the level of disdain expressed for behaviors associated with inviolable and admonitory norms decreases. Alternately, increased research activity might provide individual faculty members with experiences conducting research and publishing that resulted in negative consequences. Such negative experiences would, in turn, result in higher degrees of contempt for the behaviors associated with these normative patterns.

The failure to identify statistically significant independent effects of research activity on the espousal of the five inviolable and eight admonitory norms of graduate study generates two possibilities. First, assuming that research activity and teaching are inversely related, this relationship does not translate to less social significance being ascribed to violations of the proscriptive behaviors associated with the five inviolable and eight admonitory norms of graduate study. This contention receives reinforcement by the failure of research activity to also influence the espousal of the inviolable and admonitory normative configurations of undergraduate teaching (Braxton & Bayer, 1999).

A second possibility is that a three-year period of research activity may not be a sufficient amount of time for faculty to experience situations involving research that resulted in harmful effects on graduate students or faculty members themselves.

The failure of administrative experience to wield statistically significant independent effects on the espousal of the five inviolable and eight admonitory norms also warrants discussion. In Chapter 6, we contend that, because of their positional responsibilities, academic deans and department chairpersons may have observed personally or received reports of faculty transgressions regarding the norms of graduate study. Such experiences lead to the development of more firmly crystallized views concerning the negative consequences of such norm violations.

Because of the high value placed on individual faculty autonomy in graduate study (Fox, 2000), deans and department chairs may exercise some degree of restraint in the level of scorn they voice for such norm violations, as they do not wish to infringe on autonomy. Another possibility is that academic deans and department chairs fail to receive reports of such transgressions. Both graduate students and individual faculty members may perceive that making such reports will result in being personally stigmatized as a whistle-blower. Both graduate students and faculty members may perceive that such stigmatization might detrimentally affect their career advancement (Braxton & Bayer, 1996; Tangney, 1987).

The lack of independent effects on inviolable or admonitory norm espousal by any of the indices of participation in graduate study is also perplexing. In Chapter 6, we asserted that the number of graduate courses or seminars taught during the past three years, the number of graduate students served as their major professor during the past three years, and the number of graduate student committees served on in a nonchair role during the past three years provide opportunities for individual faculty members to directly experience or learn of incidents of violations of the norms of graduate teaching and mentoring. Graduate students may informally or formally report such incidents to individual faculty members because of their forms of participation in graduate study. As a consequence of these experiences, individual faculty members may develop views about the negative consequence of such norm violations.

Two problems may exist with these contentions. First, a three-year period may not provide a sufficient time frame for opportunities to directly or indirectly experience norm violations because of participation in graduate study. Second, graduate students may not report such incidents to faculty because of the fear of being stigmatized as a whistle-blower.

Under the earlier section "Additional Questions Pursued," we note that being an academic historian contributes the most to the differentiation of the inviolable normative pattern of *misappropriation of student work* as well as to three admonitory normative arrays: *inadequate advising/mentoring, negligent thesis/dissertation advising, and student assignment misallocation.* We also call attention to the major role professional age plays in the differentiation of the admonitory norms of *inadequate advising/mentoring* and *student assignment misallocation.* Professional age also functions as the primary source of differentiation of the admonitory norm of *neglectful teaching.* In the case of the admonitory norm of *degradation of faculty colleagues,* gender acts as the principal differentiating factor. These findings also invite the ensuing discussion in the paragraphs that follow.

The Role of History in Norm Differentiation

In his edited volume *Research Ethics: Cases and Materials,* Penslar (1995) includes a chapter that focuses on professional conduct in the discipline of history. Specifically, the *Statement on Standards of Professional Conduct* promulgated by the American Historical Association (1993) contains "A Statement of Plagiarism and Related Misuses of the Work of Other Authors" (13–16). This statement defines plagiarism as "the expropriation of another author's work, and the presentation of it as one's own." Misuses of the work of others involve the use of another historian's research findings, hypotheses, theories, or interpretations without attribution. Both plagiarism and the misuse of the work of other historians clearly reflect some of the behaviors proscribed by the inviolable norm of the misappropriation of student work. The greater degree of disdain expressed by academic historians for the behaviors associated with this normative pattern may transpire because of the desire of academic historians to follow the professional code of conduct promulgated by their academic discipline's major scholarly association.

The Role of Professional Age in Norm Differentiation

The major role professional age plays in the differentiation of the admonitory norms of *neglectful teaching*, *inadequate advising/mentoring*, and *student assignment misallocation* may stem from the opportunities to directly or indirectly experience the negative effects of violations of these norms on oneself or others. As individual faculty members advance in professional age, the likelihood of encountering the negative effects of *inadequate advising/mentoring* and *student assignment misallocation*, in particular, on graduate students seems likely. Professional age stands in contrast to the limited opportunity for such experiences presented by research activity and participation in graduate study over a three-year period of time.

The Role of Gender in Norm Differentiation

The admonitory norm of *degradation of faculty colleagues* proscribes such behaviors as making negative comments in a faculty meeting about the graduate courses offered by a colleague (G8), making derogatory remarks to graduate students about certain research methods used by other department faculty members (G6), and making negative comments about a colleague's graduate courses in public to graduate students (G9). Female academics may be more likely personally encounter such debasing behaviors from colleagues than do male academics. Female faculty members may also feel compassion for their colleagues who experience such degrading behaviors from their colleagues. The possibility of such empathy may stem from the perception of female faculty members as outsiders in academia. Such scholars as Collins (1983) and Zuckerman, Cole and Bruer (1991) refer to female academics as outsiders in the academic community. Furthermore, female academics may also perceive such behaviors as displaying a lack of care for others given that care characterizes their moral compass (Gilligan, 1977, 1982, 1993).[1] As a consequence, gender plays a major role in the differentiation of this admonitory normative configuration. Moreover, Braxton and Bayer (1999) found that female academics expressed more scorn than their male colleagues for behaviors associated with *undermining colleagues*, an admonitory norm of undergraduate college teaching. This norm also rebukes the demeaning or belittling of courses offered by colleagues (Braxton & Bayer, 1999).

Recommendations for Further Research

We present seven recommendations for further research.

1. The research conducted in pursuit of answers to the questions posed in this volume should be extended to applied academic disciplines such as education and engineering. Faculty in applied academic disciplines might express different levels of disdain for the behaviors associated with the inviolable and admonitory norms empirically delineated in this book. Because the application of knowledge to practice stands as a primary orientation of applied disciplines (Biglan, 1973), different levels of disdain might result.

2. This research should be extended to faculty members holding academic appointments in the Doctoral/Research Universities category of the 2006 Carnegie Classification of Institutions. Doctoral/Research Universities are at the lowest level of research activity among research and doctoral universities of this classification schema. Faculty members holding academic appointments in this type of university setting might have different levels of disdain for the inviolable and admonitory normative arrays described in this volume.

3. Future research on this topic should contain an item in the Graduate Teaching and Mentoring Behaviors Inventory that requests faculty members to indicate their race or ethnicity. Faculty of color may have different levels of scorn for the behaviors reflected in the inviolable and admonitory norms empirically delineated by this piece of research. Different levels of scorn may result because of the difficulties faculty of color encounter such as having a different graduate school socialization experience, weak mentoring, and few networking opportunities (Tierney & Rhoads, 1993).

4. This book concentrates on faculty perceptions of graduate teaching and mentoring regarding behaviors that meet normative criteria. However, faculty conformity to the five inviolable and eight admonitory normative patterns was not ascertained. As a consequence, future research should measure faculty conformity to the five inviolable and eight admonitory norms given that norms and behavior are never perfectly correlated (Merton, 1976; Zuckerman, 1988). Because norm violations detrimentally affect clients (Braxton, Bayer, & Noseworthy, 2004), faculty conformity to the norms of this structure is necessary. Such future research might also take into account variation in faculty conformity to these norms across academic disciplines, institutional type, and various faculty characteristics such as gender, citizenship status, and professional age.

5. The graduate school socialization process constitutes a basic mechanism for the internalization of norms (Anderson, Louis, & Earle, 1994; Zuckerman, 1977, 1988). In Chapter 8, we present formulations regarding the internalization of the five inviolable and eight admonitory norms that constitute the normative structure of graduate study as a consequence of the graduate school socialization process. We posited that internalization occurs for the five inviolable norms, but "uncertain" best characterizes the internalization of the eight admonitory norms. These formulations stand as open empirical questions and require empirical treatment. In addition to ascertaining the extent of internalization of these norms, the mechanisms of internalization should receive attention in such research. What role do such mechanisms as role-taking behaviors in the form of service as a graduate research assistant and as a teaching assistant, formal and informal relationships between faculty and students (Cole & Cole, 1973), and actual observations of graduate faculty behavior play in the internalization of the five inviolable and eight admonitory norms of graduate teaching and mentoring?

6. We also delineate outcomes of graduate student observations of norm violations by graduate faculty members in Chapter 8. As a companion to the recommendation for research described above, the effects of the observations of violations of the inviolable and admonitory norms by graduate faculty members should also receive empirical attention. Do the observations of such norm violations by graduate students lead to their departure from graduate studies? Do the observations of such norm violations by graduate students diminish their aspirations for an academic career?

7. As stated elsewhere in this volume, faculty violations of the five inviolable and eight admonitory norms constitute misconduct regarding graduate teaching and mentoring. Misconduct requires social control through such mechanisms as deterrence, detection, and sanctioning (Zuckerman, 1977, 1988). Professional self-regulation depends on the efficacy of such mechanisms of social control. Consequently, future research should focus on the identification of various mechanisms of deterrence, detection, and sanctioning. Possible research directions are:

- Because the graduate school socialization process functions as a vehicle for norm internalization, it also plays the role of a deterrent for professorial wrongdoing (Zuckerman, 1977, 1988). Thus we can acquire some knowledge and understanding of the deterrence of wrongdoing in graduate teaching and mentoring through pursuit of the fifth recommendation for research described above.

- Braxton and Bayer (1999) describe the public nature of college-level teaching. Although they were describing undergraduate teaching, graduate-level classroom teaching also has a public nature to it. Braxton and Bayer assert that the public nature of teaching as well as course rating instruments may function as mechanisms of detection of wrongdoing. Future research on graduate teaching and mentoring should focus on the role of these possible mechanisms of detection. Such research should also focus on such questions as: How often do students who are victims of norm violations discuss such incidents with either the offending faculty member or with other faculty? Do student who witness norm violations discuss these incidents with faculty members? What actions do faculties take when receiving such reports? These questions resemble those posed by Braxton and Bayer (1999, p. 175) in their recommendation for research on the detection of undergraduate teaching norm violations.
- The sanctioning of graduate teaching and mentoring improprieties also requires an empirical treatment. We echo the questions Braxton and Bayer (1999, p. 176) raised about the sanctioning of undergraduate teaching norm violations. What type of actions do individual graduate faculty members who either personally experience or receive reports of the violations of the five inviolable and eight admonitory norms of graduate study take? What type of sanctions do official sanctioning agents mete out for such norm violations?
- Because such academic administrators as graduate school deans, college deans, and provosts / chief academic affairs officers are likely sanctioning agents for graduate teaching and mentoring wrongdoing, a knowledge of their perceptions of the behaviors of the Graduate Teaching and Mentoring Behaviors Inventory requires empirical assessment. Do such academic administrators express degrees of disdain for the behaviors associated with these five inviolable and eight admonitory norms that are similar to those expressed by faculty members? The sanctioning actions such academic administrators take may depend on how disdainfully they view such proscribed behaviors.

Recommendations for Policy and Practice

The findings and formulations described in this book give rise to a set of five recommendations for policy and practice. At base, these recommended actions function as mechanisms of social control for violations of the five inviolable and eight admonitory norms of graduate study.

1. The societies of academic disciplines should add statements about graduate students to their ethical codes or develop separate documents that lay out the ground rules for ethical faculty-graduate student interactions. While various disciplines may emphasize different aspects of these norms (e.g., the American Historical Association is unlikely to address the laboratory), all should consider the agreement we found across disciplines for the five inviolable and eight admonitory norms. The AAUP, too, may wish to include statements on aspects of these norms that are not already addressed in the Redbook. The implementation of this recommendation facilitates both the deterrence and detection of wrongdoing in the form of a violation of a norm of graduate training.

2. The graduate school socialization process should seek to inculcate the five inviolable and eight admonitory norms of graduate study. As stated in the fourth conclusion, these normative patterns provide a moral compass regarding graduate teaching and mentoring for future members of the professoriate to act as stewards of their academic disciplines. We strongly endorse the notion that graduate study should prepare students for the stewardship of their academic discipline (Golde, 2006). Although the acquisition of disciplinary competence in the generation, conservation, and transformation of knowledge stands as an important component of stewardship (Golde, 2006), we, in particular, robustly support service as a moral compass for one's discipline. Moreover, the doctoral socialization process functions as a deterrent to malfeasance in graduate teaching and mentoring (Zuckerman, 1977, 1988).

Braxton and Bayer (1999) recommended that the doctoral socialization process should inculcate the inviolable and admonitory norms that constitute the proscriptive normative structure for undergraduate college teaching. We view their recommendation as complementary to this particular recommendation.

3. Universities should develop formal codes of conduct regarding graduate teaching and mentoring. The five inviolable and eight admonitory norms empirically identified in this volume should provide the foundation for the development of tenets of such a code of conduct. Like informal norms, codes of conduct act to safeguard the welfare of clients. Put differently, codes of conduct signal a profession's adherence to the ideal of service (Goode, 1969). Moreover, codes of conduct provide the basis for the deterrence and detection of wrongdoing and contribute to the exercise of professional self-regulation.

Earlier in this volume, we listed the clients served by the normative structure of graduate study: the academic discipline, the knowledge base of an academic discipline, students in groups, students as individuals, and colleagues. The promulgation of such a formal code of conduct as recommended herein communicates to the lay public, university administrators, faculty members, staff members, and graduate students that the university strives to safeguard the welfare of the clients of graduate teaching and mentoring.

At the department level, individual faculty members (in particular, tenured faculty members and those in positions of authority) should consider more formal statements about role expectations for faculty and graduate students. They also ought to make sure there are processes in place to deal with norm violations in an appropriate manner—and that students are aware of these processes. For example, do graduate students know to whom they should report research malfeasance? Is there protection for whistle-blowing? This information should be readily available on the department or university Web site, as well as communicated directly to students. Finally, individual faculty members need to ensure that when norm violations do occur, they take appropriate action.

This particular recommendation corresponds to Braxton and Bayer's (1999) recommendation calling for the development of formal codes of conduct for undergraduate college teaching by scholarly associations and individual colleges and universities. The formulation of the tenets of such codes requires careful distinctions between graduate-level teaching and mentoring and the teaching of undergraduate students. Moreover, tenets that address the proscriptions of such admonitory norms as *inadequate advising/mentoring* and *negligent thesis/dissertation advising* resonate with two recommendations regarding the advising of graduate students offered by Wulff and Austin (2004): establish standards for advising and clarify advisor responsibilities (p. 282).

4. Universities should establish formal committees to process and consider allegations of misconduct in graduate teaching and mentoring. This recommendation is comparable to one advanced by Braxton and Bayer (1999) for incidents of undergraduate teaching malfeasance. Universities could create subcommittees of such teaching integrity committees, one for graduate study and the other for undergraduate study.

Teaching integrity committees should follow the procedures recommended for use by university research integrity committees (Steneck, 1994). Such procedures entail first determining whether an allegation constitutes a form of wrongdoing. If the committee determines that the allegation meets the parameters for wrongdoing, an investigation is conducted. The committee recommends sanctions if the accused individual is found guilty. In addition, the committee must ensure that the individual making the allegation is protected from retaliation. Protection from retaliation must transpire especially for graduate students and untenured faculty members who make allegations. Without such protection, self-regulation suffers. The work of integrity committees constitutes an act of social control.

5. Universities should delineate sanctions for the various forms of wrongdoing in graduate teaching and mentoring. This recommendation augments a similar recommendation made by Braxton and Bayer (1999) for undergraduate college teaching. The delineation of sanctions facilitates the work of university teaching integrity committees. The demarcation of sanctions provide evidence of self-regulation to the lay public, university administrators, individual faculty members, staff members, and graduate students. If known and communicated, sanctions deter misconduct (Ben-Yehuda, 1985; Tittle, 1980). The negative effects and the frequency of norm violations should provide the basis for the delineation of sanctions for such occurrences. The more pervasive the wrongdoing and the greater the harm inflicted, the greater the severity of the sanction (Braxton & Bayer, 2004). The termination of the offending faculty member or graduate student represents the most severe sanction. Franke (2002) lists such less severe sanctions as a warning or a reprimand, public censure, no salary increase, a reduction in salary, and suspension. The meting out of sanctions functions as a mechanism of social control (Zuckerman, 1977, 1988).

Closing Thoughts

Graduate education occupies a position of critical importance to the work of colleges and universities. In particular, doctoral education prepares future members of the professoriate who perform the core functions of the academic profession: research and teaching (Parsons & Platt, 1973). The normative structure empirically identified in this volume safeguards the multiple clients of graduate teaching and mentoring by providing moral boundaries for the choices graduate faculty members make in their teaching and mentoring of graduate students. Without such a normative structure, graduate faculty members would be free to follow their own preferences in making such choices.

Although this volume provides empirical support for such a normative structure for graduate study, many important issues remain. First, uncertain internalization of admonitory norms during graduate study suggests that graduate students may be unprepared to make future professional choices in graduate-level teaching and mentoring regarding course design and planning, the treatment of course content, advising and mentoring, and the supervision of theses or dissertations in a way that safeguards the welfare of their graduate students as clients. Second, the extent to which the norms of graduate study identified in this book are binding on graduate faculty members remains an open empirical question. Put differently, do individual graduate faculty members conform to these norms in their day-to-day role performances? Third, violations of the norms of graduate study constitute acts of misconduct. Misconduct requires social control through such mechanisms as deterrence, detection, and sanctioning. The existence and efficacy of these mechanisms of social control stand as open empirical questions.

We close by asserting that the criticality of the normative structure of graduate study to academic work requires careful and steadfast attention to the recommendations for future research and the recommendations for policy and practice advanced in this chapter. Much work remains for the scholarly and practice communities that surround the academic profession and graduate education in general.

NOTE

1. We thank an anonymous reviewer of this book for this suggestion.

Appendix A
The Graduate Teaching and Mentoring Behaviors Inventory

Teaching and training graduate students are complex activities composed of many behaviors and expectations. Listed below are some behaviors related to faculty members who are teaching and mentoring graduate students. A number of these are worded negatively because some view them as inappropriate, and because undesirable behaviors are generally more easily identifiable than desirable ones.

We would appreciate your help in seeking to improve the future of graduate education by completing this survey. Your responses will be treated with strict confidentiality: we will delete your e-mail address from your survey responses once they are received, and we will not report any individual survey responses or summary responses for individual institutional academic departments.

Using the response codes shown below, please indicate your opinion on each of the listed behaviors as you think they might best apply to a faculty member involved in the teaching and mentoring of graduate students in your department or graduate program at your university, *whether or not you are currently involved in training graduate students.* The response categories are as follows:

1 = Appropriate behavior, should be encouraged.
2 = Discretionary behavior, neither particularly appropriate nor inappropriate.
3 = Mildly inappropriate behavior, generally to be ignored.
4 = Inappropriate behavior, to be handled informally by colleagues or administrators suggesting change or improvement.
5 = Very inappropriate behavior, requiring formal administrative intervention.

A. Supervising Graduate Research Assistants

A1. A professor who supervises graduate research assistants requires their assigned students to routinely work many extra hours per week beyond the time specified by the institution. 1 2 3 4 5

A2. A faculty member rarely gives any work to their assigned graduate assistant. 1 2 3 4 5

A3. A faculty member sometimes asks their graduate research assistant to perform personal chores such as baby-sitting or running household errands as a part of their assistantship duties. 1 2 3 4 5

1 = Appropriate behavior, should be encouraged.
2 = Discretionary behavior, neither particularly appropriate nor inappropriate.
3 = Mildly inappropriate behavior, generally to be ignored.
4 = Inappropriate behavior, to be handled informally by colleagues or administrators suggesting change or improvement.
5 = Very inappropriate behavior, requiring formal administrative intervention.

A4. A professor diverts a graduate student to work in his/her personal "start-up firm" to the detriment of the student's research progress. 1 2 3 4 5

A5. A professor instructs his/her graduate research assistant to alter databooks or lab notes to support a study's hypotheses. 1 2 3 4 5

A6. The professor instructs the research assistant to fabricate citations for a publication. 1 2 3 4 5

A7. A professor regularly cancels research team meetings/appointments that have been scheduled ahead. 1 2 3 4 5

A8. A professor's outside travel frequently interferes with regularly scheduled research team meetings/appointments. 1 2 3 4 5

A9. A professor fails to provide or ensure safe research conditions or safe laboratory environments for their graduate assistants. 1 2 3 4 5

A10. A faculty member publishes an article without offering co-authorship to a graduate assistant who has made a substantial conceptual or methodological contribution to the article. 1 2 3 4 5

A11. A professor asks a graduate student to prepare a review of a manuscript or grant proposal that the professor then represents as his/her own review. 1 2 3 4 5

A12. A professor routinely removes graduate students from research projects when they begin to show innovative results. 1 2 3 4 5

A13. A graduate student's mentor puts the student's name as co-author of a publication even though the student made no contribution to the work. 1 2 3 4 5

A14. The professor sends a research assistant to a national conference to present a paper to which the student has made minimal or no contribution. 1 2 3 4 5

A15. A faculty member fails to report a graduate research assistant who has engaged in an act of research or scholarly misconduct. 1 2 3 4 5

1 = Appropriate behavior, should be encouraged.
2 = Discretionary behavior, neither particularly appropriate nor inappropriate.
3 = Mildly inappropriate behavior, generally to be ignored.
4 = Inappropriate behavior, to be handled informally by colleagues or administrators suggesting change or improvement.
5 = Very inappropriate behavior, requiring formal administrative intervention.

A16. A professor advises his/her graduate research assistant who has personally witnessed an incident of research misconduct by another graduate assistant to ignore the incident. 1 2 3 4 5

A17. A professor advises his/her graduate assistant who has personally witnessed an incident of research misconduct by a faculty member to ignore the incident. 1 2 3 4 5

B. Mentoring and Advising

B1. A graduate advisor fails to inform his/her advisees of the requirements for completion of their degrees. 1 2 3 4 5

B2. The professor takes on more graduate advisees than he/she can handle. 1 2 3 4 5

B3. A mentor shows favoritism to those graduate students with the most academic promise and neglects those students judged to have lesser degrees of academic promise. 1 2 3 4 5

B4. A faculty advisor ignores his/her students whose academic and research interests are not similar to his/her own. 1 2 3 4 5

B5. A graduate student advisor requires all of his/her graduate students to use the same outdated methodology in preparation of their thesis or dissertation. 1 2 3 4 5

B6. The mentor fails to write a letter of recommendation that he/she had agreed to send for a graduate student. 1 2 3 4 5

B7. A graduate student's advisor fails to help the advisee make professional contacts needed to secure a position after graduation. 1 2 3 4 5

B8. A graduate student advisee is treated in a condescending manner by his/her advisor. 1 2 3 4 5

B9. A professor routinely criticizes his/her advisees to other faculty members. 1 2 3 4 5

1 = Appropriate behavior, should be encouraged.
2 = Discretionary behavior, neither particularly appropriate nor inappropriate.
3 = Mildly inappropriate behavior, generally to be ignored.
4 = Inappropriate behavior, to be handled informally by colleagues or administrators suggesting change or improvement.
5 = Very inappropriate behavior, requiring formal administrative intervention.

B10. A graduate student's advisor agrees to write a letter of recommendation for a job application, but knows it will express strong reservations for a job he/she does not think the student is qualified for. 1 2 3 4 5

B11. A professor routinely borrows money from advisees. 1 2 3 4 5

B12. A professor frequently socializes with some advisees while intentionally avoiding socializing with others. 1 2 3 4 5

B13. A professor has a sexual relationship with a graduate student in their program. 1 2 3 4 5

B14. A professor avoids giving career or job advice when asked by a graduate student. 1 2 3 4 5

B15. The graduate student's advisor does not prepare the student for their paper presentations and critique at professional conferences. 1 2 3 4 5

B16. A faculty member requires their graduate teaching assistant to grade all essay exams from their undergraduate classes without providing any guidelines to the graduate assistant or reviewing any grades assigned by the teaching assistant. 1 2 3 4 5

B17. A faculty member assigns their graduate assistant to take responsibility to teach the professor's assigned undergraduate class for the semester without administrative approval. 1 2 3 4 5

B18. A graduate student's advisor routinely fails to show up for appointments made by the graduate advisee. 1 2 3 4 5

C. Planning for a Graduate Course or Seminar

C1. Required texts and other reading materials are routinely not ordered by the professor in time to be available at the beginning of the term. 1 2 3 4 5

C2. An outline or syllabus is not prepared for the graduate course. 1 2 3 4 5

1 = Appropriate behavior, should be encouraged.
2 = Discretionary behavior, neither particularly appropriate nor inappropriate.
3 = Mildly inappropriate behavior, generally to be ignored.
4 = Inappropriate behavior, to be handled informally by colleagues or administrators suggesting change or improvement.
5 = Very inappropriate behavior, requiring formal administrative intervention.

C3. A syllabus does not contain dates when assignments are due. 1 2 3 4 5

C4. Assignment or other course requirements are not fully or accurately presented in the course syllabus. 1 2 3 4 5

C5. Objectives for the course are not specified by the professor. 1 2 3 4 5

C6. A professor will not provide information to graduate students about the content of his/her seminar for the next semester so that students might know whether it is a course they should take. 1 2 3 4 5

C7. Required course or lab materials are not kept within reasonable cost limits as perceived by graduate students. 1 2 3 4 5

C8. In-class activities are not planned or prepared in advance of each class, but are developed while the seminar or lab is in session. 1 2 3 4 5

C9. Assigned books and articles are not put on library reserve by the professor on a timely basis for graduate student use. 1 2 3 4 5

C10. The professor changes seminar meeting times immediately before the term begins and without consulting enrolled graduate students. 1 2 3 4 5

D. In-Class Practices and Behaviors

D1. The professor is routinely late for the class meetings. 1 2 3 4 5

D2. Joke-telling and humor unrelated to course content occurs routinely in the course. 1 2 3 4 5

D3. The professor frequently uses profanity in class. 1 2 3 4 5

D4. The professor meets the class without having reviewed pertinent materials for the day. 1 2 3 4 5

1 = Appropriate behavior, should be encouraged.
2 = Discretionary behavior, neither particularly appropriate nor inappropriate.
3 = Mildly inappropriate behavior, generally to be ignored.
4 = Inappropriate behavior, to be handled informally by colleagues or administrators suggesting change or improvement.
5 = Very inappropriate behavior, requiring formal administrative intervention.

D5. The professor routinely allows one or a few graduate students to dominate class discussion.	1 2 3 4 5
D6. Instructions and requirements for course assignments are not clearly described to students.	1 2 3 4 5
D7. A seminar professor requires students to purchase a book on which he/she will earn and retain royalties.	1 2 3 4 5
D8. The professor routinely holds the class beyond its scheduled ending time.	1 2 3 4 5
D9. After the first few weeks of class, the professor provides few comments and questions while requiring graduate students to conduct the class seminar sessions for the rest of the term.	1 2 3 4 5
D10. The professor cancels most seminar classes during the term, saying it is to allow more time for the graduate students to read course materials or to write a paper.	1 2 3 4 5
D11. The professor does not provide in-class opportunities for students to voice their opinion about the course.	1 2 3 4 5
D12. The professor does not follow the course outline or syllabus for most of the seminar.	1 2 3 4 5
D13. The professor does not assign some of the seminar materials that students had been told to purchase.	1 2 3 4 5
D14. Class is usually dismissed early.	1 2 3 4 5
D15. The professor's professional biases or assumptions about the seminar content are not explicitly made known to students.	1 2 3 4 5
D16. The professor frequently introduces opinions on religious, political and social issues clearly outside the realm of seminar content.	1 2 3 4 5
D17. The professor's perspective in every class is U.S.-dominated, without acknowledgment of contributions from other countries.	1 2 3 4 5

1 = Appropriate behavior, should be encouraged.
2 = Discretionary behavior, neither particularly appropriate nor inappropriate.
3 = Mildly inappropriate behavior, generally to be ignored.
4 = Inappropriate behavior, to be handled informally by colleagues or administrators suggesting change or improvement.
5 = Very inappropriate behavior, requiring formal administrative intervention.

D18. The professor does not include pertinent scholarly contributions of women and minorities in the content of the seminar. 1 2 3 4 5

D19. A professor devotes content of all of his/her seminar sessions solely to his/her own research and publications. 1 2 3 4 5

D20. Memorization of course content is stressed at the expense of analysis and critical thinking. 1 2 3 4 5

D21. Students are not permitted to express viewpoints different from those of the professor. 1 2 3 4 5

D22. The professor expresses impatience with a slow learner in class. 1 2 3 4 5

D23. The professor frequently makes negative comments in class about a student's dress, speech or manner. 1 2 3 4 5

D24. The professor does not encourage graduate students to ask questions during class time. 1 2 3 4 5

D25. The professor routinely ignores comments or questions from international graduate students. 1 2 3 4 5

D26. A professor makes condescending remarks to a student in class. 1 2 3 4 5

D27. A cynical attitude toward the seminar subject matter is expressed in class by the professor. 1 2 3 4 5

D28. The professor routinely wears dirty and sloppy clothes to class. 1 2 3 4 5

D29. The professor practices poor personal hygiene and regularly has offensive body odor. 1 2 3 4 5

D30. The professor sometimes makes racist or sexist remarks in class. 1 2 3 4 5

D31. While able to conduct the graduate class, the faculty member attends class while obviously intoxicated. 1 2 3 4 5

D32. The professor makes suggestive sexual comments to a graduate student enrolled in their seminar. 1 2 3 4 5

1 = Appropriate behavior, should be encouraged.
2 = Discretionary behavior, neither particularly appropriate nor inappropriate.
3 = Mildly inappropriate behavior, generally to be ignored.
4 = Inappropriate behavior, to be handled informally by colleagues or administrators suggesting change or improvement.
5 = Very inappropriate behavior, requiring formal administrative intervention.

D33. A faculty member criticizes the academic performance of a graduate student in front of other graduate students. 1 2 3 4 5

D34. The professor pits graduate students against each other by assigning them competing projects. 1 2 3 4 5

D35. The professor doesn't care to learn the names of the graduate students enrolled in his/her seminar. 1 2 3 4 5

D36. The professor prohibits graduate students from bringing their laptop computers to any seminar sessions. 1 2 3 4 5

E. Class/Seminar Grading and Examination Practices

E1. Graduate student seminar final grades are based on the professor's evaluation of just one term paper. 1 2 3 4 5

E2. Graded tests and papers are not promptly returned to students by the professor. 1 2 3 4 5

E3. Written comments on tests and papers are consistently not made by the professor. 1 2 3 4 5

E4. The professor changes the grading base or criteria after the course has begun. 1 2 3 4 5

E5. The professor allows some graduate students to do alternative assignments without making this option generally known to all class members. 1 2 3 4 5

E6. Individual graduate students are offered extra-credit work in order to improve their final course grade *after* the term is completed. 1 2 3 4 5

E7. The professor allows personal friendships with a graduate student to intrude on the objective grading of their work. 1 2 3 4 5

E8. Social, personal, or other non-academic characteristics of graduate students are taken into account in the assigning of grades. 1 2 3 4 5

1 = Appropriate behavior, should be encouraged.
2 = Discretionary behavior, neither particularly appropriate nor inappropriate.
3 = Mildly inappropriate behavior, generally to be ignored.
4 = Inappropriate behavior, to be handled informally by colleagues or administrators suggesting change or improvement.
5 = Very inappropriate behavior, requiring formal administrative intervention.

E9. Individual student course evaluations, where students can be identified, are read prior to the determination of final seminar grades. 1 2 3 4 5

E10. No term papers, tests, lab reports, or other criteria are used by the professor for assigning final grades. 1 2 3 4 5

E11. A professor routinely awards A's to all graduate students enrolled in his/her seminar regardless of whether the students do any assignments or attend class. 1 2 3 4 5

E12. The professor assigns a graduate student to grade the work of other graduate students. 1 2 3 4 5

F. Directing the Thesis/Dissertation

F1. A faculty member agrees to direct a thesis/dissertation only under the condition that specific other faculty members are *not* asked to serve on the graduate student's committee. 1 2 3 4 5

F2. A professor agrees to direct a thesis/dissertation only under the condition that he/she will be a co-author on all publications based on the work. 1 2 3 4 5

F3. The thesis/dissertation advisor insists that a student pursue a particular topic/problem for his/her thesis or dissertation. 1 2 3 4 5

F4. The thesis/dissertation director refuses to give his/her graduate student guidance in the selection of a thesis/dissertation topic. 1 2 3 4 5

F5. Even when a student's proposed thesis/dissertation research design appears to require it, the major professor advises bypassing animal subjects or human subjects institutional review committees. 1 2 3 4 5

F6. A student consistently cannot get an appointment with the thesis/dissertation advisor within three or four weeks to discuss issues concerning the thesis/dissertation. 1 2 3 4 5

1 = Appropriate behavior, should be encouraged.
2 = Discretionary behavior, neither particularly appropriate nor inappropriate.
3 = Mildly inappropriate behavior, generally to be ignored.
4 = Inappropriate behavior, to be handled informally by colleagues or administrators suggesting change or improvement.
5 = Very inappropriate behavior, requiring formal administrative intervention.

F7. The student's advisor often misses deadlines that affect the student's work or career. 1 2 3 4 5

F8. The thesis/dissertation advisor routinely takes more than a month to give feedback on a student's draft chapter. 1 2 3 4 5

F9. The thesis/dissertation advisor does not give any substantive feedback on drafts to any of their graduate students. 1 2 3 4 5

F10. The thesis/dissertation advisor is routinely unavailable to answer a graduate student's questions about his/her thesis or dissertation. 1 2 3 4 5

F11. The advisor fails to prepare advisees for questioning at the final oral defense. 1 2 3 4 5

F12. A thesis/dissertation advisor provides only criticism of their graduate student's work during the oral defense of the thesis/dissertation. 1 2 3 4 5

F13. The thesis/dissertation advisor fails to hold his/her students' thesis/dissertation work to the same departmental and professional standards expected of all other graduate students. 1 2 3 4 5

F14. A professor presses a graduate student to submit work for publication before the student regards the research results to be verified/confirmed. 1 2 3 4 5

F15. The thesis/dissertation advisor urges his/her graduate student to simultaneously submit the same article out of their thesis/dissertation to more than one refereed journal. 1 2 3 4 5

F16. The professor delays the graduation of his/her best graduate students, in order to keep them around longer. 1 2 3 4 5

1 = Appropriate behavior, should be encouraged.
2 = Discretionary behavior, neither particularly appropriate nor inappropriate.
3 = Mildly inappropriate behavior, generally to be ignored.
4 = Inappropriate behavior, to be handled informally by colleagues or administrators suggesting change or improvement.
5 = Very inappropriate behavior, requiring formal administrative intervention.

G. Other Behaviors Regarding Graduate Students and the Graduate Program

G1. A faculty member publishes an article using innovative ideas derived from a graduate student's term paper without acknowledging the student's contribution. 1 2 3 4 5

G2. A professor routinely blames their graduate students when his/her own research work is called into question. 1 2 3 4 5

G3. A professor accepts costly gifts from graduate students. 1 2 3 4 5

G4. A professor tells a graduate student who is in good academic standing that the student is destined to fail their preliminary or qualifying exams. 1 2 3 4 5

G5. A male professor tells a female graduate student to avoid his specialty because only men can excel in it. 1 2 3 4 5

G6. The professor makes derogatory remarks to graduate students about certain research methods used by other departmental faculty members. 1 2 3 4 5

G7. A faculty member consistently votes to not admit international students to the graduate program. 1 2 3 4 5

G8. A faculty member makes negative comments in a faculty meeting about the graduate courses offered by a colleague. 1 2 3 4 5

G9. A faculty member makes negative comments about a colleague's graduate courses in public to graduate students. 1 2 3 4 5

G10. A faculty member aggressively promotes enrollment in his/her courses at the expense of the graduate courses offered by departmental colleagues. 1 2 3 4 5

G11. A faculty member refuses to participate in departmental graduate curricular planning. 1 2 3 4 5

1 = Appropriate behavior, should be encouraged.
2 = Discretionary behavior, neither particularly appropriate nor inappropriate.
3 = Mildly inappropriate behavior, generally to be ignored.
4 = Inappropriate behavior, to be handled informally by colleagues or administrators suggesting change or improvement.
5 = Very inappropriate behavior, requiring formal administrative intervention.

G12. A faculty member refuses to serve on the departmental graduate admissions committee. 1 2 3 4 5

G13. A faculty member strongly advocates accepting a graduate student applicant who fails to exhibit minimal skills in speaking or reading English. 1 2 3 4 5

G14. A faculty member strongly advocates enrolling a graduate student applicant whose specialized interests for study are not offered by the department. 1 2 3 4 5

G15. A faculty member intentionally misrepresents graduate program requirements in order to recruit a graduate student. 1 2 3 4 5

A Few Questions About You and Your Institution

1. Are you considered a full-time faculty member by your institution for the current academic year? (check one)
   ____Yes, full-time
   ____No, part-time, but more than half-time
   ____No, half-time
   ____No, less than half-time

2. Your academic rank: (check one)
   ____Professor
   ____Associate Professor
   ____Assistant Professor
   ____Instructor or Lecturer
   ____Other (please specify: ____________________)

3. Your tenure status: (check one)
   ____Tenured
   ____Untenured, but on tenure track
   ____Untenured, and not on tenure track

4. Are you, or have you ever been, a Department Head/Chair or a Dean? (check one)
   ____No
   ____Yes, but not now
   ____Yes, and am currently

5. Information concerning your highest earned degree:
   A. Highest earned degree: ____________________________
   B. Year highest degree received: ____________________________
   C. Discipline/field of highest degree: ____________________________
   D. State/country location of degree-granting institution: ______________________

6. During the *past three years*, how many of each of the following have you published?
   A. Journal articles (circle one): None 1–2 3–4 5–10 11 or more
   B. Books and monographs (circle one): None 1 2 3 or more

7. In the *past three years*, how many *graduate* courses/seminars have you taught (please report number of *times* taught, *not* the number of different courses taught)? (circle one):
   None 1 2 3 4 5 or more

8. In the *past three years*, how many graduate students have you served as their major professor? __________________

9. In the *past three years*, how many graduate student committees have you served on for which you were not the student's major professor? __________________

10. In what year were you born? __________________

11. Current U.S. citizenship:
    ____U.S. citizen, native born
    ____U.S. citizen, naturalized
    ____Not U.S. citizen

12. Your gender:
    ____Female
    ____Male

13. Do your interests lie primarily in teaching or in research? (check one)
    ____Heavily in research
    ____In both, but leaning toward research
    ____In both, but leaning toward teaching
    ____Heavily in teaching

14. Year you were first employed at your present institution: ____________

15. Discipline of your present academic department: __________________

In the space below, please note any comments or clarifications of your answers which you would like to provide:

Please now click on the "submit" button.

THANK YOU FOR YOUR HELP AND YOUR RESPONSES

If you have additional questions or comments about this survey, you may write to:

National Graduate Training Assessment Project
Center for Survey Research
Virginia Tech
207 West Roanoke Street (0543)
Blacksburg, VA 24061

Appendix B
Means and Standard Deviations for Behaviors Included in the Graduate Teaching and Mentoring Behaviors Inventory (GTMBI)

Behaviors	Mean	Standard deviation
A. Supervising graduate research assistants		
A1. A professor who supervises graduate research assistants requires their assigned students to routinely work many extra hours per week beyond the time specified by the institution.	3.42	1.20
A2. A faculty member rarely gives any work to their assigned graduate assistant.	3.38	1.10
A3. A faculty member sometimes asks their graduate research assistant to perform personal chores such as baby-sitting or running household errands as a part of their assistantship duties.	4.63	.55
A4. A professor diverts a graduate student to work in his/her personal "start-up firm: to the detriment of the student's research progress.	4.80	.45
A5. A professor instructs his/her graduate research assistant to alter databooks or lab notes to support a study's hypotheses.	4.99	.11
A6. The professor instructs the research assistant to fabricate citations for a publication.	4.97	.23
A7. A professor regularly cancels research team meetings/appointments that have been scheduled ahead.	3.39	.88
A8. A professor's outside travel frequently interferes with regularly scheduled research team meetings/appointments.	2.97	.94
A9. A professor fails to provide or ensure safe research conditions or safe laboratory environments for their graduate assistants.	4.70	.50

Behaviors	Mean	Standard deviation
A10. A faculty member publishes an article without offering co-authorship to a graduate assistant who has made a substantial conceptual or methodological contribution to the article.	4.59	.60
A11. A professor asks a graduate student to prepare a review of a manuscript or grant proposal that the professor then represents as his/her own review.	4.40	.87
A12. A professor routinely removes graduate students from research projects when they begin to show innovative results.	4.53	.65
A13. A graduate student's mentor puts the student's name as co-author of a publication even though the student made no contribution to the work.	4.12	.78
A14. The professor sends a research assistant to a national conference to present a paper to which the student has made minimal or no contribution.	3.55	.94
A15. A faculty member fails to report a graduate research assistant who has engaged in an act of research or scholarly misconduct.	4.40	.71
A16. A professor advises his/her graduate research assistant who has personally witnessed an incident of research misconduct by another graduate assistant to ignore the incident.	4.47	.67
A17. A professor advises his/her graduate assistant who has personally witnessed an incident of research misconduct by a faculty member to ignore the incident.	4.50	.67
B. Mentoring and advising		
B1. A graduate advisor fails to inform his/her advisees of the requirements for completion of their degrees.	3.51	.91
B2. The professor takes on more graduate advisees than he/she can handle.	3.27	.82
B3. A mentor shows favoritism to those graduate students with the most academic promise and neglects those students judged to have lesser degrees of academic promise.	3.21	.92
B4. A faculty advisor ignores his/her students whose academic and research interests are not similar to his/her own.	3.49	.91
B5. A graduate student advisor requires all of his/her graduate students to use the same outdated methodology in preparation of their thesis or dissertation.	3.58	.96

Behaviors	Mean	Standard deviation
B6. The mentor fails to write a letter of recommendation that he/she had agreed to send for a graduate student.	4.21	.72
B7. A graduate student's advisor fails to help the advisee make professional contacts needed to secure a position after graduation.	3.03	.89
B8. A graduate student advisee is treated in a condescending manner by his/her advisor.	3.56	.90
B9. A professor routinely criticizes his/her advisees to other faculty members.	3.26	.94
B10. A graduate student's advisor agrees to write a letter of recommendation for a job application, but knows it will express strong reservations for a job he/she does not think the student is qualified for.	2.89	1.07
B11. A professor routinely borrows money from advisees.	4.51	3.32
B12. A professor frequently socializes with some advisees while intentionally avoiding socializing with others.	3.32	1.01
B13. A professor has a sexual relationship with a graduate student in their program.	4.58	.76
B14. A professor avoids giving career or job advice when asked by a graduate student.	3.25	.96
B15. The graduate student's advisor does not prepare the student for their paper presentations and critique at professional conferences.	3.30	.86
B16. A faculty member requires their graduate teaching assistant to grade all essay exams from their undergraduate classes without providing any guidelines to the graduate assistant or reviewing any grades assigned by the teaching assistant.	3.68	.86
B17. A faculty member assigns their graduate assistant to take responsibility to teach the professor's assigned undergraduate class for the semester without administrative approval.	4.58	.65
B18. A graduate student's advisor routinely fails to show up for appointments made by the graduate advisee.	3.97	.75

Behaviors	Mean	Standard deviation
C. Planning a graduate course or seminar		
C1. Required texts and other reading materials are routinely not ordered by the professor in time to be available at the beginning of the term.	3.63	.78
C2. An outline or syllabus is not prepared for the graduate course.	3.60	.95
C3. A syllabus does not contain dates when assignments are due.	3.29	.96
C4. Assignment or other course requirements are not fully or accurately presented in the course syllabus.	3.41	.90
C5. Objectives for the course are not specified by the professor.	3.23	.88
C6. A professor will not provide information to graduate students about the content of his/her seminar for the next semester so that students might know whether it is a course they should take.	3.24	.86
C7. Required course or lab materials are not kept within reasonable cost limits as perceived by graduate students.	2.88	.85
C8. In-class activities are not planned or prepared in advance of each class, but are developed while the seminar or lab is in session.	2.97	.97
C9. Assigned books and articles are not put on library reserve by the professor on a timely basis for graduate student use.	3.12	.83
C10. The professor changes seminar meeting times immediately before the term begins and without consulting enrolled graduate students.	3.66	.90
D. In-class practices and behaviors		
D1. The professor is routinely late for the class meetings.	3.71	.74
D2. Joke-telling and humor unrelated to course content occurs routinely in the course.	2.79	.96
D3. The professor frequently uses profanity in class.	3.66	.99
D4. The professor meets the class without having reviewed pertinent materials for the day.	3.61	.87
D5. The professor routinely allows one or a few graduate students to dominate class discussion.	2.96	.79

Behaviors	Mean	Standard deviation
D6. Instructions and requirements for course assignments are not clearly described to students.	3.49	.78
D7. A seminar professor requires students to purchase a book on which he/she will earn and retain royalties.	2.97	1.10
D8. The professor routinely holds the class beyond its scheduled ending time.	3.13	.80
D9. After the first few weeks of class, the professor provides few comments and questions while requiring graduate students to conduct the class seminar sessions for the rest of the term.	3.24	1.04
D10. The professor cancels most seminar classes during the term, saying it is to allow more time for the graduate students to read course materials or to write a paper.	3.75	.96
D11. The professor does not provide in-class opportunities for students to voice their opinion about the course.	2.89	1.03
D12. The professor does not follow the course outline or syllabus for most of the seminar.	3.28	.91
D13. The professor does not assign some of the seminar materials that students had been told to purchase.	3.21	.84
D14. Class is usually dismissed early.	2.91	.91
D15. The professor's professional biases or assumptions about the seminar content are not explicitly made known to students.	2.61	.90
D16. The professor frequently introduces opinions on religious, political and social issues clearly outside the realm of seminar content.	3.61	.94
D17. The professor's perspective in every class is U.S.-dominated, without acknowledgment of contributions from other countries.	3.12	.97
D18. The professor does not include pertinent scholarly contributions of women and minorities in the content of the seminar.	3.35	1.01
D19. A professor devotes content of all of his/her seminar sessions solely to his/her own research and publications.	3.47	.97
D20. Memorization of course content is stressed at the expense of analysis and critical thinking.	3.35	.97
D21. Students are not permitted to express viewpoints different from those of the professor.	4.01	.81

Behaviors	Mean	Standard deviation
D22. The professor expresses impatience with a slow learner in class.	3.62	.88
D23. The professor frequently makes negative comments in class about a student's dress, speech or manner.	4.43	.67
D24. The professor does not encourage graduate students to ask questions during class time.	3.38	.99
D25. The professor routinely ignores comments or questions from international graduate students.	4.16	.72
D26. A professor makes condescending remarks to a student in class.	4.17	.78
D27. A cynical attitude toward the seminar subject matter is expressed in class by the professor.	3.29	1.03
D28. The professor routinely wears dirty and sloppy clothes to class.	2.94	.97
D29. The professor practices poor personal hygiene and regularly has offensive body odor.	3.35	.99
D30. The professor sometimes makes racist or sexist remarks in class.	4.68	.56
D31. While able to conduct the graduate class, the faculty member attends class while obviously intoxicated.	4.77	.51
D32. The professor makes suggestive sexual comments to a graduate student enrolled in their seminar.	4.87	.37
D33. A faculty member criticizes the academic performance of a graduate student in front of other graduate students.	4.12	.88
D34. The professor pits graduate students against each other by assigning them competing projects.	3.18	1.17
D35. The professor doesn't care to learn the names of the graduate students enrolled in his/her seminar.	3.20	.98
D36. The professor prohibits graduate students from bringing their laptop computers to any seminar sessions.	2.42	.94
E. Class/seminar grading and examination practices		
E1. Graduate student seminar final grades are based on the professor's evaluation of just one term paper.	2.65	.99
E2. Graded tests and papers are not promptly returned to students by the professor.	3.09	.81

Behaviors	Mean	Standard deviation
E3. Written comments on tests and papers are consistently not made by the professor.	3.08	.92
E4. The professor changes the grading base or criteria after the course has begun.	3.50	.96
E5. The professor allows some graduate students to do alternative assignments without making this option generally known to all class members.	3.89	.95
E6. Individual graduate students are offered extra-credit work in order to improve their final course grade after the term is completed.	4.06	.95
E7. The professor allows personal friendships with a graduate student to intrude on the objective grading of their work.	4.41	.65
E8. Social, personal, or other non-academic characteristics of graduate students are taken into account in the assigning of grades.	4.45	.69
E9. Individual student course evaluations, where students can be identified, are read prior to the determination of final seminar grades.	4.50	.65
E10. No term papers, tests, lab reports, or other criteria are used by the professor for assigning final grades.	4.08	1.05
E11. A professor routinely awards A's to all graduate students enrolled in his/her seminar regardless of whether the students do any assignments or attend class.	4.27	.83
E12. The professor assigns a graduate student to grade the work of other graduate students.	3.62	1.07
F. Directing the thesis/dissertation		
F1. A faculty member agrees to direct a thesis/dissertation only under the condition that specific other faculty members are not asked to serve on the graduate student's committee.	2.97	1.07
F2. A professor agrees to direct a thesis/dissertation only under the condition that he/she will be a co-author on all publications based on the work.	3.43	1.35
F3. The thesis/dissertation advisor insists that a student pursue a particular topic/problem for his/her thesis or dissertation.	2.75	1.12

Behaviors	Mean	Standard deviation
F4. The thesis/dissertation director refuses to give his/her graduate student guidance in the selection of a thesis/dissertation topic.	3.46	.98
F5. Even when a student's proposed thesis/dissertation research design appears to require it, the major professor advises bypassing animal subjects or human subjects institutional review committees.	4.61	.70
F6. A student consistently cannot get an appointment with the thesis/dissertation advisor within three or four weeks to discuss issues concerning the thesis/dissertation.	4.06	.78
F7. The student's advisor often misses deadlines that affect the student's work or career.	4.18	.67
F8. The thesis/dissertation advisor routinely takes more than a month to give feedback on a student's draft chapter.	3.61	.91
F9. The thesis/dissertation advisor does not give any substantive feedback on drafts to any of their graduate students.	3.95	.81
F10. The thesis/dissertation advisor is routinely unavailable to answer a graduate student's questions about his/her thesis or dissertation.	3.95	.76
F11. The advisor fails to prepare advisees for questioning at the final oral defense.	3.38	1.00
F12. A thesis/dissertation advisor provides only criticism of their graduate student's work during the oral defense of the thesis/dissertation.	3.43	1.02
F13. The thesis/dissertation advisor fails to hold his/her students' thesis/dissertation work to the same departmental and professional standards expected of all other graduate students.	3.99	.76
F14. A professor presses a graduate student to submit work for publication before the student regards the research results to be verified/confirmed.	3.70	1.03
F15. The thesis/dissertation advisor urges his/her graduate student to simultaneously submit the same article out of their thesis/dissertation to more than one refereed journal.	4.34	.68
F16. The professor delays the graduation of his/her best graduate students, in order to keep them around longer.	4.49	.68

Behaviors	Mean	Standard deviation
G. Other behaviors regarding graduate students and the graduate program		
G1. A faculty member publishes an article using innovative ideas derived from a graduate student's term paper without acknowledging the student's contribution.	4.68	.55
G2. A professor routinely blames their graduate students when his/her own research work is called into question.	4.32	.74
G3. A professor accepts costly gifts from graduate students.	4.33	.87
G4. A professor tells a graduate student who is in good academic standing that the student is destined to fail their preliminary or qualifying exams.	3.97	1.01
G5. A male professor tells a female graduate student to avoid his specialty because only men can excel in it.	4.70	.56
G6. The professor makes derogatory remarks to graduate students about certain research methods used by other departmental faculty members.	3.38	1.01
G7. A faculty member consistently votes to not admit international students to the graduate program.	3.88	1.035
G8. A faculty member makes negative comments in a faculty meeting about the graduate courses offered by a colleague.	3.26	1.09
G9. A faculty member makes negative comments about a colleague's graduate courses in public to graduate students.	3.79	.92
G10. A faculty member aggressively promotes enrollment in his/her courses at the expense of the graduate courses offered by departmental colleagues.	3.31	.99
G11. A faculty member refuses to participate in departmental graduate curricular planning.	3.28	.94
G12. A faculty member refuses to serve on the departmental graduate admissions committee.	3.10	.99
G13. A faculty member strongly advocates accepting a graduate student applicant who fails to exhibit minimal skills in speaking or reading English.	3.26	1.01
G14. A faculty member strongly advocates enrolling a graduate student applicant whose specialized interests for study are not offered by the department.	3.48	.95
G15. A faculty member intentionally misrepresents graduate program requirements in order to recruit a graduate student.	4.38	.63

Appendix C
Respondent Bias Assessment

t-Test Comparisons between Initial and Subsequent Survey Mailings

	Mean initial mailing	Mean subsequent mailing	t-Value
Normative patterns			
Inviolable norms			
Disrespect toward student efforts	4.25	4.26	0.44
Misappropriation of student work	4.47	4.45	0.55
Harassment of students	4.54	4.54	0.06
Whistle-blowing suppression	4.54	4.41	2.86*
Directed research malfeasance	4.98	4.98	0.26
Admonitory norms			
Neglectful teaching	3.47	3.48	0.25
Inadequate advising/mentoring	3.38	3.45	1.33
Degradation of faculty colleagues	3.41	3.45	0.73
Negligent thesis/dissertation advising	3.68	3.68	0.02
Insufficient course structure	3.43	3.45	0.25
Pedagogical narrowness	3.34	3.45	1.87
Student assignment misallocation	3.43	3.47	0.67
Graduate program disregard	3.24	3.29	0.93
Faculty characteristics			
Articles published	3.59	3.47	1.26
Books/monographs published	1.46	1.46	0.01
Graduate seminars/courses taught	3.91	3.91	0.08
Graduate students' major professor	4.59	4.43	0.58
Member student committee	7.72	7.50	0.46
Professional age	19.53	19.87	0.37

*$p < .001$

Chi-Square Tests of Independence between Initial and Subsequent Survey Mailings

	Initial mailing	Subsequent mailing	Chi-square statistic
Variables			
Academic discipline			
Biology	18.4%	23.2%	2.86
Chemistry	28.2	25.8	
History	27.8	28.2	
Psychology	25.7	22.7	
Institutional type			
Very high research	49.4	50.6	0.47
High research	52.0	48.0	
Faculty characteristics			
Academic rank			
Professor	47.3%	47.7%	0.17
Associate professor	26.1	27.1	
Assistant professor	26.5	25.2	
Administrative experience			
Yes	27.3	21.0	3.88*
No	72.7	79.0	
Citizenship status			
U.S. citizen, native born	85.5	82.8	0.94
U.S. citizen, naturalized	6.2	7.2	
Not U.S. Citizen	8.3	10.0	
Gender			
Female	37.8	33.8	1.12
Male	62.2	66.2	
Tenure status			
Tenured	71.8	74.5	0.64
Untenured, but on tenure track	28.2	25.5	

*$p < .05$

References

Abbott, A. (1983). Professional ethics. *American Journal of Sociology, 88(5)*, 855–885.

Adams, H. (pseudo.). (2009). Academic bait-and-switch, part 4. *Chronicle of Higher Education*, December 18.

Aguinis, H., Nesler, M. S., Quigley, B. M., Lee, S.-J., & Tedesch, J. T. (1996). Power bases of faculty supervisors and educational outcomes for graduate students. *Journal of Higher Education, 67(3)*, 267–297.

American Association of University Professors. (2006). *AAUP policy documents and reports* (10th ed.). Washington, DC: Johns Hopkins University Press.

American Historical Association. (1993). *Statement on standards of professional conduct*. www.historians.org/pubs/free/professionalstandards.cfm (accessed May 24, 2010).

Anderson, M., & Louis, K. (1994). The graduate student experience and subscription to the norms of science. *Research in Higher Education, 35(3)*, 273–299.

Anderson, M., Louis, K., & Earle, J. (1994). Disciplinary and departmental effects on observations of faculty and graduate student misconduct. *Journal of Higher Education, 65(3)*, 331–350.

Association of American Universities. (1998). *AAU Committee on Graduate Education report and recommendations*. Washington, DC: Association of American Universities.

Austin, A. (2002). Preparing the next generation of faculty: Graduate school as socialization to the academic career. *Journal of Higher Education, 73(1)*, 94–122.

Austin, A. E., & McDaniels, M. (2006). Preparing the professoriate of the future: Graduate student socialization for faculty roles. In J. C. Smart (Ed.), *Higher education: Handbook of theory and research* (Vol. 21, pp. 397–456). Boston: Springer.

Austin, A. E., & Wulff, D. H. (2004). The challenge to prepare the next generation of faculty. In D. H. Wulff, A. E. Austin, & Associates (Eds.), *Paths to the professoriate: Strategies for enriching the preparation of future faculty* (pp. 3–16). San Francisco: Jossey-Bass.

Baldridge, J., Curtis, D., Ecker, G., & Riley, G. (1978). *Policy making and effective leadership*. San Francisco: Jossey-Bass.

Baron, D. (2003). Professors behaving badly. *Chronicle of Higher Education*, October 24.

Bartlett, T. (2003). Historical association will no longer investigate allegations of wrongdoing. *Chronicle of Higher Education*, May 23.

Bartlett, T. (2008). Columbia U. professor denies plagiarism, saying accusers instead stole her work. *Chronicle of Higher Education*, February 22.

Bayer, A., & Astin, H. (1975). Sex differentials in the academic reward system. *Science, 188(4190)*, 796–802.

Becker, H. S. (1968). On labeling outsiders. In E. Rubington & M. S. Weinberg (Eds.), *Deviance:The Interactionalist Perspective* (pp. 13–17). New York: Macmillan.

Bender, T. (2006). Expanding the domain of history. In C. M. Golde, G. E. Walker, & Associates (Eds.), *Envisioning the future of doctoral education: Preparing stewards of the discipline. Carnegie essays on the doctorate* (pp. 295–310). San Francisco: Jossey-Bass.

Ben-Yehuda, N. (1985). *Deviance and moral boundaries.* Chicago: University of Chicago Press.

Bernstein, D. A., & Lucas, S. G. (2004). Tips for effective teaching. In J. M. Darley, M. P. Zanna, & H. L. I. Roediger (Eds.), *The compleat academic: A career guide* (2nd ed., pp. 79–115). Washington, DC: American Psychological Association.

Biglan, A. (1973). The characteristics of subject matter in different academic areas. *Journal of Applied Psychology, 57(3)*, 195–203.

Birnbaum, R. (1988). *How colleges work: The cybernetics of academic organization and leadership.* San Francisco: Jossey-Bass.

Black, D. (1976). *The behavior of law.* New York: Academic Press.

Blackburn, R. T., & Lawrence, J. H. (1995). *Faculty at work: Motivation, expectation, satisfaction.* Baltimore: Johns Hopkins University Press.

Blau, P. (1973). *The organization of academic work.* New York: Wiley.

Boice, R. (2000). *Advice for new faculty members: Nihil nimus.* Boston: Allyn and Bacon.

Braxton, J. (1986). The normative structure of science: Social control in the academic profession. In J. Smart (Ed.), *Higher education: Handbook of theory and research* (Vol. 2, pp. 309–357). New York: Agathon Press.

Braxton, J. (1990). Deviancy from the norms of science: A test of control theory. *Research in Higher Education, 31(5)*, 461–476.

Braxton, John M. (1993). Deviancy from the norms of science: The effects of anomie and alienation in the academic profession. *Research in Higher Education, 34*, 213–228.

Braxton, J. (1995). Disciplines with an affinity for the improvement of undergraduate education. In N. Hativa & M. Marincovich (Eds.), *Disciplinary differences in teaching and learning: Implications for practice* (pp. 59–64). San Francisco: Jossey-Bass.

Braxton, J. (1999). Toward a guiding framework of professional self-regulation in the community of the academic profession. In J. M. Braxton (Ed.), *Perspectives on scholarly misconduct in the sciences* (pp. 139–161). Columbus: Ohio State University Press.

Braxton, J. (2010). The criticality of norms to the functional imperatives of the social action system of college and university work. *Journal of Higher Education, 81(3)*, 416–429.

Braxton, John M., & Baird, Leonard L. (2001). Preparation for professional self-regulation. *Journal of Science and Engineering Ethics*, 7, 593–610.

Braxton, John M., & Bayer, Alan E. (1996). Personal experiences of research misconduct and the response of individual academic scientists. *Science, Technology and Human Values, 21*, 198–213.

Braxton, J., & Bayer, A. E. (1999). *Faculty misconduct in collegiate teaching.* Baltimore: Johns Hopkins University Press.

Braxton, J. M., & Bayer, A. E. (2004). Toward a code of conduct for undergraduate teaching. In J. Braxton & A. E. Bayer (Eds.), *Addressing faculty and student classroom improprieties: New directions for teaching and learning* (no. 99, pp. 47–55). San Francisco: Jossey-Bass.

Braxton, John M., Bayer, Alan E., & Noseworthy, James A. (2004). The effects of teaching norm violations on the welfare of students as clients of college teaching. In John M. Braxton & Alan E. Bayer (Eds.), *Addressing faculty and student classroom improprieties: New directions for teaching and learning* (no. 99, pp. 41–16). San Francisco: Jossey-Bass.

Braxton, J., Eimers, M., & Bayer, A. (1996). The implications of teaching norms for the improvement of undergraduate education. *Journal of Higher Education, 67(6)*, 603–625.

Braxton, J., & Hargens, L. (1996). Variation among academic disciplines: Analytical frameworks and research. In J. Smart (Ed.), *Higher education: Handbook of Research and Theory* (Vol. 11, pp. 1–46). New York: Agathon Press.

Braxton, J., & Mann, M. (2004). Incidence and student response to faculty teaching norm violations. In J. M. Braxton & A. E. Bayer (Eds.), *Addressing faculty and student classroom improprieties: New directions for teaching and learning* (no. 99, pp. 35–40). San Francisco: Jossey-Bass.

Braxton, J. M., Proper, E., & Bayer, A. E. (2011). Towards a normative structure for graduate teaching and mentoring. In J. Hermanowicz (Ed.), *The American academic profession: Changing forms and functions.* Baltimore: Johns Hopkins University Press.

Bucher, R., & Stelling, J. (1977). *Becoming professional.* Beverly Hills, CA: Sage Publications.

Cahn, S. M. (2008). *From student to scholar: A candid guide to becoming a professor.* New York: Columbia University Press.

Caplan, P. J. (1993). *Lifting a ton of feathers: A woman's guide for surviving in the academic world.* Toronto: University of Toronto Press.

Carlin, J. (1966). *Lawyers' ethics.* New York: Sage.

Carnegie Foundation for the Advancement of Teaching. (2005). *A classification of institutions of higher education.* Princeton, NJ: Princeton University Press.

Chan, T. F. (2006). A time for change? The mathematics doctorate. In C. M. Golde, G. E. Walker, & Associates (Eds.), *Envisioning the future of doctoral education: Preparing stewards of the discipline. Carnegie essays on the doctorate* (pp. 120–134). San Francisco: Jossey-Bass.

Chubin, D. (1983). Misconduct in research: An issue of science policy and practice. *Minerva, 23*, 175–202.

Cole, J., & Cole, S. (1973). *Social stratification in science* (Vol. 42). Chicago: University of Chicago Press.

Collins, P. H. (1983). Learning from the outside from within: The sociological significance of black feminist thought. *Social Problems, 33(6)*, 514–532.

Creamer, E. G. (1998). *Assessing faculty publication productivity: Issues of equity.* Washington, DC: Graduate School of Education and Human Development, George Washington University.

Cronon, W. (2006). Getting ready to do history. In C. M. Golde, G. E. Walker, & Associates (Eds.), *Envisioning the future of doctoral education: Preparing stewards of the discipline. Carnegie essays on the doctorate* (pp. 327–349). San Francisco: Jossey-Bass.

Demsetz, H. (1967). Toward a theory of property rights. *American American Economic Review, 57*, 347, 351–353.

Deneef, A. L. (2007). Some thoughts on faculty mentoring (with a focus on graduate students). In A. L. Deneef & C. D. Goodwin (Eds.), *The academic's handbook* (3rd ed., pp. 229–235). Durham, NC: Duke University Press.

Durkheim, E. (1982). *The rules of sociological method.* New York: Free Press. Original work published 1895.

Durkheim, E. (1995). *The elementary forms of religious life.* New York: Free Press. Original work published 1912.

Ehrenberg, R., Jakubson, G., Groen, J., So, E., & Price, J. (2007). Inside the black box of doctoral education: What program characteristics influence doctoral students' attrition and graduation probabilities? *Educational Evaluation and Policy Analysis, 29(2),* 134.

Ethington, C. A., Thomas, S. L., & Pike, G. R. (2002). Back to the basics: Regression as it should be. In John C. Smart (Ed.), *Higher education: A handbook of theory and research* (Vol. 17, 263–293). Dordrecht, The Netherlands: Kluwer Academic Publishers.

Filene, P. (2005). *The joy of teaching: A practical guide for new college instructors.* Chapel Hill: University of North Carolina Press.

Finkelstein, M. J. (1984). *The American academic profession: A synthesis of social scientific inquiry since World War II.* Columbus: Ohio State University Press.

Fox, M. (1985). Publication, performance, and reward in science and scholarship. In J. Smart (Ed.), *Higher education: Handbook of theory and research* (Vol. 1, pp. 255–282). New York: Agathon Press.

Fox, M. (1992). Research, teaching, and publication productivity: Mutuality versus competition in academia. *Sociology of Education, 65(4),* 293–305.

Fox, M. (2000). Organizational environments and doctoral degrees awarded to women in science and engineering departments. *Women's Studies Quarterly, 28(1),* 47–61.

Franke, A. (2002). Faculty misconduct, discipline and dismissal. Paper presented at the annual meeting of the National Association of College and University Attorneys, New Orleans.

Fulton, O., & Trow, M. (1974). Research activity in American higher education. *Sociology of Education, 47(1),* 29–73.

Gaston, J. (1978). *The reward system in British and American science.* New York: Wiley.

Gibbs, J. (1981). *Norms, deviance, and social control: Conceptual matters.* New York: Elsevier.

Gilligan, C. (1977). In a different voice: Women's conceptions of self and moraliity. *Harvard Eductional Review, 47,* 481–517.

Gilligan, C. (1982). *In a different voice: Psychological theory and women's development.* Cambridge, MA: Harvard University Press.

Gilligan, C. (1993). *In a different voice: Psychological theory and women's development* (29th printing). Cambridge, MA: Harvard University Press.

Givres, J. E., & Wemmerus, V. (1988). Developing models of graduate student degree progress. *Journal of Higher Education, 59(2),* 163–189.

Golde, C. M. 2006. Preparing stewards of the discipline. In C. M. Golde, G. E. Walker, & Associates (Eds.), *Envisioning the future of the doctoral education: Preparing stewards of the discipline. Carnegie essays on the doctorate* (pp. 3–20). San Francisco: Jossey-Bass.

Golde, C. M., & Dore, T. M. (2004). The survey of doctoral education and career preparation. In D. H. Wulff, A. E. Austin, & Associates (Eds.), *Path to the professoriate: Strategies for enriching the preparation of future faculty* (pp. 19–45). San Francisco: Jossey-Bass.

Golde, C. M., Walker, G. E., & Associates. (2006). *Envisioning the future of doctoral education: Preparing stewards of the discipline. Carnegie essays on the doctorate.* San Francisco: Jossey-Bass.

Goldsmith, J. A., Komlos, J., & Gold, P. S. (2001). *The Chicago guide to your academic career: A portable mentor for scholars from graduate school through tenure.* Chicago: University of Chicago Press.

Goode, W. (1969). The theoretical limits of professionalization. In A. Etzioni (Ed.), *The semi-professions and their organization* (pp. 266–313). New York: Free Press.

Goode, W. J., and Hatt, P. K. (1952). *Methods of social research*. New York: McGraw-Hill.

Goodwin, L., & Stevens, E. (1993). The influence of gender on university faculty members' perceptions of "good" teaching. *Journal of Higher Education, 64(2)*, 166–185.

Gray, P., & Drew, D. E. (2008). *What they didn't teach you in graduate school: 199 helpful hints for success in graduate school.* Sterling, VA: Stylus.

Hagstrom, W. (1965). *The scientific community*. New York: Basic.

Handler, J. (1967). *The lawyer and his community*. Madison: University of Wisconsin Press.

Hirschy, A., & Wilson, M. (2002). The sociology of the classroom and its influence on student learning. *Peabody Journal of Education, 77(3)*, 85–100.

Horne, Christine. 2001. Sociological perspectives on the emergence of social norms. In Michael Hechter & Karl-Dieter Opp (Eds.), *Social Norms* (pp. 3–34). New York: Russell Sage.

Kish, L. (1957). Confidence intervals for clustered samples. *American Sociological Review, 22(2)*, 154–165.

Kuhn, T. S. (1962). *The structure of scientific revolutions* (1st ed.). Chicago: University of Chicago Press.

Kuhn, T. S. (1970). *The structure of scientific revolutions* (2nd ed.). Chicago: University of Chicago Press.

Lang, J. M. (2005). *Life on the tenure track: Lessons from the first year.* Baltimore: Johns Hopkins University Press.

Lee, B. A. (1999). Legal aspects of scholarship misconduct. In J. M. Braxton (Ed.), *Perspectives on scholarly misconduct in the sciences* (pp. 189–210). Columbus: Ohio State University Press.

Leslie, D. W. (1973). The status of the department chairpersonship in university organization. *AAUP Bulletin, 59*, 419–426.

Leslie, L. L. (1972). Are response rates essential to valid surveys? *Social Science Research, 1*, 323–334.

Lovitts, B. (2001). *Leaving the ivory tower: The causes and consequences of departure from doctoral study.* Lanham, MD: Rowman & Littlefield.

Lovitts, B. (2004). Research on the structure and process of graduate education: Retaining students. In D. H. Wulff, A. E. Austin, & Associates (Eds.), *Paths to the professoriate: Strategies for enriching the preparation of future faculty* (pp. 115–136). San Francisco: Jossey-Bass.

Lucas, C. J., & Murray, J. W., Jr. (2007). *New faculty: A practical guide for academic beginners.* New York: Palgrave Macmillan.

Merton, R. (1942). Science and technology in a democratic order. *Journal of Legal and Political Sociology, 1*, 115–126.

Merton, R. (1968). *Social theory and social structure*. New York: Free Press.

Merton, R. (1973). *The sociology of science: Theoretical and empirical investigations.* Chicago: University of Chicago Press.

Merton, R. (1976). The sociology of social problems. In R. Merton & R. Nisbet (Eds.), *Contemporary social problems* (pp. 3–43). New York: Harcourt Brace.

Merton, R., Reader, G., & Kendall, P. (1957). *The student physician.* Cambridge, MA: Harvard University Press.

Monastersky, R. (2008). Purdue punishes professor who led disputed fusion experiment. *Chronicle of Higher Education*, August 28.
Mullins, N. (1973). *Science: Some sociological perspectives*. Indianapolis, IN: Bobbs-Merrill.
Nettles, M., & Millett, C. (2006). *Three magic letters: Getting to Ph.D.* Baltimore: Johns Hopkins University Press.
Nyquist, J. D., Woodword, B. J., & Rogers, D. L. (2004). Re-envisioning the Ph.D.: A challenge for the twenty-first century. In D. H. Wulff, A. E. Austin, & Associates (Eds.), *Paths to the professoriate: Strategies for enriching the preparation of future faculty* (pp. 194–216). San Francisco: Jossey-Bass.
Nyquist, J. D., and Wulff, D. (1996). *Working effectively with graduate assistants*. Thousand Oaks, CA: Sage Publications.
Opp, K. (1982). The evolutionary emergence of norms. *British Journal of Social Psychology, 21(2)*, 139–149.
Parsons, T. (1939). The professions and social structure. *Social Forces, 17(4)*, 457–467.
Parsons, T., & Platt, G. (1973). *The American university*. Cambridge, MA: Harvard University Press.
Parsons, T., & Smelser, N. (1956). *Economy and society*. New York: Routledge.
Penslar, R. (1995). *Research ethics: Cases and materials*. Bloomington: Indiana University Press.
Research gone wrong. (2008). *Chronicle of Higher Education*, May 16.
Reskin, B. (1979). Academic sponsorship and scientists' careers. *Sociology of Education, 52*, 129–146.
Rockquemore, K. A., & Laszloffy, T. (2008). *The black academic's guide to winning tenure—without losing your soul*. Boulder, CO: Lynne Rienner Publishers.
Rossi, P., & Berk, R. (1985). Varieties of normative consensus. *American Sociological Review, 50(3)*, 333–347.
Ruscio, K. (1987). Many sectors, many professions. In B. Clark (Ed.), *The academic profession: National, disciplinary, and institutional settings* (pp. 331–368). Los Angeles: University of California Press.
Schein, E. (1972). *Professional education: Some new directions*. Hightstown, NJ: McGraw-Hill.
Schoenfeld, A. C., & Magnan, R. (1992). *Mentor in a manual: Climbing the academic ladder to tenure*. Madison, WI: Magna Publications.
Scott, W. Richard. (1970). Professionals in bureaucracies—areas of conflict. In H. M. Vollmer & D. L. Mills (Eds.), *Professionalism* (pp. 265–275). Englewood Cliffs, NJ: Prentice-Hall.
Smart, J. (1991). Gender equity in academic rank and salary. *Review of Higher Education, 14(4)*, 511–526.
Stacy, A. M. (2006). Training future leaders. In C. M. Golde, G. E. Walker, & Associates (Eds.), *Envisioning the Future of Doctoral Education: Preparing Stewards of the Discipline. Carnegie Essays on the Doctorate* (pp. 187–206). San Francisco: Jossey-Bass.
Steneck, N. (1994). Research universities and scientific misconduct: History, policies, and the future. *Journal of Higher Education, 65(3)*, 310–330.
Strain, B. D. (2007). Publishing in science. In A. L. Deneef & C. D. Goodwin (Eds.), *The academic's handbook* (3rd ed., pp. 306–314). Durham, NC: Duke University Press.
Tangney, J. (1987). Fraud will out—or will it? *New Scientist, 115(1572)*, 62–63.

Tierney, W., & Rhoads, R. (1993). *Enhancing promotion, tenure and beyond: Faculty socialization as a cultural process.* Washington, DC: George Washington University.

Tinto, V. (1993). *Leaving college: Rethinking the causes and cures of student attrition* (2nd ed.). Chicago: University of Chicago Press.

Tittle, C. (1980). *Sanctions and social deviance: The question of deterrence.* New York: Praeger.

Toth, E. (1997). *Ms. Mentor's impeccable advice for women in academia.* Philadelphia: University of Pennsylvania Press.

Toth, E. (2005). Ms. Mentor advice column. Students or serfs? *Chronicle of Higher Education,* April 4.

Toth, E. (2009). *Ms. Mentor's new and ever more impeccable advice for women and men in academia.* Philadelphia: University of Pennsylvania Press.

Tucker, A. (1993). *Chairing the academic department: Leadership among peers.* Washington, DC: American Council on Education.

University of Illinois at Urbana-Champaign. (2010). Department of English Faculty Directory. www.english.illinois.edu/people/ (accessed October 8).

Vesilind, P. A. (2007). The responsible conduct of academic research. In A. L. Deneef & C. D. Goodwin (Eds.), *The academic's handbook* (3rd ed., pp. 112–119). Durham, NC: Duke University Press.

Vick, J. M. and Furlong, J. S. (2010). Dealing with a difficult advisor. "Career Talk" advice column. *Chronicle of Higher Education,* February 9.

Wagner, P. A. (1996). *Understanding professional ethics.* Bloomington, IN: Phi Delta Kappa Educational Foundation.

Walker, G., Golde, C., Jones, L., Bueschel, A., & Hutchings, P. (2008). *The formation of scholars: Rethinking doctoral education for the twenty-first century.* San Francisco: Jossey-Bass.

Walker, M., & Thomson, P. (2010). *The Routledge doctoral supervisor's companion: Supporting effective research in education and the social sciences.* London: Routledge.

Wasley, P. (2006). Review blasts professors for plagiarism by graduate students. *Chronicle of Higher Education,* June 16.

Weidman, J. C., Twale, D. J., & Stein, E. L. (2001). *Socialization of graduate and professional students in higher education: A perilous passage?* (Vol. 28). San Francisco: Jossey-Bass.

Whicker, M. L., Kronenfeld, J. J., & Strickland, R. A. (1993). *Getting tenure.* Newbury Park, CA: Sage Publications.

Wilson, R. (2002). Music's open secret. *Chronicle of Higher Education,* June 7.

Wilson, R. (2009). Notoriety yields tragedy in Iowa sexual-harassment cases. *Chronicle of Higher Education,* February 20.

Winston, R. B., Jr., & Polkosnik, M. C. (1984). Advising graduate and professional school students. In R. B. Winston Jr., T. K. Miller, S. C. Ender, T. J. Grites, & Associates (Eds.), *Developmental academic advising: Addressing students' educational, career, and personal needs* (pp. 287–314). San Francisco: Jossey-Bass.

Woolston, C. (2002). When a mentor becomes a thief. *Chronicle of Higher Education,* April 1.

Wulff, D. H., & Austin, A. E. (2004). Future directions: Strategies to enhance paths to the professoriate. In D. H. Wulff, A. E. Austin, & Associates (Eds.), *Paths to the professoriate: Strategies for enriching the preparation of future faculty* (pp. 267–292). San Francisco: Jossey-Bass.

Wulff, D. H., & Nerad, M. (2006). Using an alignment model as a framework in the assessment of doctoral programs. In P. L. Maki & N. A. Borkowski (Eds.), *Assessing learning at the doctoral level* (pp. 83–108). Sterling, VA: Stylus.

Zacks, J. M., & Roediger, H. L. I. (2004). Setting up your lab and beginning a research program. In J. M. Darley, M. P. Zanna, & H. L. I. Roediger (Eds.), *The compleat academic: A career guide* (2nd ed., pp. 135–152). Washington, DC: American Psychological Association.

Zanna, M. P., & Darley, J. M. (2004). Mentoring: Managing the faculty-graduate student relationship. In J. M. Darley, M. P. Zanna, & H. L. I. Roediger (Eds.), *The compleat academic: A career guide* (2nd ed., pp. 117–131). Washington, DC: American Psychological Association.

Zuckerman, H. (1977). Deviant behavior and social control in science. In E. Sagarin (Ed.), *Deviance and social change* (pp. 87–138). Beverly Hills, CA: Sage Publications.

Zuckerman, H. (1988). The sociology of science. In N. Smelser (Ed.), *Handbook of sociology* (pp. 511–574). Thousand Oaks, CA: Sage Publications.

Zuckerman, H., Cole, J., & Bruer, J. (1991). *The outer circle: Women in the scientific community*. New Haven, CT: Yale University Press.

Index

Page numbers in *italics* refer to tables.